CARRYING
THE COLORS

CARRYING THE COLORS

The Life and Legacy of Medal of Honor Recipient

ANDREW JACKSON SMITH

W. Robert Beckman and Sharon S. MacDonald

With Andrew S. Bowman and Esther L. Bowman

WESTHOLME
Yardley

Facing the title page: Andrew Jackson Smith as color sergeant, 55th Massachusetts Volunteer Infantry, 1865, the only known photograph of Smith in wartime service or as a young man. (*Alfred S. Hartwell Collection, State Library of Massachusetts, Boston*)

©2020 W. Robert Beckman and Sharon S. MacDonald
Maps by Paul Rossmann.

Westholme Publishing, LLC
904 Edgewood Road
Yardley, Pennsylvania 19067
Visit our Web site at www.westholmepublishing.com

ISBN: 978–1–59416–341-8
Also available as an eBook.

Printed in the United States of America.

In memory of
Color Sergeant Robert H. King,
55th Massachusetts Volunteer Infantry,
KIA, Battle of Honey Hill, SC,
November 30, 1864.
He nearly did carry the flag into the fort.

And Esther L. Bowman
November 3, 1937—June 19, 2018

And for
Katherine Dhalle
Willis J. Keith
Ray Parish

"Much depends on the courage and daring of the color-sergeant. Wherever he will carry the flag, the men will follow to protect and defend it; and no non-commissioned officer occupies a post that is so likely to bring distinction and promotion if he does his duty; whilst none is more certain to bring disgrace if he proves recreant to his trust."

—Captain August V. Kautz, 6th US Cavalry,
Brigadier General US Volunteers

"Will you come with me? I am going to carry the flag into the fort or die."

—Color Sergeant Robert H. King,
55th Massachusetts Volunteer Infantry

CONTENTS

ILLUSTRATIONS

MAPS

ILLUSTRATIONS

PREFACE

CARUTH SMITH WASHINGTON had a simple request, or so it seemed: she wanted someone to write about the life of her father, Andrew "Andy" Jackson Smith. He had bequeathed documents containing the basics of a fascinating story of his service in a black Civil War regiment and the denial of a Medal of Honor. In 1984, Caruth organized these papers into an album with commentary to produce her own, short account of Andy Smith's life.[1] She then presented the album to historians in search of finding an author, but therein she encountered a problem.

Few written sources existed to document individual lives among a people emerging from slavery. As an escaped slave and illiterate soldier, Smith did not leave behind a diary, journal, or letters to his family back home, and few records reinforced his family's memory of his postwar life in Kentucky. This paucity of information discouraged the historians whom Caruth approached, and Andy Smith's life seemed relegated to obscurity.[2]

Caruth remained hopeful that research into her father's military career would yield more documents, but for more than two years she made little progress until her nephew, Andrew S. Bowman, took up the cause to begin his own journey in search of Andy Smith's history. Surely, Bowman believed, a way could be found to preserve the story of his grandfather's life and the perils he faced. Of particular interest to Bowman was the government's claim it did not possess records to substantiate Smith's recommendation for the Medal of Honor. Perhaps, Bowman thought, these and additional documents could be found, not only to reveal the actions meriting the Medal of Honor recommendation but also to document other aspects of an interesting life.

About thirty years before Caruth organized her album, Civil War historians found a way to preserve the history of black soldiers. Abundant information did survive, if not in depth about individual soldiers then about their collective experiences as detailed in military and government records, letters and diaries, and in accounts written by newspaper correspondents and other observers. The result was to meld the voices of many, creating a common history of black military service emphasizing black soldiers' shared struggles, sacrifices, and contributions to the Union war effort.[3]

If Smith's story were to be told, it would be necessary to adopt the methodology of those who first began to write collectively about the lives of black soldiers, but with the focus on one individual. The survival of letters and diaries by officers and enlisted men in the 55th Massachusetts Volunteer Infantry, as well as the regimental books, helped to make such a process possible. In particular, the papers of Dr. Burt G. Wilder, a surgeon of the 55th Massachusetts, yielded letters dictated by Smith, including a few short accounts of his life in the army. All of these sources combined not only to provide information about Smith's military service but to reveal his character, his steadfast determination, and his courage.

Smith also led an interesting postwar life in Kentucky that merits a place in the social history of all Americans, but its recovery entailed special challenges. The devastating flood of 1937 destroyed much of the Lyon County's historical record, including public documents, newspapers, letters, diaries, and wills. Still, information about the activities of Andy Smith and others in the local black and white communities may be teased from the pages of those public records that survived the flood, the result of herculean efforts by county officials to move their documents to safety. The deed books, many of the tax assessment books, and other public records in the Lyon County Clerk's Office were preserved, as were records of the Lyon County Circuit Court and the deed books in adjacent Livingston County.

Working closely with his mother, Geneva Shelton, and with Caruth, Andrew Bowman proved to be a careful custodian of his grandfather's history, preserving both remembrance and documentation while gathering new information wherever possible. In particular, he sought out and secured interviews with individuals possessing remarkable memories who had known and interacted with Andy Smith during the last decade of his life. Together these sources and the surviving public records allowed the history of Smith's postwar life and achievements to be recovered. Thus, Andy Bowman had been correct: it took years of research and unwavering dedication, but there was a way to tell his grandfather's story.

This work is the first to reconstruct the life of an individual, illiterate black soldier, whom the authors believe to have been a significant American figure. Andrew Jackson Smith was one of nearly two hundred thousand like individuals who formed a vital resource for the Union during the Civil

War. He was also among those black servicemen who built interesting and successful postwar lives in often difficult environments—lives that, where possible, historians should try to recover.

ABOUT THE TEXT

Corrections of capitalization, spelling, or grammar conflicting with modern usage have not been made in quotations. Use of the apostrophe as well as its absence in place names can be idiosyncratic. We have chosen to follow the established usage of the Civil War era, which often remains the spelling used today, for example, Rivers' Causeway, James Island, Johns Island, Coles Island, Bulls Bay, Sisters Ferry, St. Johns River, and St. Marys River.

Andrew Jackson Smith was so insistent on being called Andy that not only family and friends but also officers and men of the 55th Massachusetts used only his nickname. The authors have chosen to respect Smith's choice when referring to him in the text. Similarly, the authors often refer to Smith's daughters, Geneva and Caruth, and to his grandson, Andrew "Andy" Bowman, by their given names. This is not intended to be in any way disrespectful but is in accord with family preference.

PROLOGUE: MARCH 6, 1932

CARUTH STOOD QUIETLY, somberly, watching as the pastor intoned the last prayer that would be spoken over her father. The grave opened the ground within a stand of trees. If there was ever a place for eternal rest, it was this remote corner of western Kentucky. The pines and cedars stood as sentinels about the small cemetery, their branches softly sighing as the breeze wound through them, their needles littering the ground, deadening the sounds of movement.

Graves of friends surrounded the plot of Andy Smith, which was oddly appropriate, since he had been at the center of his local community, even donating the land for this cemetery. No graves were closer, however, than those of his wife, Gertrude, and infant daughter Laculian: their names shared the same headstone. Nearby lay his first wife, Amanda, and not far away his mother, Susan. Her gravestone read "aged about seventy years." Hard to tell her age—they did not always keep accurate birth dates for slaves.

Caruth's birth in 1907 came late in Andy Smith's life. When her mother died unexpectedly, he sent Caruth to live with her maternal grandparents in nearby Paducah, but they soon moved to Indiana. Family and friends closer to home helped raise Caruth's older sister, Geneva, until, approaching age seven, she too joined her sister and grandparents in Indiana. Smith did not believe that as a man in his sixties he could adequately raise two little girls alone.

His visits to Indiana could not come often enough for Caruth's liking, but life there gave Caruth and Geneva an advantage their father wanted them to have: an education. Schooling for black children in Kentucky ended in the sixth grade, and Smith knew the value of education as only a person who had been denied one could. In Indiana, Caruth and Geneva were able to attend high school, and in later years Caruth became a teacher of young children. An accomplished person, her achievements would have been no surprise to those who knew her father, for he was successful in his own right.

It was amazing, all that Andy Smith had achieved in his life, with no formal schooling, amid the imposition of segregation. After he escaped from slavery, at the beginning of his life as a free man, he survived a gunshot wound to the head to become a highly regarded soldier in the 55th Massachusetts Volunteer Infantry. He was later recommended for the nation's highest military award, the Medal of Honor. After the war, he returned home to become a prominent member of his community in the land separating Kentucky's Tennessee and Cumberland Rivers.

Despite the obstacles, as a black man in a segregated world, Andy Smith managed to buy and sell several thousand acres of land, including land for people wanting their own farms. A successful farmer and businessman, he prevailed in court on occasion, during the heyday of Jim Crow, in cases against white men and companies.

Although he made a mark on his world, his daughter Caruth felt she never really got to know her father while she was growing up in Indiana. She knew he had been a soldier in the Union army and was successful in farming and business. Beyond that she knew little, creating a void she could never fill. Consciously, or unconsciously, she idolized her father and mourned the loss of his memory as much as his actual physical loss.

Even before his death, the vestiges of his life were fading, the land sold, his community changing, and the contributions he and other black soldiers had made in the Civil War were minimized by white historians. It seemed the memory of Andy Smith was destined to fade and slowly disintegrate, just as his way of life was slowly disappearing. By the 1960s, even Between the Rivers was gone, much of it, including most of Andy Smith's farm, covered by two lakes created by Tennessee Valley Authority dams, with the remainder now known as the Land Between the Lakes. It seemed the life of Andy Smith would be lost forever.

On the day of her father's funeral, Caruth was informed there was something he expressly desired her to have. It was a cardboard case, and, as it was handed to Caruth, she was told it contained letters and papers Andy Smith had saved during the course of his life. Here was what she wanted more than almost anything else on this day. Here was her father's story, contained within these pages. Here was a vehicle for knowing and preserving her father's life and deeds. With bittersweet anticipation, Caruth opened the case.[1]

PART 1

HEROISM

CHAPTER 1

ESCAPE BETWEEN THE RIVERS

September 1842–January 1862

ANDREW JACKSON SMITH was born a slave on September 3, 1842, in a region of Kentucky bounded by the Tennessee and Cumberland Rivers, locally known as Between the Rivers. His owner and father, Elias P. Smith, was a farmer, wealthy enough to accumulate about twenty slaves and several sizable parcels of land, selling nearly two thousand acres on one occasion. At the time of Andy's birth, Elias was a widower with a large extended family, but his immediate white family was small, consisting of his teenage sons William and Harrison.[1]

Little is known of Elias Smith's activities or the lives of his slaves and their treatment. Historians often encounter a dearth of written sources when researching the life of an ordinary person, especially when that person was illiterate, as was Elias, and only snippets of information are gained from Andy Smith, who had precious little to say about his life in slavery. In a letter dictated in 1913, he revealed, "I was born in [what would become] Lyon County Ky about five miles South East [actually southwest] of Eddyville. My Mother's name was Susan. She came from Virginia when she was a small girl about 12 years of age. A man by the name of Debinport brought her to Kentucky. My father was a white man."[2]

In these few words, Andy Smith described his parents. White slave owners typically did not acknowledge children they fathered with slave women, and his father's apparent refusal to recognize him must have contributed to a disconcerting childhood for Andy. The effect of such estrangement is also evident in Frederick Douglass's account of his parentage, in which he used the same words to identify his father as did Andy Smith: "My father was a white man. . . . The opinion was also whispered that my master was my father. . . . The whisper . . . may or may not be true; and, true or false, it is of but little consequence to my purpose whilst the fact remains, in all its glaring odiousness, that slaveholders have ordained, and by law established, that the children of slave women shall in all cases follow the condition of their mothers."[3]

Andy did not specify Elias was his father, and there is no evidence Elias ever acknowledged his paternity of Andy and his three sisters, but that Elias was their father remains common knowledge among the white and black members of the family to this day. The only written evidence is contained in Elias's will, wherein he affirms a special affinity for Andy's mother and another of his slaves, Hilary:

> I desire that my son Harrison P. Smith shall take care of and provide for my negro woman Susan during her life, and that my son William J. Smith, shall take care of and provide for my negro woman Hilary during her life, and I hereby require my said sons to treat said negroes differently from other slaves, and keep them each comfortable and with all the necessaries of life as long as they live.[4]

Susan and Hilary are the only slaves mentioned by name in the will. All others are merely dealt with as property. The affection and concern Elias Smith exhibited for Susan and Hilary suggests the presence of personal relationships, and both may have had children by him. It is not known if Andy's sisters were his full or half-sisters, and we only have a name, Lucy, for one sister.

Elias's extended white family included his brother Edward's nine children, with whom Andy was well acquainted. While young, Andy and some of his cousins formed lifelong bonds. He even became responsible for the care of a younger cousin, John Rucker Smith. John Rucker's granddaughter, Joanne Smith Evans Carnes, relates that Andy "slept on a pallet on the floor by John Rucker Smith, and it was his [Andy's] job to play with him and keep him occupied while all the family worked in the fields. . . . This was the story that was handed down through the family. They played together, and he slept on a pallet next to John's bed."[5]

Around 1850, when Andy was about eight years old, Elias moved with his slaves across the Cumberland River close to Eddyville. Andy recalled

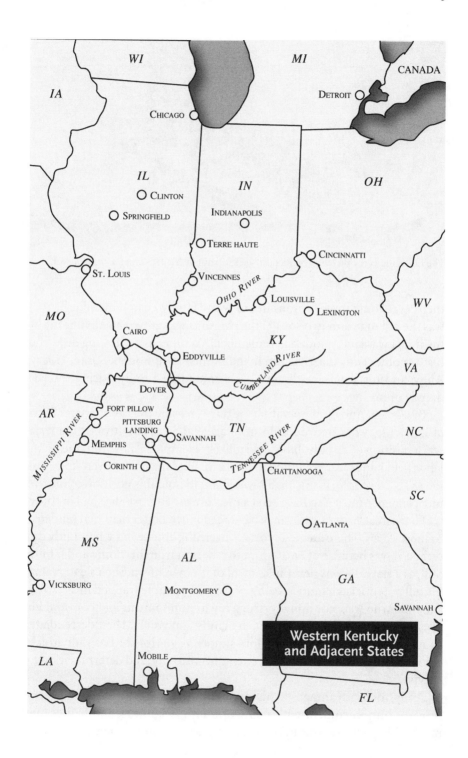

Western Kentucky
and Adjacent States

The Eddyville Ferry sketched by Richard McKinney. (*Richie McKinney, Princeton, KY*)

there were "only three persons in our white family I can remember[:] that was the old man and two sons[;] the two sons was grown and left home by the time I was large enough to remember."[6] With Elias's wife long dead and his two older sons married and living in their own homes, Susan, Hilary, Andy, and his sisters made up Elias's immediate family during the last decade of his life.

By age ten, Andy was operating the ferry crossing the Cumberland River at Eddyville, work he would do until age eighteen.[7] Control of the ferry was a position of responsibility, and it likely exempted Andy from the heavy labor field hands were required to perform. Elias may have given Andy this job as an act of favoritism, but allowing him to hold this position of relative independence must also have been a measure of the trust Elias had in Andy.

Elias's treatment of Andy may have been much better than that rendered to most slaves. There are no reports concerning abuse, and when Andy did escape, it was because of an attempt to take him from his home and family. Still, as a slave, he was never in control of his own life, never able to realize his full potential as a human being. Slaves were people trapped in a terrible situation who were continually struggling to gain some influence over their lives and manage them with as much dignity as possible. Their descendants should not imagine their ancestors simply as victims but as individuals who exhibited remarkable spirit, strength, creativity, and determination to survive.

Andy took advantage of his opportunities. Operation of the ferry brought him in contact with many of Elias's neighbors, and he became more widely known within the local white community than would normally be expected of a slave. He also moved among the farms owned by Elias, Edward, and their children, either to help with fieldwork or other tasks or to play with his young white cousins. He thereby came to know the northern regions of Between the Rivers exceptionally well. As matters turned out, knowledge of the land, its people, and their activities aided him not only in his escape but also after the war when he engaged in real estate speculation to become one of Lyon County's largest landowners.

Elias Smith died in late 1860 or early 1861. By terms of his will, his sons William and Harrison Smith divided his property equally. Susan went to Harrison. Andy, taken by William, moved back to Between the Rivers to live on William's farm near the bank of the Cumberland River. As the Smith family partitioned Elias's property, the United States approached its own division, a devastating civil war that would pull his family apart.[8]

AS SEVEN STATES OF THE DEEP SOUTH seceded from the Union during winter 1860–61, eight other slave states, including Andy Smith's home state of Kentucky, remained loyal. Following the Confederate attack on Fort Sumter on April 12, 1861, four more slave states joined the newborn Confederacy, but Kentucky was not among them. Settled by immigrants from both the North and the South and with strong economic ties to both regions, Kentucky had divided loyalties, but there was little disagreement over slavery. No citizen of any Confederate state endorsed slavery more vehemently than those making up Kentucky's Unionist majority.

Kentucky's loyalists believed remaining in the Union provided the best protection for slavery, and thus Kentucky joined Delaware, Maryland, and Missouri to become one of the border states—slave states that remained loyal to the Union. Meanwhile, Kentucky's Southern sympathizers saw secession as the best means to ensure slavery's continuation. In the western region of the state, where such sentiment was most substantial, Confederate proponents began to vie with Unionists for Kentucky's loyalty, thereby creating the circumstances leading to Andy Smith's escape.

After the attack on Fort Sumter, Kentucky's governor did not answer President Abraham Lincoln's call for troops. In May, the legislature declared the state to be neutral, but Kentucky's neutrality was short lived, ended ironically by a Confederate blunder. On September 3, 1861, Confederate Major General Leonidas Polk, in violation of orders, seized the heights on the Mississippi River at Columbus, Kentucky. Polk's invasion was of little value to the Confederates, but it gave Union commanders the justification they needed to enter the state. Brigadier General Ulysses S. Grant quickly responded by seizing Paducah, Kentucky, on September 6 and then the town of Smithland, located at the confluence of the Ohio and Cumberland Rivers, near Andy Smith's home.

The people of western Kentucky began to take sides. A young Lyon County resident, William J. Stone, became an early convert to the secessionist cause and actively recruited others to join the Confederate army. Andy Smith's owner, William Smith, was among 120 men who left home with Stone in September 1861 to enlist for one year in Company G of the 1st Kentucky Cavalry. Confederate sympathizers in the area also joined the 8th Kentucky Infantry, but Union support remained firm in the state as a whole, and other Kentuckians began to fill Union regiments.[9]

In October, the war came to Lyon County. With the end of neutrality, Union gunboats began patrolling the lower Tennessee and Cumberland Rivers to show the flag, encourage Union supporters, and gather intelligence. In particular, the *Conestoga*, under Lieutenant Commander Seth Ledyard Phelps, became a familiar sight to locals as it traversed the rivers, routinely stopping at Eddyville and other settlements. Andy Smith had ample opportunity to observe the *Conestoga* negotiate the Cumberland.[10]

Phelps described Eddyville as "a strong secession town and a neighborhood where Union men have been driven from their homes." On October 14, he "found it necessary to use strong language to the citizens in regard to the persecution of Union people." Two days later a punitive Union cavalry raid came within four miles of Eddyville. A Confederate officer reported, "25 cavalry . . . took all the double-barreled guns they could find, robbed some women of their jewelry, seized several horses and mules, destroyed some property, insulted some women, captured one citizen as prisoner, and returned to Smithland, from whence they came."[11]

The raid was intended to intimidate local secessionists, but it also prompted Confederate leaders to send the 1st Kentucky Cavalry's Company G to Lyon County. William Smith and the others who had left in September with William Stone now returned to defend their homes. They established a camp four miles north of Eddyville, but a local Union loyalist quickly reported their presence to U. S. Grant at his headquarters in Cairo, Illinois. Thereupon Grant wrote Brigadier General C. F. Smith, the Union commander at Paducah and Smithland, "you may, if you deem it prudent, take steps to secure these fellows."[12]

Late on the afternoon of October 25, the transport *Lake Erie*, carrying three hundred men from the 9th Illinois Volunteer Infantry, departed Paducah with the gunboat *Conestoga*. Phelps took considerable care to disguise their destination from the network of spies at Smithland as the navy's plan to deceive the Confederates unfolded. The *Lake Erie* bypassed Smithland and the entrance to the Cumberland River to continue up the Ohio. The *Conestoga* stopped in Smithland, took two barges in tow, and an hour later continued along the Ohio. Miles upriver at night, beyond the reach of Smithland's spies, the *Conestoga* rendezvoused with the *Lake Erie*. Phelps released the empty barges and, taking the *Lake Erie* in tow, "with all lights out, fires screened, and engines stopped," headed back down the Ohio. As the *Conestoga* turned up the Cumberland River in the dark of night, the Smithland spies mistook the *Lake Erie* for a barge and, unaware of the impending attack, issued no early warning.[13]

At 3:30 AM on October 26, the 9th Illinois disembarked from the *Lake Erie* a few miles north of Eddyville and moved overland toward the Confederate cavalry camp. To avoid detection, their guides led them down a back road for three miles, along the bed of a dry watercourse for five miles, and finally across country for another five miles to reach their destination. Arriving after daybreak, the Illinois troops surprised and captured the enemy pickets without firing a shot. They then advanced to within six hundred yards of the camp before the Confederates, who were at breakfast, spotted their approach.

Dismounted, the surprised and green Confederate cavalry tried to organize a defense, but the Union, with twice as many troops, pressed the attack. The Confederates "broke for their horses, though many took shelter behind fences, trees, or houses. We charged to within fifty yards, halted, delivered a volley," recalled Major Jesse J. Phillips, "and then charged bayonet, driving them from the houses and from their place of cover, and they fled in every direction—some on foot, others on horseback."[14]

Union troops took as prisoners twenty-one Confederate soldiers and several civilian secessionists who lived near the camp. The civilians were captured to maintain secrecy, and in the process, Union soldiers discovered and also took seven slaves. William Smith was not with his company for the fight and may have been across the Cumberland River at his home.[15]

Meanwhile, the *Conestoga* and *Lake Erie* continued up the Cumberland toward Eddyville. Phelps concealed the *Lake Erie* from view "behind a wooded point" and "quietly anchored [the *Conestoga*] off the main street." He waited until the 9th Illinois had time enough to reach the Confederate cavalry camp and then "threw a force on shore and surrounded the town with picket guards to prevent the escape of rebel citizens or the entrance and concealment of refugees from the rebel camp."[16]

Phelps held Eddyville until about 10:00 AM, when the 9th Illinois "reached town with a number of prisoners, horses, wagons, arms, etc." The

Union troops, their prisoners (soldiers and civilians), and the seven slaves embarked on boats for Paducah along with animals and other confiscated property. Before the *Conestoga* departed Eddyville, Phelps threatened secessionists living there and along the length of the Cumberland River in Kentucky: they would be held "responsible for any violence Union people might be subject to after our departure."[17]

Local slaves must have been encouraged by these events and saw as potential friends and liberators the Union troops who attacked Confederate soldiers, arrested slave owners, and took away slaves. Andy Smith was cognizant of these actions and realized a Union force was fortuitously present at Smithland. Its arrival had coincided with a troublesome time for area slaves.[18]

Confederate authorities were appropriating local slaves to construct defenses at Fort Donelson about forty miles south of Eddyville. Slaves dreaded the hard and dangerous labor at the forts, where disease was prevalent and the approaching winter would only aggravate the already poor living conditions. The situation was all the more onerous as slaves were separated from their families and forced to work in support of the Confederacy. Slave owners also disliked the appropriations. They lost the service of slaves whom they might eventually get back in a weakened condition or never recover. One owner complained the seizures of his slaves was "most villainous . . . the beginning of a despotism worse than any European monarchy."[19]

Confederate cavalry scoured the countryside in search of slaves to labor at the forts. Lieutenant Commander Phelps reported from the Cumberland River in December 1861, "Union men and secessionists alike are telling their slaves to escape to the woods to avoid the rebel cavalry engaged in seizing them. I am informed that union men have been seized and carried off to work in place of their escaped Slaves." Phelps protected one slave, belonging to a Confederate sympathizer, who had been warned by his owner's sons to escape: "Just before dark a Negro ran down to the river bank, near the boat, chased by bloodhounds in full cry after him, and begged to be taken on board. I sent a boat to his rescue, and learning by his statement confirmed by Kentuckians on board, that he was being chased by rebel cavalry—he had run 18 miles—with the intent of seizing him and taking him to Dover [Fort Donelson] to work upon the fortifications."[20]

On the morning of January 4 or 5, 1862, Andy Smith was gathering corn in a field with his nephews, William Smith's young sons, William and Harrison, when their father unexpectedly returned home. Andy recalled, "We looked down the road and thought that we recognized him, and when

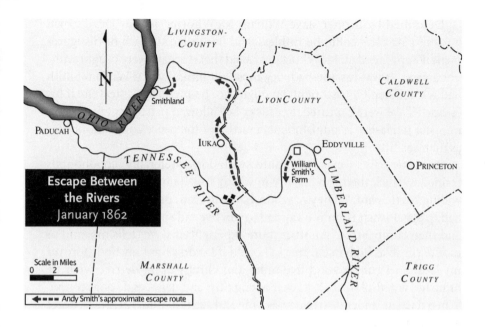

we drove the wagon to the barn, sure enough, it was he. We all shook hands with him." But Andy soon learned the purpose behind his owner's surprise visit. About 10:00 AM, William went to his house where another slave, Alf Bissell, "overheard a conversation between my owner and another man. Our owners had come to take us to the Confederate army."[21]

A while later, when William Smith dispatched his sons on an errand, Andy "suspected that he had sent them to get help to take us away." This must have been a chilling moment for him, realizing he was about to be put in shackles (possibly for the first time in his life), taken from his family, and placed under the control of Confederate soldiers to labor at Fort Donelson. He and Bissell immediately decided to escape. "We left the wagon with the team hitched and climbed over the fence into the woods. We knew that Smithlands Landing was about 25 miles away and we struck out for that point, where we expected to find the Union Army."[22]

Smith and Bissell entered a dangerous world the moment they went over the fence. They had to avoid not only Confederate cavalry but also patterollers—slave catchers or patrollers who roamed the countryside looking for runaway slaves, especially at night. Kentucky's counties were divided into districts, with each district scoured by a separate team of mounted patrollers. Thus, Smith and Bissell needed to avoid multiple patrols as their route took them southwest and then north through a portion of Lyon County and the length of Livingston County.

Described by former slave William McWhorter as the "Devil's own hosses," patrollers could be ruthless, and Smith faced death or disfigurement if apprehended. McWhorter recalled that if a slave were caught without a pass, "it was jus' too bad; dey most kilt him." Even if William Smith had wanted benign treatment, he might not be present to intervene if his escaped slave were captured. Kentucky law allowed patrol captains to administer ten lashes as punishment; a justice of the peace could administer as many as fifty.[23]

Runaway slaves were often hunted with dogs, preferably bloodhounds trained to track them, an activity in which slave James Green was an unwilling participant: "[D]ey . . . chooses me to train de dogs with. I's told I had to play I [was] runnin' away and to run five mile in any way [direction] and then climb a tree." Another more experienced slave "tells me kind of nice to climb as high in dat tree as I could if I didn't want my body tore off my legs. So I runs a good five miles and climbs up in de tree whar de branches is gettin' small. I sits dere a long time and den sees de dogs comin'. When dey gits under de tree dey sees me and starts barkin'. After dat I never got thinkin' of runnin' away."[24]

Being caught by slave trackers and dogs was a horrifying experience, as described by another slave, Henry Waldon, who depicted what awaited runaways like Smith if caught:

[They would] send for a man that had hounds to track you if you run away. They'd run you and bay you, and a white man would ride up there and say, "If you hit one of them hounds, I'll blow your brains out." He'd say "your damn brains." Them hounds would worry you and bite you and have you bloody as a beef, but you dassent to hit one of them. They would tell you to stand still and put your hands over your privates. I don't guess they'd have killed you but you believed they would. They wouldn't try to keep the hounds off of you; they would set them on you to see them bite you. Five or six or seven hounds bitin' you on every side and a man settin' on a horse holding a doubled shotgun on you.[25]

Keeping to woods as much as possible, Smith and Bissell traveled a longer route than they had anticipated. From his years of working on the river, Smith knew the distance of the Cumberland from the Bend, the river's turn near the northwestern corner of Between the Rivers, to Smithland to be roughly twenty-five miles, but William's farm was in the northeastern corner, forcing Smith and Bissell to follow the Cumberland's south bank for at least an additional five miles to reach the Bend. This first portion of Smith's escape route took him across land he would one day own.

During the afternoon, Smith and Bissell turned north to cross through a narrow neck of land, perhaps one and three-quarters miles wide, separating the Tennessee and Cumberland Rivers. There, in daylight, they had to bypass the first of three white communities on their route, a small settlement on the Tennessee River side of the neck. The increased risk of being seen or encountering dogs could only be mitigated by moving rapidly and staying in woods close to the Cumberland.

Beyond the settlement, the courses of the two rivers soon diverged from one another. Smith and Bissell kept the Cumberland over their right shoulders to turn northeast with the river for five more miles to arrive near the second white settlement, Iuka. Though Iuka consisted of only a small group of families, its farms were directly in the escapees' path and thus presented a greater danger than did the first settlement.

Their arrival coincided with an approaching weather front, its clouds obscuring the sun's twilight from the west and the first quarter moon in the east. In such low-light conditions, it was difficult to make out houses, farm buildings, and cultivated fields, but the darkness shielded their movements. Without the stars, the Cumberland was their only guide. They continued to avoid people and dogs by moving through woods close to the riverbank, which was now all the more important to keep in sight.[26]

"We had left home in our shirtsleeves," Smith related. "It was a bright, sunshiny morning," but "about nightfall it began to rain a slow drizzle." With the onset of "constant rain there came a sudden change in temperature and our clothes, having become soaking wet by the rain, began to freeze upon us."[27] Unpleasant as it was, the freezing rain may have been a boon to the two fugitives, diminishing chances of incidental contact with whites and discouraging searches by patterollers.

The escapees followed the twisting course of the river beyond Iuka, making the remainder of their journey nearly twice as long as the direct overland route to Smithland, but it provided a sure and less inhabited path to their destination. There was only one more settlement, Tiline, to avoid, and they moved around it late at night.

Averaging more than two miles an hour, they traveled at least fifteen hours to arrive at Smithland and locate the Union camp about 2:00 AM. Unwilling to expose themselves to potentially trigger-happy guards, the fugitives waited until daybreak to gain admittance, having "walked around the picket line half frozen."[28] Smith and Bissell had escaped assuming that if they could only reach the Union army, they would have a place of refuge; they had not realized the Union army guaranteed them neither sanctuary nor freedom.

Waiting outside the picket line of the 41st Illinois Volunteer Infantry, they might not have been so hopeful had they known the fates of other fugitive slaves who had recently surrendered to the regiment. At Paducah the previous December, three lieutenants of the 41st "gave up fugitive slaves who had placed themselves under their care to the ... custody of their owners, and consented to receive ... sums varying from one hundred and thirty to twenty dollars each. In one case, the negroes (two of them) were decoyed from the camp lines under pretense of being put over on the Illinois side, and there delivered to their master."[29]

Escape had special peril for people enslaved in the border states, where federal authorities were committed to slavery's protection, both officially and personally. The North's military leadership and most of the thousands of volunteer soldiers saw themselves engaged in a war to save the Union, not to destroy an institution recognized by the Constitution they had sworn to uphold. Accentuating Kentucky's perilous conditions, the state's commanding brigadier generals—Robert Anderson (of Fort Sumter fame), William T. Sherman, and Don Carlos Buell—all endorsed slavery, and slave owners filled Kentucky's Union regiments.[30]

Still, there were officers and men who opposed slavery, and abolitionist sentiment was strong in some of the volunteer regiments. Over time, exposure to the evils of slavery converted others. Efforts were made to shelter escaped slaves, but the reasons for doing so were often a mixture of humanitarianism and self-interest: officers and men quickly discovered that escaped slaves were marvelous servants.[31]

In the absence of owners or their agents arriving to recapture them, fugitive slaves like Smith could claim to be free and hope to blend in at army camps with other refugees, a mix of people including free blacks, escaped slaves from Confederate states, and escaped slaves from Kentucky, some belonging to Confederate sympathizers, others to loyal Unionists.

In late November 1861, however, just seven weeks before Smith and Bissell arrived at the Union picket line in Smithland, western Kentucky came under the authority of Major General Henry Wager Halleck, commander of the new Department of the Missouri. Halleck was sensitive to the political quagmire the fugitive slave issue posed for the army and the Lincoln administration.

Sheltering slaves might precipitate a political crisis and turn border states against the Union, but returning slaves to their owners was unpopular with many supporters of the president's war effort, including the Republican leadership in Congress. Halleck, hoping to avoid the problem by keeping the army and fugitives apart, ordered that no escaped slaves were to "be hereafter permitted to enter the lines of any camp or of any forces on the march, and that any now within such lines be immediately excluded therefrom."[32]

There was resistance to Halleck's order within the army, and compliance was uneven as fugitive slaves continued to pour through Union lines followed by owners demanding access to army camps to recover their property. Some officers persevered in efforts to protect escaped slaves while others were eager to return them. Fugitives who made their way to camps housing Kentucky's Union regiments discovered they had merely fled into the clutches of slave owners. It was simply a matter of chance whether escaped slaves found soldiers who would help them, turn them away, or return them to slavery.

Dr. John Warner. (*John Warner IV*)

In the morning, after having spent the night in the freezing rain, and as soon as it was light enough to approach the Union camp safely, Smith and Bissell walked up to pickets of the 41st Illinois, unaware the soldiers were ordered not to admit them. Luckily, the pickets disobeyed their orders. Escorted to Captain Benjamin B. Bacon, the two men were warmed, fed, and allowed to remain. Shortly thereafter, Smith met Major John Warner.

Warner, a volunteer from Clinton, Illinois, commanded the two companies of the 41st Illinois assigned to Smithland. It was here Smith began his long association with Warner, who undoubtedly sought to utilize Smith's knowledge of the area. When the companies rejoined the remainder of the regiment at Paducah, Smith and Bissell accompanied them. Warner protected Smith by hiring him as a personal servant, and Bissell similarly found protection and employment as the servant to Colonel Isaac C. Pugh, the 41st's commander.[33]

Andy Smith and Alf Bissell were indeed fortunate to have been found by soldiers who would protect them. We do not know if William Smith attempted their recovery, but U. S. Grant's forces were preparing to advance south, taking the escaped slaves out of the state and enabling them to disappear in the confusion.

CHAPTER 2

FORT HENRY, FORT DONELSON, AND SHILOH

February–April 1862

ANDY SMITH AND ALF BISSELL settled in with the 41st Illinois Volunteer Infantry as Ulysses S. Grant was preparing his first campaign of the war. The seizure of Fort Henry on the Tennessee River and Fort Donelson on the Cumberland River in western Tennessee would open the middle South to invasion. Grant's initial objective was to capture Fort Henry together with Fort Heiman, an unfinished earthwork high on the bluffs of the Tennessee River's west bank. Once these forts were secured, Union forces were to converge on Fort Donelson. The 41st Illinois would participate in the campaign, assigned to Colonel John McArthur's brigade. Ironically, Smith and Bissell found themselves going to Fort Donelson after all.

Grant's operation commenced on February 3, 1862, a mild winter day that quickly turned cold with the approach of thunderstorms in the evening. Awaiting their transport, Smith and Bissell endured the inclement weather with the 41st Illinois for more than twenty-four hours, finally boarding the steamer *Minnehaha* about 10:00 PM on February 4.[1] Away from home for the first time in their lives, seeing a world previously denied to them, and traveling with an army of invasion—one can only imagine what their thoughts must have been, feelings likely shared by the soldiers who, typically, had not traveled far from their own homes before the war.

They voyaged through storms, with the boat so crowded men had no place to sleep. Many gave up any hope of rest or staying dry and chose to stand and talk all night with fellow soldiers, but Smith and Bissell likely had better accommodations as they attended Major Warner and Colonel Pugh. When dawn broke through overcast skies, the *Minnehaha's* passengers found themselves on the Tennessee River surrounded by hills suspended in fog.[2]

Three miles north of Fort Heiman, they disembarked with Brigadier General C. F. Smith's troops into deep mud on the Tennessee's west bank. The mud, with the reddish tinge characteristic of much southern soil, would be an obstacle to Union troop movements and created difficult living conditions, "No bottom!" being the cry as soldiers trudged among their tents.[3]

Heavy rain returned that night, exacerbating the misery of those in both armies. As unpleasant as the rain made conditions for Union soldiers, the situation was worse for the Confederates. Fort Henry had been constructed on low ground. Recent rains had flooded the fort, and the river was continuing to rise,[4] leaving many of its defenders literally in water up to their knees.

Confederate Brigadier General Lloyd Tilghman, struggling to deal with the dual calamities of invasion and flooding, decided to withdraw his forces first from Fort Heiman and then from Fort Henry to redeploy to Fort Donelson. Tilghman remained behind with fewer than ninety men to delay the Union advance with artillery, allowing the remainder of Fort Henry's garrison to escape early on February 6. That morning, to the relief of both sides, the sky cleared and a breeze arose strong enough to sweep away smoke from cannon fire and afford artillerists unobstructed views.[5]

Unaware Tilghman's garrison was evacuating, Grant did not commence operations until 11:00 AM. He ordered the infantry to advance south along both banks of the Tennessee to escort Flag Officer Andrew H. Foote's gunboats as they steamed toward Fort Henry. On the west bank, Andy Smith and Alf Bissell accompanied the 41st Illinois as part of C. F. Smith's column, advancing up a road paralleling the river, striving to keep pace with Foote's ironclads.[6]

One of the Union gunboats occasionally fired shells into the woods ahead of the column, bringing cheers from the men each time. For an hour and a half, the soldiers moved through standing water and knee-deep mud. Fording backwaters and bridging as needed, the column followed a route into dense woods, blocking the men's view of the river as Foote's ironclads—the *St. Louis, Carondelet, Cincinnati,* and *Essex*—closed on Fort

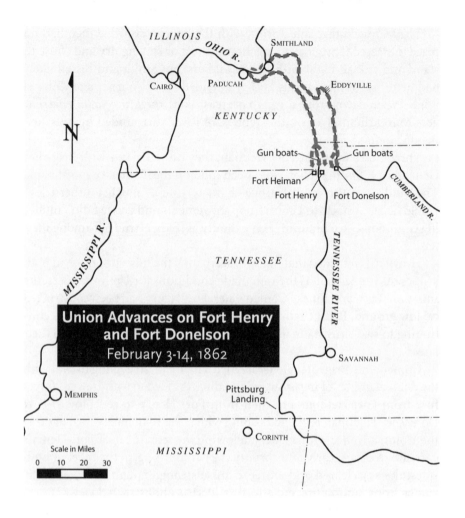

Henry. Around noon the ironclads, staying abreast, spread out across the river to form a line of battle.[7]

Suddenly, the men in C. F. Smith's command were "startled by the report of a heavy gun."[8] The *Cincinnati* had begun to shell Fort Henry, inaugurating the artillery battle between the gunboats and the fort—a conflict occurring beside the men in C. F. Smith's column that they could not see. Thus it was by sound, a cacophony of cannon fire, that Andy Smith experienced his first battle—a noncombatant unable to witness horrific scenes unfolding nearby, yet close enough to be in danger.

Brigadier General Lew Wallace, riding near the head of the column, found the noise unrelenting: "[W]ith the cannonading of the fleet and that of the fort, the interchange became an almost unintermittent thunder. . . . And to make the situation more peculiar, we could see nothing of the fight on the river—to us hastening through the woods, it was all smoke, sound, and fury." The climactic moment was a tremendous eruption and repercussion signaling one of the gunboats had received a devastating hit, but neither Andy Smith nor anyone else could know a Confederate shell had disabled the *Essex*, exploding one of its boilers and scalding more than thirty officers and crew.[9]

The gunboats moved into position between Fort Henry and C. F. Smith's column, placing his men in the Confederate line of fire, but fortunately the artillerists overelevated their guns. Andy Smith could look overhead and see the shells "roaring and screaming into the tree-tops, darkening the air with fragments of limbs." The infantry column moved away from the river, passing around Fort Heiman to attack its west side. Finally, at a turn in the road, the fort came into view. C. F. Smith reined in his horse, ordered a halt, and listened. Then he realized, "The firing has stopped."[10]

Fort Henry's artillery had scored fifty-nine hits against the Union ironclads but had succeeded in disabling only the *Essex*. In exchange, Union fire soon reduced the Confederates to just four serviceable guns. Tilghman raised a white flag, obligating the surrender of himself and his small band of defenders, and ordered an officer to strike the Confederate colors. Flooding required Union Commander Henry Walke to enter Fort Henry by boat to take its surrender and raise the US flag.[11]

Confederate cavalry at Fort Heiman had escaped only minutes before the arrival of C. F. Smith's troops. Near the Confederate headquarters tent, Lew Wallace found dinner waiting to be served. A boiling kettle contained "a block of fresh pork 'done to a turn.' By the kettle a pot simmered, spraying the air with the aroma of coffee. A pone of corn-bread freshly baked adorned a bench nearby." Before sharing the Confederates' meal with C. F. Smith, Wallace looked down to see the Stars and Stripes flying over at Fort Henry. Andy Smith and Alf Bissell later witnessed the scene, providing at least some images for the battle they had only heard.[12]

Private Job Roberts and others in the 41st Illinois were not as fortunate as the generals. Ordered to stack their knapsacks during the bombardment so they might move more quickly, they arrived at Fort Heiman "without blankets or tents," Roberts wrote. This was especially unpleasant as "the night was cold and stormy. We had been without sleep for three nights and in order to make the best of a bad case, we built fires of log rails and bushes. . . . I slept standing with the others that did not have a hotel."[13]

Because Smith and Bissell accompanied officers, they again likely had better sleeping arrangements than did Roberts and the other soldiers. Colonel Pugh was exhausted as well, writing to his wife, "I lost five nights sleep[,] that is I did not sleep more than five or six hours in that time," but "the men are generly in good health & fine spirits." Pugh also noted the men were "vexed a little that the boats done all the work at the fort & the enemy run away on this side but I expect thy will have their curiosity satisfied before this thing is setled."[14]

SMITH AND BISSELL BEGAN their journey to Fort Donelson on the morning of February 12. They left Fort Heiman to cross over the Tennessee River with the 41st Illinois on an improvised bridge of log poles and brush. Once ashore on higher ground, the 41st formed with Colonel McArthur's brigade at the rear of Grant's army. Union troops began to advance in long columns on narrow roads passing through the wooded area Between the Rivers separating Fort Henry from Fort Donelson.[15]

It was a pleasant march in warm weather. Along the way, soldiers captured small parties of Confederates. One group of prisoners included a sutler from whom the 41st liberated a treat: boxes of gingerbread. Private Roberts and his fellow soldiers "made a very good marching column with the squares of ginger bread hanging on the bayonet[s] of the gun[s] as we marched on to Fort Donelson."

For Andy Smith and the men of the 41st, the march to Fort Donelson in warm weather with their gingerbread surprise would be the highlight of their experience for the next few days. They soon encountered wounded along their path, leading Job Roberts to reflect, "Here I was taught for the first time what war was for."[16]

As Grant's columns emerged from the woods, Smith and Bissell saw a portion of the extensive earthworks on which they might have been forced to labor had they not escaped: a two-and-a-half-mile ring of rifle pits encompassing the fort, protected by abatis (trees felled so their tops lay pointed outward with their limbs trimmed and pointed).

They were not yet able to see the other earthworks to which they might have been consigned. Fort Donelson sat on a hill near the river surrounded by earthen walls ten feet high and nearly ten feet thick at the base. The most menacing structure slaves worked to build lay beyond the fort: river batteries carved into the high bluff on the Cumberland's west bank then mounting twelve guns.

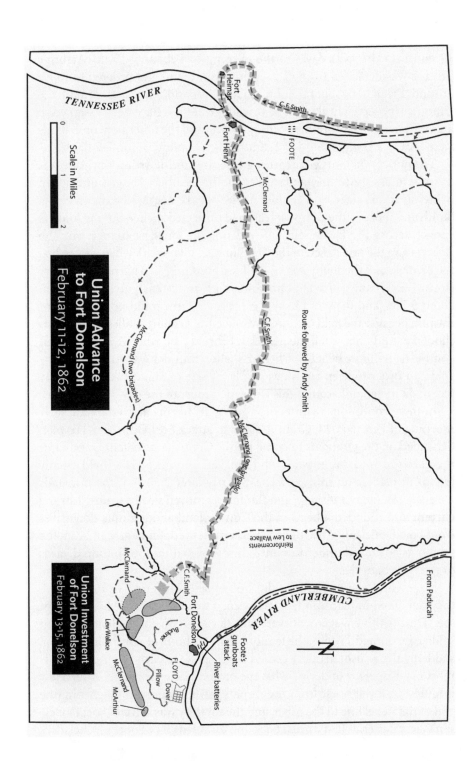

Union Advance
to Fort Donelson
February 11-12, 1862

Union Investment
of Fort Donelson
February 13-15, 1862

TENNESSEE RIVER

Scale in Miles

Fort
Heiman

Fort Henry

McClernand

FOOTE

C.F. Smith

McClernand (two brigades)

C.F. Smith

Route followed by Andy Smith

McClernand (one brigade)

Reinforcements
to Lew Wallace

From Paducah

CUMBERLAND RIVER

McClernand

Lew Wallace

C.F. Smith

Fort Donelson

Buckner

FLOYD

Pillow

Dover

McClernand

McArthur

Foote's
gunboats
attack

River batteries

N

Smith and Bissell continued with the 41st Illinois the night of February 12 and into the next day. On the evening of February 13, McArthur's brigade was detached from C. F. Smith's command and ordered to move around Brigadier General John A. McClernand's lines to defend the Union's exposed right flank. The brigade could not have been assigned to a more dangerous position, so Smith, Bissell, and the other noncombatants were sent to a camp behind C. F. Smith's lines on the Union left flank.[17]

The noncombatants were fortunate because as McArthur's brigade was moving to assist McClernand's division, the weather changed drastically, bringing snow, sleet, and temperatures twenty degrees below freezing. Smith and those in the camps at least had protected shelter, but the soldiers spread across the battlefield enjoyed not the smallest luxury. For Job Roberts and the other men in the 41st Illinois, "It was dark when we reached the bivouac and the night was . . . cold, without fire. . . . This night was very stormy. . . . It commenced to rain about dark and it was a great sleet storm about 9 PM, and the wind blew a great gale." Fires could not be used for warmth because the light or smoke would attract enemy artillery and sharpshooter rounds. Snow fell the next day, February 14, when Roberts and his comrades, without benefit of fire or shelter, found a way to fight off the cold: "In order to keep warm, we made a circle of about twenty to thirty feet in diameter and around this we trotted most of the day."[18]

In these conditions, with Foote's gunboats having arrived by the early morning of February 14, Grant decided to attack Fort Donelson. His plan depended on the gunboats to bombard the Confederate defenses and force the garrison into submission while his surrounding army held enemy troops in place, preventing escape. Shortly after 2:30 PM, the ironclads *Louisville*, *St. Louis*, *Pittsburg*, and *Carondelet* moved slowly against a strong current and rounded a bend in the Cumberland about a mile downriver from Fort Donelson. An artillery duel commenced; for nearly an hour, the gunboats advanced under fire until they were within four hundred yards of the river batteries.

Meanwhile, the two armies did not engage. Shivering from the cold, they remained in place, and Smith listened to another battle he could not see. "During this engagement every gun along our lines was silent," a Union soldier recounted. "After a little more than an hour of continuous firing, suddenly the roar of artillery ceased. Men spoke to each other quietly, almost in whispers, wondering what the ominous silence meant. After a few minutes . . . a yell burst from the throats of thousands, ringing from one end of the Rebel line to the other, and the mystery was solved." Fort Donelson's river batteries had turned back and disabled all of Foote's ironclads.[19]

For the remainder of the fighting at Fort Donelson, Smith and Bissell were in relative safety behind the lines in C. F. Smith's camps, but the same would not be true for their companions in the 41st Illinois. After dark, about 7:00 PM on February 14, McArthur's brigade moved farther into an exposed position on McClernand's far right flank. At daybreak on February 15, more than six thousand Confederates hit McArthur's and McClernand's brigades. The attackers included men from Smith's home of Lyon County who assailed McClernand's flank from two directions: the 8th Kentucky Infantry from the left, and Company G of the 1st Kentucky Cavalry, serving in Lieutenant Colonel Nathan Bedford Forrest's command, from the right.[20]

The Confederate breakout ultimately failed, and their leaders decided to surrender Fort Donelson, but several thousand of its garrison determined to escape, including most of the cavalry, who were led out of the fort before daylight by Forrest. A few cavalry officers chose to remain and surrender their commands, including Captain Morrison D. Wilcox of Company G of the 1st Kentucky Cavalry. Wilcox's decision was not universally popular, and some men of Company G did manage to slip away, including Private William J. Stone.[21]

At daybreak on Sunday, February 16, the Confederates raised a white flag over Fort Donelson. As Union soldiers moved into Donelson's environs, warmer temperatures melted the snow, contributing to the return of the ubiquitous red mud that made conditions miserable for all.

McArthur's brigade was among those assigned to guard prisoners, but Union supervision was not overly strict. Confederates were permitted to go outside the lines to bury their dead, and mingling occurred between the soldiers of both armies, allowing Smith to have a chance encounter: "I shook hands with the captain of my master's company about 11 o'clock Sunday morning. Quite a number of the men had been reared around my home town of Eddyville, Ky." Smith shook hands with Company G's Captain Wilcox, but his master was not among the prisoners. If William Smith had been with his company at Fort Donelson, he was among those who escaped with William J. Stone. Only a few hundred yards may have separated master and former slave, but, symbolic of the change the nation was undergoing, it might as well have been miles. William Smith would not be recovering this runaway.[22]

FOLLOWING THE SURRENDER of Fort Donelson, Smith recalled, "we laid around the camp a week or so then marched down [to] the Tennessee River and took boats to Savannah, Tenn., just below Pittsburg Landing." Actually, the 41st Illinois remained in the area of Fort Donelson a couple of weeks longer than Smith remembered. Reassigned to the 1st Brigade of Brigadier General Stephen A. Hurlbut's 4th Division, the regiment returned to the Tennessee River on March 9 to board the steamer *Aleck Scott* for its trip south with Ulysses S. Grant's army to Shiloh.[23]

Smith and Bissell traveled with an army of soldiers who, predominately, having yet to fight, were eager to experience battle. Many remained frustrated by missed opportunities at either Fort Henry, where the navy had done the fighting, or at Fort Donelson, where fewer than half of the troops had engaged in actual combat. Similarly, Smith and Bissell were on the fringes of military actions at Fort Henry and Fort Donelson, and Smith, at least, remained inquisitive about the experience of combat. The week-long trip to Shiloh allowed ample time for Smith, as well as green soldiers eager "to see the elephant," to think about the adventure ahead, one that would soon assuage everyone's curiosity.

Just two months after escaping slavery, Smith found himself part of an immense operation, the war's largest on western rivers, entailing 173 transports and their gunboat escorts. The travelers were generally in high spirits on their voyage south in delightful weather, and Job Roberts enjoyed the musical accompaniment. "Some [of the steamers] had calliopes and they played the 'Starry Flag,' 'The Red, White, and Blue,' 'The Old Folks at Home,' 'The Girls I Left at Home,' 'My Old Kentucky Home, Far Away,' and a number of other songs." Roberts also took in the scenery. "The weather is fine, the birds singing and all things are beautiful in the soft air on these spring days in this southern clime. Up the river we go. . . . The boats are loaded to their capacity with soldiers of all kinds, with all their supplies for all branches of the service. . . . I will say here that there were no state rooms for the privates. We had to make our beds on the cabin floor, for anything is good enough for the private to sleep on. Anything is good enough to eat also."[24]

Unlike the officers, who had sleeping accommodations and hot meals, troops had to subsist on uncooked food and river water, the ingestion of which contributed to diarrhea that quickly became endemic in Grant's army. Given their proximity to Major Warner and Colonel Pugh, Smith and Bissell likely managed to share in the hot meals available to officers, but virtually all those at Shiloh eventually endured intestinal distress. "[F]or about six weeks," Private Leander Stillwell, 61st Illinois Volunteer Infantry, recalled, "everybody suffered, more or less, the difference being only in degree."[25]

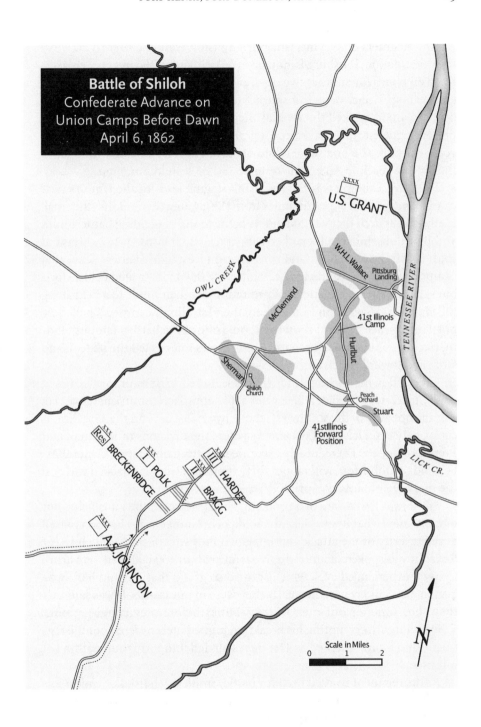

Battle of Shiloh
Confederate Advance on
Union Camps Before Dawn
April 6, 1862

U.S. GRANT

OWL CREEK

W.H.L.Wallace

Pittsburg Landing

McClernand

41st Illinois Camp

Hurlbut

Sherman

TENNESSEE RIVER

Shiloh Church

Peach Orchard

Stuart

41st Illinois Forward Position

LICK CR.

BRECKENRIDGE

Res.

I POLK

II

III HARDEE

BRAGG

A.S.JOHNSON

Scale in Miles
0   1   2

N

The steamers conveying Hurlbut's division were the first to arrive at their destination, Pittsburg Landing, on March 15, but the troops were confined on board for another two days, awaiting the return of Brigadier General William T. Sherman's transports from a mission upstream. Meanwhile, other steamers packed the river as they converged on Pittsburg Landing, presenting what must have been a grand sight for Smith to observe after years working as a boatman: a line of steamers at a standstill, "[a]s far as the eye can reach . . . their smokestacks can be seen looming up."[26]

Pittsburg Landing was the riverbank staging area for the Union's next campaign. Two and a quarter miles from the landing was Shiloh—the small Methodist church that would lend its name to the impending battle. Smith and Bissell disembarked together with approximately forty-two thousand soldiers of Grant's command, dispersing to establish widely separated camps on a heavily wooded plateau intersected with cultivated fields. Hurlbut's division moved inland southwest for more than a mile to a field along the Hamburg–Savannah Road. There the 41st Illinois camped a half-mile north of a peach orchard soon to become one of the battle's famous landmarks. East of the peach orchard, deep ravines intersected the plateau and stretched toward the river.

Creeks flowing through marsh and scattered ravines protected much of the plateau's perimeter. The one viable approach for an enemy attack was the opening to the southwest, about two miles beyond the 41st Illinois camp, between Lick and Owl Creeks where the divisions of Sherman and Prentiss camped. There, nearly three weeks later, Confederate General Albert Sidney Johnston, with about forty thousand troops, attacked early on the morning of Sunday, April 6.

Smith was first aware of a problem when "we heard the guns firing but did not know what it was." Like the soldiers in Grant's army, he was amazed at the severity of the attack and imagined they were facing a much larger force: "It was spoken of among us . . . as an army of 150,000 men—an army, to my inexperienced eyes, which seemed so grand that it could hardly be beaten. On Sunday morning early they were in our camps. It was said that they shot some of our men in their bunks before they could get out." Colonel Pugh, interrupting his breakfast, immediately ordered out the regiment, and Smith watched as 41st men scurried into formation within ten minutes.[27]

As the regiment readied itself for battle, Smith saw hordes of Union soldiers running through the camp in flight from the front lines and heading in the direction of Pittsburg Landing. Intermingled among these troops were the walking wounded, "men . . . straggling through the wood, singly, and in squads. Some with blood running from their heads, walking briskly. Others pale, from loss of blood, leaning on their comrades for support."[28]

Smith remained in camp as the 41st Illinois joined Hurlbut's brigades about 8:00 AM and formed battle lines to advance against the flow of frightened and wounded troops and toward the sound of combat. They went forward for about half a mile, halting their line beyond the peach orchard on the far side of a cotton field. Once again, the 41st Illinois was placed on a flank of the Union line, this time on the left of Hurlbut's command. A quarter-mile farther east, near the river, Colonel David Stuart's two brigades held the Union's far left flank. Hurlbut's troops began exchanging artillery and skirmishing fire with Confederates in the woods ahead.[29]

The Confederates were advancing on a three-mile front, but the Union left flank was the focus of General Albert Sidney Johnston's attack. If the brigades of Hurlbut and Stuart did not hold their positions, Johnston's troops could envelop the Union left and cut Grant's army off from Pittsburg Landing. With a Confederate force blocking its line of retreat and reinforcement, Grant's command would be in a desperate strait. Meanwhile, Sherman's and McClernand's divisions engaged in the other critical fight that day, on their right flank, where Confederates were slowly driving Union troops from the vicinity of Shiloh Church.

The Confederate movement against the Union left flank became evident to Hurlbut when he saw "the glimmer of bayonets on the left and front" of the 41st's position. He pulled the 41st and the remainder of its brigade back one hundred yards to establish another line in front of the peach orchard. Hurlbut then placed Colonel Pugh in command of the 1st Brigade, and Lieutenant Colonel Ansel Tupper took command of the 41st Illinois. Tupper strengthened the new line, ordering his troops to rip down nearby fences and pile up the rails to create a breastwork so soldiers might fight behind it from prone positions. About this time, Andy Smith went "out on the field just to look at the soldiers."[30]

Smith had wanted to see the battle, but the battlefield was a particularly dangerous place for him. As a black man with Union forces, he was a prime target for Confederates. If he were captured, it meant at the least a return to slavery, but Smith did not want to leave. Major Warner "told Andy to keep him in sight with a canteen of water, and if he . . . should fall, to come to him with water." Warner was forced to dismount when his horse was wounded, "and turning around found Andy standing close to him and giving the wounded horse to Andy, told him to take it to the rear and stay there." Smith began to move away with the horse, and, he later recalled, "as

I was doing so I was knocked down by a [minié] ball. This was my first wound, though nothing serious." He must have been hit by a spent round that "struck me in [my] right temple and knocked me down but did not enter my head."[31]

As Smith returned to camp, Brigadier General John McArthur's 9th and 12th Illinois Volunteer Infantry Regiments arrived about 10:30 AM, soon followed by the 50th Illinois Volunteer Infantry. These regiments deployed on the left of the 41st Illinois and helped fill the gap between Hurlbut and Colonel Stuart's brigades on the Union far left flank.

Thus strengthened, Hurlbut's command continued to hold its line in front of the peach orchard while, Private Job Roberts related, the regiment engaged "in a desperate struggle. They [the Confederates] charged and charged until they had made five charges at this time. I was now getting very tired, for we had been out in the early morning and had been fighting for about four hours, loading our guns and firing as fast as we knew how."[32] Colonel Tupper was killed, shot through both temples by a musket ball, and Major Warner assumed command of the 41st.

Warner caught and mounted a riderless horse that had run out between the lines from the Confederate side. When this horse, too, was wounded, Warner "again dismounted and turning, found Smith standing close to him again and handing the second horse to Smith, told him to take it back and keep out of danger."[33] Smith resisted:

> "Maj. Warner saw that the fight was raging and he told me to go to the rear, but [I] begged . . . to stay and watch the soldiers fight a little longer. After he saw that he was in danger of being killed he told me where he lived and asked me to promise to take his trunk to Clinton, Ill., to his family, and assured me that I would be well taken care of. After much persuasion I took his horse and started to the rear. I was in full view of the whole Southern army. When I had gone about 50 yards from him he called to me, 'Hurry: don't stop, but go like hell!'"[34]

Smith turned to hurry away from the fighting. Then he felt a tremendous impact: "a round ball struck me in or about my left temple entering my head . . . This is the ball that hurt me." This round, the second to hit him that day, traveled under the skin around the outside of his skull and lodged in the center of his forehead: "I went back to the hospital and the doctor took the ball out and screwed a piece of sponge in my forehead." Smith later told his family that "the [doctor] sat down and I laid my head in his lap and he cut it out. This being the only medical attention I ever received." The doctor inserted the sponge into the wound over Smith's ear, forced it along the bullet's path, and removed it through the incision. Although shot twice in one day, Smith was lucky indeed. Except for a distinctive scar in the middle of his forehead, he suffered no lasting effects. Years later, he wrote to Burt Wilder, "The scar can be plainly seen where the ball entered my head and where it was taken out."[35]

While Smith was receiving medical treatment that afternoon, the Union left flank was collapsing. Stuart's brigades were "driven in" and withdrew by 3:00 PM. Job Roberts watched as the flank crumbled: "I'll tell you it look[ed] very bad for Uncle Sam about that time.... [We were] Fighting like Trojans and to see the Ninth and Twelfth Illinois with their flag flying, their battle line afire and again see them double quick to the rear leaving the field covered with their dead and wounded. It makes my heart ache today, although years have passed since then." The 50th Illinois also abandoned the field, losing "Seventy-nine men killed and wounded, and that in fifteen moments time.... The rebels came on us before we knew it. The undergrowth being so thick we could not see them until they got within twenty yards of us."[36]

Job Roberts surveyed the scene, "the woods on fire, the Rebels charging, and the Ninth and Twelfth Illinois going to the rear. It looked like I would soon be taken in but we kept throwing lead at them from our front line.... At last General Hurlbut ordered [us] to fall back." Major Warner guided the 41st's withdrawal, passing through the camp they had left that morning. In anticipation of returning to the fight, he directed the men to a brook to clean their fouled weapons and replenish ammunition.[37]

There would be no return to the battlefield that day. By 4:00 PM, the Confederates were moving to consolidate their success. The Union right had also given way as Sherman's and McClernand's divisions fell back toward Pittsburg Landing. Soon after 5:00 PM, Confederates closed behind the regiments remaining near the center of the Union line and cut off their escape. These troops had no choice but to surrender.

The Confederates had attacked relentlessly throughout the day and nearly driven the Union army off the field, but their battle plan ultimately failed. Instead of driving the Union forces away from their base at Pittsburg Landing, the Confederate attack had driven them back to their base, where they could be supplied and reinforced.

Grant's retreating soldiers halted to establish a strong defensive line extending about a mile and a half inland from Pittsburg Landing. Concentrated Union infantry and artillery fire gave the defenders an advantage over attacking Confederates, but the Confederates opened a terrifying, two-hour artillery barrage against the Union position. After surviving in one of the most desperately contested areas in the battle, Smith endured this last stage of the Confederate assault with the 41st near the center of Grant's line. "[W]e were lying on our faces," a soldier of the regiment recalled, "the earth was trembling as though it was being convulsed by a heavy earthquake."[38]

On the morning of April 7, reinforced by the arrival of Major General Don Carlos Buell's thirty thousand troops of the Army of the Ohio, Grant launched an attack that battered the exhausted Confederate army until it withdrew. The 41st Illinois participated, without Major Warner, who had been wounded. Smith likely remained with Warner and probably did not witness the second day's fighting.

The battlefield presented a gruesome aftermath to the Battle of Shiloh that Smith could not avoid, sights such as those described by Chaplain John M. Garner of the 18th Missouri Infantry. Smith, like Chaplain Garner, would have seen that when there was fighting in woods, artillery fire brought the canopy down on its victims, "timbers [were] torn down by shot and shell, piled on mangled men who lie here, not by scores but by hundreds. Union and rebel soldiers lie cross and pile in indiscriminate mass, and many of them partly covered with dirt and litter thrown upon them by plowing shot and exploding shells."[39]

Near the southern end of the battlefield Garner saw "[t]imber shot to splinters, dead men, dead horses and mules, wagons knocked to pieces, gun carriages demolished, clothing scattered on the ground, muskets and canteens here and there and, once in a while, a poor wounded soldier. . . . [T]he dead are in horrid conditions—bloated till the buttons have given way on their waistbands, bloody froth oozing from their mouths, flies buzzing about them like bees and the air charged with putrid odors."[40]

Smith would also have discovered soldiers, perhaps some known to him, in conditions such as those Garner described: the bodies of two lieutenants from his regiment, each shot through the head, and another with a broken thigh, still alive, having lain for two days in the sun and the rain; or at the Hornet's Nest, a friend, "shot just back of his right ear," and nearby, six men "almost in a pile were killed by the same shot from a rebel battery." Smith surely also observed soldiers, as did Garner, searching for their comrades, "moving about among the dead and narrowly peering into their faces."[41]

There were also especially horrible sights for Smith to witness, such as Garner reported when hearing "someone in deep distress," one of Hurlbut's soldiers, "wildly calling out 'Seventeenth Kentucky!' A poor federal in a broken down ambulance—team killed and driver gone . . . and the soldier

"The Battle of Pittsburg Landing, The Engagement of the Left Wing," *Supplement to Frank Leslie's Illustrated Newspaper*, May 17, 1862. The 41st Illinois formed part of the Union defense line in front of the peach orchard that can be seen in the center background of this illustration (note the placement of battle flags). These Union troops were engaged with Confederate forces in the woods on the far side of the open field where clouds of smoke emanated from Confederate artillery. Andy Smith moved from the tree line to the right and rear of the peach orchard when he twice ventured forward to the position of the 41st Illinois and would have seen the engagement represented in this scene. But Andy Smith did not see a Union line as presented in the foreground extending left from the peach orchard. This was the artist's attempt to compress other Union actions that day into the image. (*Library of Congress*)

smeared with blood and dirt—both legs and one lower arm shot off, but all hanging to him by leaders [tendons] and strips of torn flesh. Bones of legs and arm gone. In this condition how large his feet and hand look! All that we can get him to say is that he belongs to the 17th Kentucky and he wants some of his regiment to come to him. By some oversight he has been here a long time. And can he survive? Possibly, but hardly."[42]

Soldiers were not the only victims for Smith to encounter. The suffering of horses and mules was appalling, as Garner also observed: "There you can see a gun carriage knocked to pieces; three of the horses lie there dead and the fourth one stands hitched to the wreck by one tug, quivering with pain, a large portion of one ham having been shot away, and under one of the dead horses lies his rider, fatally crushed but still alive!"[43]

On Thursday, after burying its dead, the army disposed of the remains of horses and mules, a sickening experience for Smith and every soldier remaining at Shiloh. Chaplain Garner related, "[T]he last item in the order, was to clear the field of dead animals and all other offensive debris. A shocking undertaking. The dead animals were drawn together in piles, and ricks of logs, limbs and leaves stacked on them; and then fire was applied. It is safe to say there were hundreds of such fires in full blast at the same time. The fumes from such quantities of burning, putrid flesh were almost unbearable, and it took so long to reduce these piles to ashes!"[44]

At Shiloh, Andy Smith had found himself in the midst of one of the most terrible battles of the Civil War. Soon afterward, he traveled to the home of Major Warner in the free state of Illinois. There, without blame or reproach, he could have turned his back on the horrors of war and, with the protection of the Warner family, made a new life for himself in the North. Instead, he would volunteer to fight for the Union and against the life he had left behind.

CHAPTER 3

ILLINOIS TO NORTH CAROLINA

April 1862–July 1863

A NDY SMITH MAY HAVE PLAYED an unwitting role in moving his life to its next stage in Illinois when he captured an old goose and prepared it as a fine meal for Major Warner. Whether it was that meal or the same affliction many in the army suffered that spring from bad water, the major soon suffered a debilitating intestinal disorder requiring a leave of absence to recover at his home in Clinton, Illinois—an opportunity Warner used to smuggle Smith out of the South.[1] In mid-April 1862, Smith parted with Alf Bissell (who stayed behind with Colonel Pugh) to journey north with Warner on one of the many steamers transporting casualties from Shiloh to Cairo, Illinois, the southern terminus of the Illinois Central Railroad.

At Cairo, Smith stepped onto free soil for the first time in his life—but more likely he stepped onto free mud. Devoid of trees, hot, humid, and rank with foul odors from stagnant water and dead animals in the streets, Cairo's squalor was infamous among travelers—"the biggest mudhole in the country" according to an army physician who was there in April. Cairo was built on low ground at the confluence of the Ohio and Mississippi Rivers; flooding was a persistent problem, and the town's existence depended on its massive levee. Before they could board the train, Smith and Warner had to pass "cargo loads of wounded and sick and disabled soldiers, who lay for hours upon the jetty, waiting for transport northward" and "piles . . . of coffins" from Shiloh "with the dead men's names inscribed upon them, left standing in front of the railway offices."[2]

Smith might have come to a free state, but racist attitudes were common, and much of wartime Illinois was chaotic and violent. Bordered by two loyal slave states, Illinois had long served as a prime destination for escaped slaves and slave catchers from Kentucky and Missouri. Support for the South and slavery was strong in southern and western Illinois. Even in areas staunchly loyal to the Union, racism often prevailed. Encounters with whites in Illinois were, therefore, uncertain for fugitive slaves. As in the border states, they could not know if the next person they met would assist them, leave them alone, or try to reenslave them.

Further complicating matters for Smith, his presence in Illinois was illegal. Major Warner had violated the Illinois exclusion law, designed to prevent black immigration, when he brought Smith into the state. White violators of the law were subject to fines of $100 to $500 and imprisonment for one year; blacks faced fines of $50. If unable to pay the fine, their labor was to be sold at public auction, the work to be exacted until the fine was paid in full. Enforcement of the law was uneven and largely ignored in some areas, especially in northern regions of the state, but the act was popular with voters. They affirmed a new exclusion provision in 1862 by a greater than two-to-one majority, and citizen complaints could move authorities to enforce the law when contrabands or free blacks arrived in a locality.[3]

Major Warner appears to have been little concerned about violating the law, trusting that his standing in the community and his political alliances would shield him and Smith from the law's application. Absent such protection, the legal niceties of Northern states mattered little to escaping slaves. It was enough to know that on reaching a free state, their flight from slavery was not finished, and they had to avoid both slave catchers and legal authorities to maintain their freedom.

Threats to Smith's safety were not absent in north-central Illinois. Minorities of Copperheads were to be found, including Knights of the Golden Circle in Randolph, just twelve miles north of Clinton. Other proslavery Democrats were scattered about the countryside and in Bloomington, twenty-two miles north, but a strong antislavery Republican presence served to curb the excesses of these groups in Clinton and Bloomington. Slave catchers roaming the cities, towns, and surrounding rural areas were not accepted as in southern and western Illinois. A month before Smith's arrival at Warner's home, the *Bloomington (IL) Daily Pantagraph* castigated a slave catcher lurking in the vicinity to kidnap "a little mulatto boy about

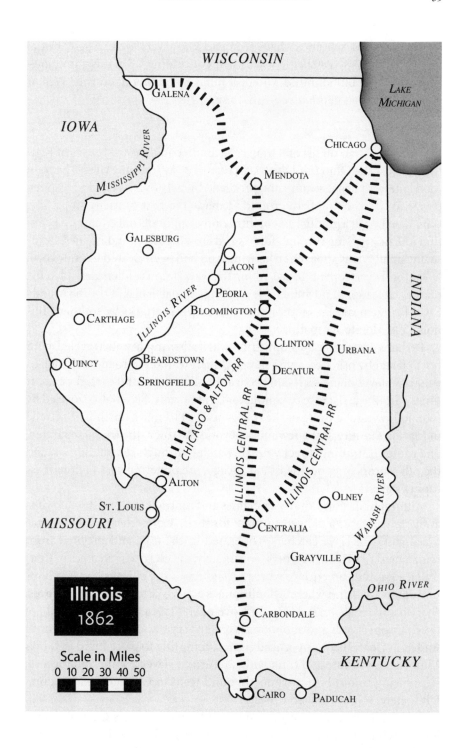

WISCONSIN

LAKE
MICHIGAN

GALENA

IOWA

MISSISSIPPI RIVER

CHICAGO

MENDOTA

GALESBURG

LACON

PEORIA

ILLINOIS RIVER

BLOOMINGTON

CARTHAGE

CLINTON

URBANA

INDIANA

DECATUR

QUINCY

BEARDSTOWN

SPRINGFIELD

CHICAGO & ALTON RR

ILLINOIS CENTRAL RR

ILLINOIS CENTRAL RR

ALTON

OLNEY

ST. LOUIS

WABASH RIVER

MISSOURI

CENTRALIA

GRAYVILLE

Illinois
1862

OHIO RIVER

CARBONDALE

Scale in Miles
0 10 20 30 40 50

KENTUCKY

CAIRO   PADUCAH

twelve years old, whom we have seen and know very well." The editorial instructed the slave catcher to leave town, concluding, "You miserable, low-lived, sneaking bloodhound, you deal in flesh and blood, do you? Well, if you do you won't get *that boy*—that's sure."[4]

DEPARTING CAIRO on his first train ride, Smith could see the forests of Kentucky across the Ohio until the tracks turned away from the river. The train soon entered a dense swamp and proceeded slowly over a creaking wooden trestle until, reaching firm ground, it made the first of many stops. The train then began a gradual ascent into southern Illinois hill country, a beautiful journey passing through forests and crossing rivers and ravines. Eventually, small farms appeared where the land had been cleared to grow corn, wheat, and even some tobacco. Along the way, Union soldiers defended the railroad at stations and vulnerable crossings, in particular at the Big Muddy River Bridge near Carbondale, to protect against attacks by southern Illinois Confederate sympathizers.[5]

Perhaps it occurred to Smith he was following a well-traveled path north taken by other escaping slaves. Underground Railroad stories tell of runaway slaves being secluded aboard the Illinois Central's freight cars, at times with the assistance of conductors and porters. Slaves also traveled by foot, following the route of the tracks nearly 115 miles north to Centralia in Marion County. Just a few miles beyond the town, the tracks separated, one route continuing directly north, passing through central Illinois, and the other branching northeast to Chicago, the preferred destination of escaping slaves.

Although Marion County's rail lines and central location attracted runaway slaves, it was a dangerous place for them. Copperhead clubs—organized gangs of slave catchers—operated in the area and profited from returning slaves to their owners. Fortunately, the escapees had allies in Centralia, a Republican enclave where a majority of the citizens had voted for Lincoln in 1860 and wherein abolitionists actively assisted escaping slaves.

Two and a half years earlier, in November 1859, a fight had ensued between Copperheads and abolitionists on the very tracks where Smith's train waited in Centralia: Copperheads were attempting to place fugitive Tobias Minor on a southbound train with a return to slavery, while abolitionists were trying to put him on a northbound train to Chicago and freedom. Ultimately, Minor reached Chicago.[6]

Smith and Warner continued due north on the Illinois Central's other line, moving into loyal Union country where soldiers no longer guarded railroads and the terrain began to change. The hills diminished, large fields appeared, and stands of timber became restricted to the lines of watercourses. As they traveled farther, the land leveled out, revealing a scene Smith had likely never imagined: the Grand Prairie of Illinois. The work of glaciers, the land was flat to the horizon in all directions with fertile, black soil, not the red soil with which he was familiar. Travelers were typically startled by their first view of the prairie: "It is impossible to conceive a country more hopelessly and irredeemably flat and bare and unbroken," author Edward Dicey told his readers. "As far as the eye could reach, the rich green pasture-lands of Illinois stretched away unchequered by a single tree, like the surface of a vast billiard-board."[7]

Where the land was not yet disturbed by cultivation, Smith may have seen prairie grass tall enough to conceal a man on horseback. He likely enjoyed the variety of brightly colored prairie flowers, and he probably saw his first prairie chickens (large grouse) alongside the railroad track. These birds had impressed English correspondent William Russell the previous June as he rode the train north from Cairo, watching them rise "in flocks from the long grass at the side of the rail or from the rich carpet of flowers on the margin of the corn fields." Along much of the railway, however, the prairie was being farmed, and Smith certainly would have noted that the people laboring in these fields were white.[8]

After the train entered DeWitt County, the prairie gave way in places to streams and groves of trees. Smith and Warner soon concluded a trip of 226 miles and more than fourteen hours to arrive in Clinton, a small farming community in central Illinois, which had prospered with the coming of the railroad in 1854. They were deep in the Land of Lincoln.

The president was well known to the people of Clinton, a county seat on the Illinois Eighth Judicial Circuit, to which he had traveled twice a year for more than two decades. The court attracted other notable people to Clinton, including future US Supreme Court Justice David Davis, Stephen A. Douglas, and George B. McClellan. Davis traveled the judicial circuit with Lincoln to preside over court sessions, and Douglas, like Lincoln, represented clients in court. When cases involving the Illinois Central Railroad arose, McClellan, as its chief engineer and vice president, would be present to confer with Lincoln, who also served as an attorney for the railroad.

In 1843, just four years after Lincoln began appearing in the circuit court, John Warner arrived in Clinton. He was warmly welcomed, not only because he was a physician but also because his Whig political sympathies fitted nicely with the political leanings of prominent local citizens. His path and Lincoln's crossed within the next few years, certainly no later than

1848, when Warner began a four-year tenure as Dewitt County circuit clerk. In 1852, Warner gave up the practice of medicine and became successful in business and real estate. Later in the year, Lincoln represented Warner in *Campbell v. Warner*, a civil case concerning land for which the outcome is not known. In 1855, Lincoln served as opposing counsel in *Warner and Moore v. Slatten et al.*, another case involving land that reached a settlement.[9]

Warner was an early member of the new Republican Party, as were many other community leaders and legal associates whom Lincoln had encountered at the county seats of the Eighth Judicial Circuit. The counties encompassing the circuit became, according to historian Guy C. Fraker, "the center of the formation of the Republican Party in Illinois. The organizers, leaders, and core strength of the new party came from the area of the circuit." John Warner was one of these individuals, and in 1856, he attended the meeting in nearby Bloomington that organized the Illinois Republican Party. In 1860, Judge Davis and attorneys from the Eighth Judicial Circuit were instrumental in obtaining the presidential nomination for Lincoln at the Republican National Convention in Chicago.[10]

In the interim, Warner prospered in Clinton. Close family and professional ties to the town's leading citizen and foremost Republican, attorney Clifton H. Moore, made Warner an even more formidable figure in the community. He enlisted in April 1861, promptly after the declaration of war, and used his standing to raise a company of men for the 41st Illinois Volunteer Infantry.[11] Yet only a year later, bringing Smith to Clinton may have placed Warner at variance with some among his fellow Republicans who loathed the presence of escaped slaves within the state.

Many Republicans opposed the expansion of slavery, not slavery itself. Before the war, they had viewed slavery's extension into the territories as a threat to free (nonslave) labor. With the war came the concern escaped slaves would crowd into free states and take jobs at lower wages. In Illinois, Governor Richard Yates and Judge David Davis had espoused this view, as had other prominent Republicans—in particular, Leonard Swett—who had helped Lincoln secure the presidential nomination.[12]

There was local opposition to Smith's presence, but these people were not identified in a May 7, 1863, *Clinton (IL) Public* article, the information presented as if their names were common knowledge. Copperheads and others in nearby townships surely objected to Smith's illegal status, but his opponents appear to have limited their actions to verbal protests.[13]

John Warner's position and connections in the community protected Smith well when Warner rejoined the 41st in May 1862. In November, he returned permanently to Clinton, forced to end his military service (he had risen to lieutenant colonel) by the persistent illness he had contracted prior to the Battle of Shiloh. His return could only have enhanced Smith's security.[14]

In late summer and autumn 1862, the influx of contrabands into Illinois swelled as thousands more fled the South, heightening fears the refugees would consume white jobs. Turbulence arose, and Alf Bissell could not have chosen a worse time to enter Illinois.

Fearful he might be separated from the 41st Illinois during its many movements and forced marches, Bissell decided to follow Smith's example and go to Illinois. On October 14, Colonel Pugh wrote his wife from Bolivar, Tennessee, "I have sent Alfred to you by Mr. [Lieutenant George R.] Steele . . . he did not like to leave me but he was afraid that he might be taken prisoner . . . he had liked to have tired out when we had to retreat."[15]

Pugh thought Bissell would be safer in Decatur, and given the labor shortage in Illinois, he could certainly help on the family farm. Indeed, Pugh had additional plans for Bissell, that he marry and then he and his wife live and work at Pugh's farm, but these received a temporary setback, as Pugh explained in his letter: "I could not send a wench[;] if I could get home I could bring one with me[;] the trouble is to get one that is worth any thing[;] there are plenty that are good house girls but I have no chance to tell who they are." Pugh tried to arrange a marriage for Bissell on several occasions, always intending to send the bride and groom to his farm in Illinois, but Bissell managed to maintain his bachelor's status.[16]

It is unlikely Pugh realized he was sending Bissell home at such a dangerous time, and Bissell quickly decided life at the front lines was safer than life in Decatur. Pugh's son Rinaldo, also a member of the 41st, wrote his mother just eight days later on October 22: "Old Alfred is here. He arrived on Sunday morning. Pa and I were very mad, when we saw him. Is it true that those infernal traitors at home scared him back? The old fellow was scared almost to death when he came in."[17] Unfortunately, Bissell did not realize Smith resided just twenty miles to the north, at the next stop on the railroad, where he likely would have met a far better reception. Clinton appears to have no recorded incidents of violent actions against its black residents.

Only six free blacks lived in Clinton in 1860, one of whom, Henry Mann, remains a figure in the community's memory. Local lore maintains he served under Lincoln in the Black Hawk War, and years later, Mann's obituary in the *Clinton Public* related he had once bested Lincoln: "In the early days of this county during court week the lawyers and people from the country who attended court used to vie with each other in the evenings, in jumping long distances. Mr. Lincoln could beat any man till Henry Mann came upon the green one afternoon and left Mr. Lincoln so far behind that Uncle Henry was declared to be the champion."[18]

Apocryphal or not, the story suggests Henry Mann was at least safe and accepted by the local population. He worked at the homes of white families, apparently saved his money, and prospered: according to the *Clinton Weekly Register*, he "owned some valuable property in Clinton." Mann and his wife, Nancy, each had sufficient standing in the community for the local newspapers to publish their obituaries.[19]

During the year Smith remained with the Warner family in Clinton, momentous changes were underway that altered the course of his life. The North's war effort, having failed to convince the South to return to the Union with slavery intact, turned to one of conquest. To prevail, Northern armies not only had to make war against Southern armies but also seize Southern territory and property. They also had to demolish the institution of slavery, which underpinned the South's war effort. Increased manpower became essential.

On July 17, 1862, Congress passed the Militia Act authorizing the president "to receive into the service of the United States, for the purpose of constructing entrenchments, or performing camp service, or any other labor, or any military or naval service for which they may be found competent, persons of African descent."[20] Lincoln avoided the matter of black military service in his Preliminary Emancipation Proclamation on September 22, but quietly, on the fringes of the war, in Kansas, Louisiana, and South Carolina, blacks entered the US Army. They did so in such a way that Lincoln could avoid responsibility in the anticipated voter backlash in the coming autumn elections.

Once beyond the elections, with his congressional majorities intact and the border states still in the Union, Lincoln issued the Emancipation Proclamation on New Year's Day 1863, freeing the slaves in disloyal territory and providing for their service in the military: "that such persons of suitable condition, will be received into the armed service of the United States to garrison forts, positions, stations, and other places, and to man vessels of all sorts in said service."[21]

The president's phrasing seemingly allowed only a limited support role for former slaves inducted into the army—a reflection of Lincoln's political concern to appease those voters who opposed black military service.[22] But Lincoln had opened the door, and this narrow access to black military enlistment soon widened. Among the first to break the restrictions were Massachusetts abolitionists, who used the president's acceptance of former slaves as justification to enroll and train a regiment of free blacks for front-line service.

Massachusetts recruiters were active in central Illinois in spring 1863, the *Bloomington (IL) Daily Pantagraph* reported, holding successful drives in Bloomington and Springfield. As an escaped slave from the loyal state of Kentucky, Smith was not freed by the Emancipation Proclamation, but he was ready to enlist in the army when he heard John Warner "reading [in the newspaper] about the 54th Mass. being formed. He learned that I was eager to join, so he wrote for transportation money for me."[23]

A short article on the front page of the *Clinton Public* reported Smith's departure by train for Chicago on May 7. He had evidently become a controversial local celebrity during his year in the community:

THE CONTRABAND QUESTION SETTLED. Andy, a contraband, brought to this town by Col. Warner, and who has, for some months past, been a thorn in the side of certain citizens, because of his unconstitutional presence in this State, has settled the difficulty, and relieved their minds by going to Chicago, where he will enlist in a black regiment. May his bayonet be felt more keenly by the rebels, than was his presence, by a certain clique, here.[24]

Smith traveled by the Illinois Central Railroad to Bloomington, where he changed trains for Chicago. Once there, he joined about thirty others traveling to Buffalo, New York, the first stop for prospective recruits, where they were to receive a medical examination. Smith, being judged fit to serve, was among those who went the remainder of the way to Massachusetts. His train stopped about ten miles from Boston at Readville. There, only a few hundred yards in the distance, was Camp Meigs, the training ground for Massachusetts regiments.[25]

SMITH AND HIS FELLOW RECRUITS passed between two large trees framing the entrance to Camp Meigs. Nearby was the guard tent, and ahead the camp's center where barracks faced the parade ground. Perhaps it was at the guard tent, or from the officer of the day, that Smith learned he would not be joining the 54th Massachusetts Volunteer Infantry. Its ranks had filled just days before, leaving nearly one hundred extra recruits in camp. With more men scheduled to arrive and the recruiters still active, the organizing committee quickly decided to raise a second black regiment, the 55th Massachusetts Volunteer Infantry.[26]

Smith began the process preparatory to enlisting in the 55th Massachusetts. He was escorted into camp with other recruits to await a final physical examination, a more rigorous procedure than the physical inspection administered at Buffalo. He was next directed to a pond where the recruits disrobed, bathed, and then received their uniforms, their civilian clothes having been burned. On May 16, Smith and twenty-nine other men reported to Lieutenant Leonard C. Alden to be mustered in the regiment. Alden, a devout abolitionist, had only four days earlier become the first officer commissioned in the 55th; he would also become the first officer of the regiment to die.[27]

The Descriptive Book of the 55th recorded Smith's height to be five feet six inches, his complexion brown, his eyes hazel, and his hair black. The process of enlistment required each recruit to provide his name, age, occupation, and place of birth. Smith gave his full and correct name, his age as twenty, and his occupation as boatman, but when asked to give his birthplace, he told Alden he was from Clinton, Illinois. Smith dared not disclose the truth. If discovered to be an escaped slave from the loyal Union state of Kentucky, he faced the possibility of being returned home in chains. It was a risk even to use his name.[28]

Camp Meigs, named for Union Quartermaster General Montgomery Meigs, encompassed 139 acres astride two rail lines near the Neponset River. Augustus S. Lovett, who trained at Camp Meigs as a corporal of the 45th Massachusetts Volunteer Infantry, recalled that the camp's "ten new barracks, each arranged for some 100 men . . . stood on a line facing the sunrise. A space called the company street ran between the buildings, where the different companies formed for drill, parade, or guard mounting [ceremonial changing of the guard]. Just back of each building was a small building occupied as a cook house, and the quarters of the different line officers were just in rear of the latter."[29]

Recruits arrived steadily. On some days enrollments were few, but more often the numbers ranged from around ten to more than seventy, continuing until the 55th reached a strength of 980 men. Twenty-five percent (247) of the recruits acknowledged to have been slaves, but it is not possible to know how many additional individuals, like Smith, concealed this information. The four border states were well represented by 166 men (perhaps fifty-nine of whom, not including Smith, were free) with more than sixty each from Kentucky and Missouri; 188 other recruits were born in Confederate states. Thirty-four officers and two chaplains left Camp Meigs with the regiment.[30]

Colonel Alfred S. Hartwell, left, commander of the 55th Massachusetts Volunteer Infantry Regiment and Major Charles B. Fox, the regiment's second in command. (*Massachusetts Historical Society*)

Two days after Smith mustered in the 55th, Lieutenant Burt Green Wilder, who in later years became one of Smith's staunchest allies, joined the regiment as its assistant surgeon. Wilder had sought an appointment as a field surgeon while serving in a New York City hospital for wounded soldiers. There, on Sunday morning, May 10, he received a letter from Massachusetts Surgeon General William J. Dale offering him "a position in the 55th Mass." Wilder wrote in his diary "father is very desirous that I should accept." He arrived at Camp Meigs to find "a lot of men who had been passed by a surgeon in Buffalo; I rejected five of them, one had a sore leg, another weak lungs, and most of them were under size."[31]

In the beginning, with a few exceptions among units in Kansas and Louisiana, officers of black regiments were white. Governor John A. Andrew determined the officers of Massachusetts regiments would be exemplary abolitionists,[32] and the 55th's field officers, Colonel Norwood P. Hallowell, Lieutenant Colonel Alfred S. Hartwell, and Major Charles B. Fox, were men of the character Governor Andrew desired. A wound received at Antietam forced Hallowell's retirement in December, whereupon Hartwell became the regiment's commander. Unfortunately, Hartwell, though much concerned about the care of his troops, had little battlefield experience. Fox, the regiment's most experienced officer, became the 55th's second in command. He also became the regimental historian.

Smith's days at Camp Meigs were busy as the regiment's officers prepared their charges for military service. Reveille was at 5:00 AM for Smith and his fellow recruits, followed by roll call and a march to a nearby dam for personal washing. Upon returning, Smith participated in policing the barracks, performing regimental fatigue duty such as cutting wood, and afterward engaged in an hour of squad drill. Then came breakfast, which was announced by a bugle call known as "Peas Upon a Trencher." After breakfast, the bugler announced guard mounting. Each company led a detail of men to the parade ground from where the adjutant assigned them to stand guard in two-hour rotations.

Smith drilled with the entire regiment two more times each day, in the morning from 9:00 to 11:00 AM, and in the afternoon from 2:00 to 4:00 PM, the drills separated by the midday meal. The recruits initially drilled using fifty old US Springfield muskets that had to be passed around among the men. Finally, on June 27, they were issued British Enfield rifled muskets and could begin to train with the weapon they would take into battle. Afternoon drill was concluded by an hour and a half of dress parade, followed by the evening meal, announced by a bugle call known as "Roast Beef." Beating of tattoo (a drum call to return to quarters) preceded roll call at 8:00 PM and taps at 8:30, after which Smith and his fellow recruits were confined to barracks, where they collapsed, exhausted, onto their bunks.[33]

July 16, 1863, was a proud day in the history of the regiment when Governor Andrew presented the 55th Massachusetts with its colors—its national and state flags.[34] Andrew's presentation marked the formation of the 55th's first color guard, the heart and soul of the regiment.

The flags were the most cherished symbol of a regiment and a critical marker on the battlefield. In the midst of the battlefield's smoke and confusion, the highly visible flags were often the only means troops had of determining their location, whether they were to advance or retreat. Capture of the flags by the enemy could disorganize and demoralize a regiment, and any soldier worthy of his fellow troops would be willing to die to protect his regiment's colors.

The color guard was led by the color sergeant, a soldier carefully selected for his courage and discipline under fire, who was accompanied by a guard of distinguished corporals.[35] Just once in a regiment's term of service, the day when its flags were first issued, a soldier was named color sergeant without showing prowess in battle. Once named, the color sergeant retained his office unless he failed in some way or was seriously wounded or killed—an event that was sadly common. In battle, the color guard would be in the midst of the heaviest fighting, and the color bearer—whether the

Opposite: the 55th Massachusetts' regimental colors. Top, the national regimental flag, bottom, the state regimental flag. (*State House Art Commission, Commonwealth of Massachusetts, Boston*)

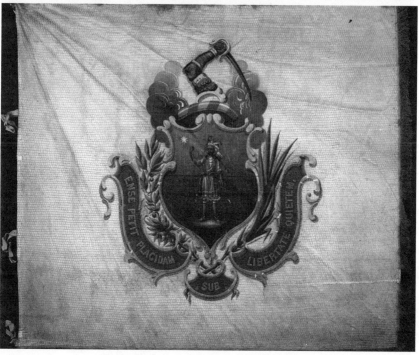

color sergeant, a corporal of the color guard, or another soldier who took the colors from a fallen comrade—was a prime target for the enemy. It was not uncommon for multiple color bearers to be wounded or killed in a single battle. Smith's career in the 55th Massachusetts would climax in the color guard.

The presentation ceremony signaled that the 55th's time to depart Camp Meigs was near, but Secretary of War Edwin Stanton and Governor Andrew disagreed about where the regiment was to be deployed. Stanton wanted to send it to an area in great need of troops, particularly southern Louisiana. Andrew favored sending the regiment to New Bern, North Carolina, where it would serve under Brigadier General of Volunteers Edward A. Wild, a physician turned infantry commander.[36]

Wild, a noted Massachusetts abolitionist, had recently organized his African Brigade of former slaves in North Carolina. Andrew believed that under Wild's command, the soldiers of the 55th Massachusetts would be allowed the opportunity to demonstrate their equality to white troops in combat. This matter was important to Andrew, not only as a politician who needed this experiment to succeed but also as an abolitionist who wanted to press for equal treatment and rights for black Americans. He considered it essential, therefore, to prevent these regiments from being placed under the control of commanders who considered black troops inferior and might not allow them to participate in combat. Andrew exerted his considerable political influence and prevailed. On July 16, Stanton acceded by telegram: "The [F]ifty fifth Massachusetts is to go wherever governor Andrew wants it to go. I understand he wants it to go to New Bern."[37]

On July 17, Colonel Hallowell ordered the regiment to be ready to depart Camp Meigs on July 20. The 55th was to march to New York City and board a steamer for New Bern. Three days' rations were distributed, but then departure was delayed.[38]

Northern racism, long simmering just below the surface, had erupted in an orgy of violence: the New York City Draft Riots. After learning of the depredations of the mobs and crimes against members of their race, the men of the 55th Massachusetts were, Major Fox recorded, "carefully drilled in street firing" and eager to march through New York and exact vengeance on anyone who dared attack them.[39]

The Lincoln administration decided the 55th Massachusetts would not depart from New York, and on July 21, Smith boarded a train to Boston with the regiment. Local authorities, concerned about the potential for public acts of violence, canceled a review on Boston Common by Governor Andrew. Instead, Smith marched with his fellow soldiers through the streets of Boston in the rain with their muskets loaded, bayonets fixed, and five extra rounds. The excessive caution was unnecessary. Fox saw "no signs of disapprobation . . . made by the spectators who thronged the route of the regiment, and . . . frequent cheers and applause greeted them. . . . The men marched and appeared well."

The 55th reached Boston Harbor without incident. Once on the dock, to avoid an accidental discharge of his loaded weapon, Smith fired his musket into the harbor in unison with his company before they boarded the steamer *Cahawba*. When the gangplanks had been drawn up, "such friends as the rain had not disbursed, came upon the wharf and witnessed the departure." At about 2:00 PM, the *Cahawba* fired "two guns by way of salute," and Andy Smith began his journey south.[40]

Private Smith's first ocean voyage was not a pleasant one. Rough seas and cramped quarters forced many to endure seasickness belowdecks; others more fortunate found open space on deck. After more than three days, the *Cahawba* entered calmer waters off North Carolina's Outer Banks and dropped anchor at low tide off Morehead City at 2:30 AM on July 25. All endured more than ten additional hours on board waiting for high tide to enable the steamer to dock, which was followed by even more hours of waiting for the regiment's horses and baggage to be unloaded.[41]

At 5:00 PM, Smith boarded a flatcar of a train to travel inland for about two hours to New Bern and the headquarters of the African Brigade. Brigadier General Wild greeted the regiment on arrival, as did the soldiers of the 1st North Carolina Volunteer Infantry, commanded by Colonel James C. Beecher, brother of Harriet Beecher Stowe. Smith's first dinner in the South consisted of hot coffee and hardtack.[42]

Service with the African Brigade entailed days of hard work coupled with morning and evening drills, including firing practice, and nights of too little sleep. The routine ended abruptly on the third night when Smith awoke with the brigade at 3:00 AM. Wild's regiments were under urgent orders to disembark quickly by sea without their baggage. Smith and everyone else in the regiment departed with only the clothes they were wearing. Rumors identified their destination as Charleston, South Carolina.[43]

After daylight, Colonel Hartwell and four companies departed on the schooner *Recruit*, leaving most of the regiment, including Smith's Company B, to stand for hours in heavy rain awaiting the steamer *Maple Leaf*. They finally boarded to learn that an attack led by the 54th Massachusetts against Charleston Harbor's Battery Wagner had failed on June 18. Smith was now among ten thousand Union reinforcements descending on Charleston's Sea Islands. This duty was supposed to be a temporary assignment for the regiments of the African Brigade, but Wild would return to North Carolina without the 55th Massachusetts (and the 1st North Carolina). Reassigned to the Department of the South and the X Corps, Charleston and its Sea Islands became the home base for Smith and the 55th for the duration of the war.[44]

CHAPTER 4

BATTERY WAGNER, THE SEA ISLANDS, AND FLORIDA

August 1863–June 1864

L ATE ON THE AFTERNOON of August 2, Andy Smith and his comrades passed safely around Charleston Harbor aboard the *Maple Leaf*. From the steamer's deck, Smith could see the city in the distance, a seemingly peaceful view with towering church spires, but the harbor was a war zone. Fort Sumter was receiving artillery fire; numerous vessels, most notably Union warships and several monitors, were on station in the ocean beyond the harbor; a seemingly endless number of army tents covered the beaches.[1]

Smith disembarked from the *Maple Leaf* the following day onto the dock at Folly Island's Stono Landing to join in a march of more than six miles along the length of the beach. Their destination was the 55th's bivouac site near Lighthouse Inlet on Folly's northeastern corner, and their trek served as a tour of the island and military installation that was to be their base for much of the war. The next morning, the men of the 55th learned the spade, not the musket, would be the infantry's weapon of war.[2]

Smith's arrival at Charleston coincided with the early stages of Brigadier General Quincy Adams Gillmore's siege of Battery Wagner. Undertaken in the wake of the failed infantry assault led by the 54th Massachusetts on July 18, the army was constructing a series of interconnecting trenches on the Morris Island beach to shield soldiers in their next advance against Wagner's walls.[3]

Simultaneously, Gillmore's engineers were erecting heavy artillery batteries on the beach, interposed among the trenches, and on the Union left flank, a peninsula-shaped rise of land extending west from Morris Island into the marshes where Smith would do most of his work. Battery fire was directed not only at Wagner and Battery Gregg, on the tip of Morris Island, but also against Fort Sumter at a distance of more than two miles.[4] These operations depended on the infantry, both black and white regiments, to provide the heavy labor required to erect batteries, transport ammunition, move guns into place, and, in conjunction with engineering regiments, serve as sappers, the men who dug the trenches.

Smith received his introduction to siege work and artillery fire on the first morning after his arrival on Folly Island. At 6:30 AM, he crossed Lighthouse Inlet as part of a four-hundred-man fatigue (labor) detail. Landing on adjacent Morris Island, the men continued north on foot along the beach for nearly two miles. Smith saw the rear of Gillmore's first siege trench come into view, and soon their line of march turned inland. Before long, looking to the horizon on his right, Smith realized his column was crossing in front of Wagner's face, roughly a mile in the distance.

Reaching their destination, some of the men began repairing a bridge while Smith joined with the remainder to fill between three thousand and four thousand sandbags. Meanwhile, Wagner's gunners had seen the detail and eventually fired three shells but caused no injuries. Captain Charles B. Bowditch described the sound Smith, as a member of the detail, also heard: "It was the first time I had ever heard the whizz of a shell coming toward me, I heard it when it first left the gun and then lost the sound, but caught it again as it came nearer when it sounded just as I supposed a solid shot would have sounded if sent through water." Unnerving as it was to be the target of artillery, soldiers soon learned to use direction and sound to know when to take cover. The sandbags were to be used in construction of the Union's Marsh Battery that would support a massive, 8-inch Parrott gun, known as the "Swamp Angel," aimed at Charleston, more than four miles distant.[5]

Smith resumed work on Morris Island the night of August 6, this time to help haul heavy guns to the left batteries. His detail began on the beach at Morris's southern shore after crews had unloaded the guns from ships. Each gun was hung under a sling cart with large wheels to elevate their axles to a height of about four feet, thereby allowing the cannons' barrels to clear the ground by a few inches. Long ropes extended from the front of these carts. Smith was among several hundred men who each took hold of a portion of one of the long ropes, shifted it over his shoulder, and began pulling the sling cart and the gun as far as two miles to its battery.[6]

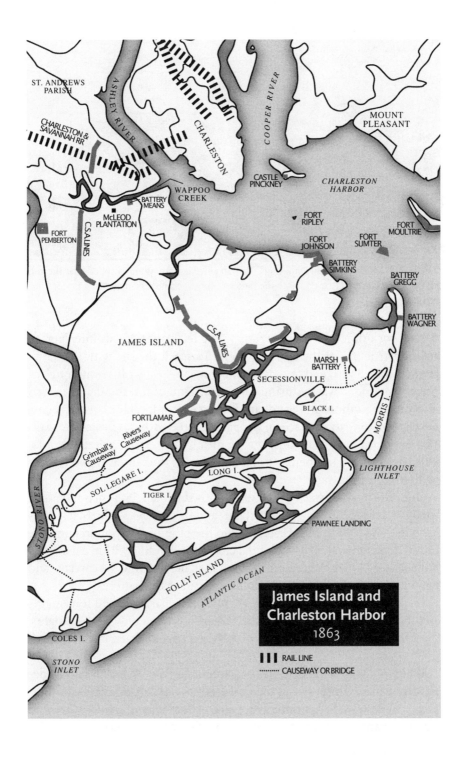

ST. ANDREWS
PARISH

ASHLEY RIVER

COOPER RIVER

CHARLESTON

MOUNT
PLEASANT

CHARLESTON &
SAVANNAH RR

CASTLE
PINCKNEY

CHARLESTON
HARBOR

WAPPOO
CREEK

BATTERY
MEANS

McLEOD
PLANTATION

C.S.A. LINES

FORT
PEMBERTON

FORT
RIPLEY

FORT
JOHNSON

FORT
SUMTER

FORT
MOULTRIE

BATTERY
SIMKINS

BATTERY
GREGG

BATTERY
WAGNER

C.S.A. LINES

JAMES ISLAND

MARSH
BATTERY

SECESSIONVILLE

BLACK I.

MORRIS I.

FORT LAMAR

Rivers'
Causeway

Grimball's
Causeway

SOL LEGARE I.

LONG I.

LIGHTHOUSE
INLET

TIGER I.

STONO RIVER

PAWNEE LANDING

FOLLY ISLAND

ATLANTIC OCEAN

James Island and
Charleston Harbor
1863

COLES I.

STONO
INLET

||| RAIL LINE
········· CAUSEWAY OR BRIDGE

The "Marsh Battery" and "Swamp Angel" Parrott rifled cannon photographed after the gun exploded on August 22, 1863. Note the battery's massive sandbag walls. (*Library of Congress*)

The work of hauling heavy guns to the left batteries was interspersed with construction of the Marsh Battery. To reach the site with the 55th's fatigue detail, Smith had to cross over a long, unsteady causeway, much of which was under water during high tide. One night, the detail moved nearly thirteen thousand sandbags from a mound, each man conveying one bag at a time to its place on the parapet (the battery's protective wall) and then repeating the process. During the night, the detail raised the parapet's height by two feet before crossing back over the causeway and returning to camp by dawn.[7]

Once the parapet was built, Captain Bowditch led 55th men in fatigue details to deliver the 8-inch Parrott gun and its carriage to the Marsh Battery. First, the 8,000-pound carriage and then the 16,300-pound gun were moved slowly by water through tidal creeks to a landing within a half-mile of the battery. Once at the landing, 55th men helped drag the carriage and then the gun over the half-mile length of road to the battery.

Engineers mounted the 8-inch Parrott on its carriage, and four nights later the Swamp Angel began to shell Charleston, but only for two nights. The gun exploded on the evening of August 23, while firing its thirty-sixth shell.[8]

When not preparing batteries or hauling guns to the front, fatigue details from the 55th served in the construction and maintenance of Gillmore's siege trenches. Confederate sharpshooter and artillery fire had halted forward progress in the trenches, but Gillmore regained the initiative

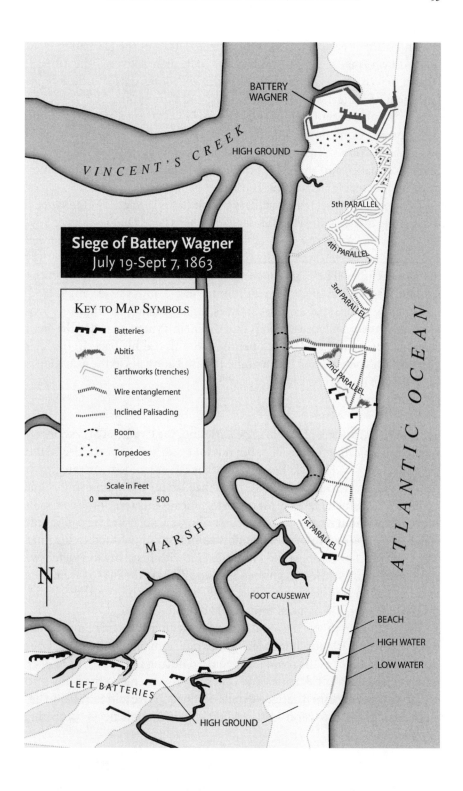

BATTERY WAGNER

VINCENT'S CREEK

HIGH GROUND

5th PARALLEL

4th PARALLEL

3rd PARALLEL

2nd PARALLEL

1st PARALLEL

ATLANTIC OCEAN

Siege of Battery Wagner
July 19-Sept 7, 1863

KEY TO MAP SYMBOLS

Batteries

Abitis

Earthworks (trenches)

Wire entanglement

Inclined Palisading

Boom

Torpedoes

Scale in Feet

0   500

MARSH

N

FOOT CAUSEWAY

BEACH

HIGH WATER

LOW WATER

LEFT BATTERIES

HIGH GROUND

due in no small part to the work of fatigue details in the left batteries. At 5:30 AM on August 17, just hours after 55th men delivered the 10-inch Parrott to its battery, Gillmore unleashed a week-long, dawn-to-dusk bombardment of Batteries Wagner and Gregg and Fort Sumter.[9]

The bombardment demolished the fort's walls, but Union fire could not drive off Confederate infantry. They remained to protect a log-and-chain obstruction stretching across the harbor waters between the fort and Sullivan's Island, and thereby Fort Sumter continued to deter the Union navy from entering Charleston Harbor.

Gillmore now directed all artillery fire on Battery Wagner as the sappers digging the trenches advanced closer to Wagner's base. On the night of September 7, 55th men were among the sappers who broke through the wall of Wagner's moat to discover the Confederates had abandoned the battery just hours earlier. These 55th men were also among the first Union troops to enter Wagner, but there is no indication Andy Smith was among them.[10]

Utilizing traditional siege techniques, Gillmore and his engineers provided informed, skilled leadership, and the infantrymen provided the labor required for a successful siege operation. Smith did his part: In his later years, Smith's pension record attributed painful ailments to the heavy labor he had done on Morris Island.[11]

THE POLITICAL GLORY of capturing Charleston, the Cradle of Secession, remained an objective for the navy, but not for the army's commander, Major General Henry W. Halleck. Possession of the city offered little strategic advantage for the army and required troops needed for operations in Virginia and the West, which Halleck saw as the significant theaters of the war. Gillmore was without orders to support naval operations, and he could only watch as troops and resources from his command transferred to Virginia. The siege of Charleston would continue, but with his army in a defensive stance. Gillmore turned to engineering and fatigue details to strengthen existing Union positions in the Sea Islands, constructing earthworks behind which even his reduced force could defend its ground.

Thus, far from preparing to take Charleston after Wagner's capture, soldiers on the Sea Islands, both black and white, remained mired in fatigue details, though not at the frequency required during the siege. By October, with strengthening of defenses and other improvements to the army's installations accomplished, fatigue details declined in size and number to become less of an intrusion into soldiers' lives, though never vanishing completely.[12]

Smith's day now began with his fellow soldiers under arms and in line on the beach before dawn, at the expense of much-needed sleep, ready to repel attacks that never materialized. Some regimental commanders used this time for drill, necessary if the troops were to perform successfully in battle, but drill also served a special function for the 55th and North Carolina troops of the African Brigade. They were without any clothing except what they wore departing New Bern, and General Wild, pressing for a swift return to North Carolina, had prohibited the transfer of his regiments' baggage to Charleston. With their summer uniforms nearly in rags and the nights getting colder, drilling helped the men fight off September's predawn chill. Finally, on the last day of the month, their baggage arrived, the result of Hartwell and Colonel Beecher of the 1st North Carolina intervening with Gillmore to circumvent Wild's directive.[13]

After sunrise, the regiments broke their formations to bathe in the ocean, have breakfast, and report for their assignments. Perhaps once or twice a week, Smith served fatigue duty with Company B at Wagner and Gregg where they worked to turn the batteries' fire against the defenses of Charleston. The transformation was carried out under hideous circumstances, in the midst of the sights and smells of the dead, both human and animal. The work was also dangerous, done under converging artillery fire from Fort Johnston and Fort Moultrie.[14]

When not delegated to fatigue details, Smith and his comrades had other responsibilities. Among these was picket duty, often served on Long Island for a rotation of three days. As in all areas isolated from strong sea breezes, mosquitoes on the inner islands posed a greater threat to all soldiers than did their enemy.

The enlisted men's first line of defense was to wrap themselves as completely as possible in thick clothing, a solution that did not work well for many, including Smith, who contracted malaria. The problem was serious, and it became "necessary to issue whiskey to the men who come off picket on the interior islands after three days duty, to overcome the effects of Malaria and it is mixed with quinine," but Smith would not accept whiskey with his quinine. Years later, Doctor Burt Wilder wrote approvingly of Smith, "He never took liquor, even when prescribed by me."[15]

Also in October, Smith began to emerge from the obscurity of the enlisted ranks. In response to an order from headquarters, Captain Grant selected Smith for detached duty with Quartermaster George B. Mussey. Grant described the duty as that of a servant, but it may have entailed something more. Regardless, the assignment was a mark of Grant's confidence in Smith, that he would perform well, and also of trust: service with the quartermaster would ease access to the supplies of the regiment, which unscrupulous individuals perpetually sought to steal. On November 21, Colonel Hartwell detailed Smith as a private servant to the assistant adjutant, Lieutenant Leonard B. Perry, but on November 22, the new African Brigade commander, Wild's replacement Colonel M. S. Littlefield, ordered him to report again to Quartermaster Mussey. Smith became an intermittent presence at headquarters during the fall, long enough to become known among the officers of the regiment.[16]

Smith similarly came to the notice of his superiors through his service in the brigade's provost guard, essentially the military police, to which Company B was assigned. He became quite proficient in the duty, which at times could be far more demanding than that of pickets. In a sanitized account published in the regimental history, Smith received credit for helping to quell an incident the following November (after his promotion to corporal): "A disturbance among some members of the band and drum corps . . . was prevented by the coolness and soldierly conduct of Corp. Andy Smith, Company B, of the provost guard."[17]

The events amounted to more than a "disturbance," as Fox intimated in his unpublished manuscript of the regimental history. "[Q]uite a disturbance was created near Hd. Qs. by two members of the band and principal musicians Moore and Pelette—arising from the use of intoxicating liquor. The affair would have been more serious but for the soldierly conduct of the Corporal of the Provost Guard—Smith of Co. B. who arrested Pelette at the tent of the colored laundress of the 54th New York, who had remained after the regiment had moved, and where the first difficulty occurred from his insulting and abusing the woman." Fox revealed additional details in a letter to his wife: "One [Pelette] was so violent that I was obliged to chain him and tie his hands behind his back; I came very near cutting him down with my sword."[18]

Smith's duty with the provost guard continued for the duration of his service with the regiment. In March 1865, Lieutenant Colonel Fox entrusted Smith with apprehending a deserter, and his final duty with the regiment in summer 1865 was with the provost guard maintaining the delicate peace between soldiers and civilians in South Carolina's interior.

As 1863 drew to a close, the 55th came under new leadership. Colonel Hallowell, disabled by his wound from Shiloh, resigned his commission in November. Hartwell became the regiment's new commander with promotion to colonel in December, and Fox became the lieutenant colonel. Brigadier General Wild returned to his command in North Carolina, but without the 55th Massachusetts and the 1st North Carolina (soon to be renamed the 35th United States Colored Troops, or USCT), now brigaded in the Department of the South.

DURING WINTER 1864, the 55th Massachusetts participated in an expedition to Florida where the army was, ostensibly, to encounter little resistance among citizens eager to return to the Union. The false claim was advanced by corrupt Republican businessmen eager to profit from Florida's hastened return to the fold. Federal forces managed to secure a portion of northeastern Florida, but on February 20, the expedition climaxed at the Battle of Olustee, forty-five miles west of Jacksonville, in a terrible Union defeat marked by atrocities committed against wounded and captured black troops.[19]

Smith did not fight at Olustee. A chance occurrence, being the last of Gillmore's regiments to depart Folly Island for Florida, relegated the 55th to rear-echelon duty on its arrival at Jacksonville, thereby sparing the men the harrowing ordeal of the battle. All regiments engaged at Olustee suffered terribly, their total casualty rate reaching 36 percent, one of the highest proportions of the war.[20]

In Jacksonville, where fate spared the 55th, at least for the time being, the regiment settled into camp and commenced fatigue duties. Then, on February 19, six companies departed for the front with Colonel Hartwell, only to assist the Union retreat as it reached the St. Marys River. Lieutenant Colonel Fox commanded the four companies, including Smith's Company B, remaining at Jacksonville, dividing their time between fatigue duty on the fortifications—"very hard work," according to Fox, "but little danger accompanies it"—and picket duty. On February 28, Fox led two of his companies, including Company B, to Yellow Bluff, a peninsula on the north bank of the St. Johns River commanding the channel about halfway between Jacksonville and the ocean. Their assignment was to fortify and defend the peninsula and aid engineers in the construction of a signal tower.[21]

A single case of smallpox at Yellow Bluff precipitated a significant development in Smith's life—his introduction to Surgeon Burt Wilder. To care for the patient, Wilder assigned a smallpox survivor, his aide, Private George C. Akers, and Smith was detailed as Akers's replacement. "During the past week I have had a new servant, Andrew Smith of Co. B. . . . 'Andy' had been Q. M. [quartermaster] Mussey's servant but was returned to his company when we ceased to be in Littlefield's Brigade [on Folly Island]; he is very bright, quick and clean, real[l]y to[o] good a soldier to be a servant."[22]

Wilder's assignment was light duty, allowing him time to pursue exotic creatures for scientific study. His desire to catch an alligator rose almost to the level of obsession, and Yellow Bluff was prime territory for Wilder to seek his new quarry: "We bathe in the river, but do not venture far from shore; partly because it deepens rapidly and partly because the region is called 'Little Alligator Swamp' from the abundance of those animals." Wilder undertook alligator hunts accompanied by Smith—the first on March 9, within a day or two of their meeting: "This afternoon, with . . . a man of Co. B, I made an expedition about two miles out to what was said to be the haunt of alligators. It was a creek in the midst of the swamp west of us; we saw several young ones run into the water but could not secure any; we caught a young raccoon that is now upstairs with a piece of beef; also a black pig that the soldier [Smith] hopes to fatten enough to be eatable."

Wilder was rapidly accumulating an assortment of animals—"Our last pet is a bat, already quite reasonable. We have had quite a varied assortment of creatures, including flying squirrels, lizards and a scorpion"—when two days later an alligator was brought into camp. "This afternoon an alligator about t[w]o feet long was shot in the head so that the brain had been destroyed, but when I dissected it the heart was beating and the muscles quite active. The man that killed it guided me this morning to a nest in the swamp where on a pile of soft earth 2 feet high and three or four wide were about 50 eggs and 20 little alligators, all dead, perhaps from cold."

Five days later, after the death of the smallpox patient, Akers joined Wilder and Smith on an expedition to the home of a supposed Unionist, "This afternoon I took Smith and Ackers (the latter fumigated and provided with new clothes) armed with their guns and went where no one has been before, viz., around the marsh west of us to another bluff where stands a house, said to have been occupied by a Union man and his daughter, driven away by the rebels. It is a nice house and the garden is tastefully laid out; from it I gathered a fleur de lis. The men fired at some ducks, but hit none. We heard the deep bellow of a large alligator, but could not see it."

Wilder decided to hunt the alligator the next day: "This afternoon, accompanied by Capt. Gordon and Lt. Ellsworth and Andy, I went again in search of the big alligator; not finding it we kept on along the bank of the river by a path between it and the woods." Wilder then described an event foreshadowing an accident that was to occur nearly a week later: "Suddenly we found the fresh footprints of men, and presently reached a house; no one was in it, but on looking over the bank Ellsworth saw Lt. Jones and one of the signal officers sitting on a log; we separated so as to be on either flank and then Ellsworth fired his revolver over their heads. On looking over the bank again we saw our friends crouched under the edge, their . . . pistols cocked as if intending to sell their lives dearly; it was a rather dangerous practical joke for if either of us had worn a gray hat he might have been shot before the error was discovered."

Two days later, Wilder and Smith went on yet another gator hunt, this time joined by Captain John Gordon. Wilder procured a dugout canoe, and the three went off paddling through the marsh: "We were all well armed in case the alligators should attack our boat. Besides guns and pistols we had an axe and hatchet. We came upon two sunning

Dr. Burt G. Wilder, a surgeon of the 55th Massachusetts, in 1868. (*Cornell University Library*)

themselves on the bank; but they slid off before we came within accurate shooting distance; after waiting in vain for them to reappear, about half an hour, we rowed further up the creek and saw a third, but he also escaped."

Smith did not take part in Wilder's hunts much longer. On March 22, the soldiers at Yellow Bluff thought they might be coming under enemy attack. A detail of engineers sent out from camp began firing at pigs. Another detail nearby, consisting of the 55th's Captain Charles B. Soule, Lieutenant Dennis H. Jones, and two soldiers, "had found a boat at a house on the river at the east side of the marsh believed to have been recently occupied by rebel pickets; they were dragging it to the water when they heard the firing of the engineers."

Soule's party, believing they were under enemy fire, "renewed [their] efforts to drag the boat and so escape the supposed enemy, both officers fell, and Soule's pistol, being cocked in anticipation of the attack, exploded and the ball pierced Jones' heart. The two soldiers supposing the shot to have come from the enemy, leaped into the river and by swimming and wading over the marsh reached camp . . . and it was naturally concluded that the rebels had killed Jones and taken Soule prisoner; all was excitement and expectation of attack. But . . . a party went in a boat and found Soule and the body."

In the midst of the excitement, Smith left Dr. Wilder's service: "When the alarm occasioned by the death of Lt. Jones occurred Andy Smith begged permission to join his company in case of action; afterward I learned from his captain that he is trying to perfect himself with a view to promotion as a corporal." Smith successfully secured new assignments, and a few weeks later Wilder noted his accomplishments: "[Brigadier General John P.] Hatch has ordered that the river be patrolled tonight lest the rebels plant torpedoes in the path of our now frequent boats. Lt. Gannet goes in charge of the patrol and one of the men is my former servant, 'Andy' Smith; he is a splendid man and soldier. He is also one of nine men selected to manage the cannon in Redoubt Jones."

ON THE AFTERNOON of April 17, Smith was waiting on the dock at Yellow Bluff, his Florida excursion about to conclude. The previous two months, which had been a difficult if not terrible period for many Union soldiers, had for him been one of opportunity. As part of a small garrison, his character, dependability, and efforts to improve as a soldier were more easily recognized, not only by Burt Wilder but also by other officers. Promotion would soon come, during difficult times, but the regiment first had to return to Folly Island. As Smith waited, the transport *Sentinel* passed by conveying Colonel Hartwell and the companies from Palatka where they had been protecting the southern flank of the Union's defense line. Eventually, the transport *Neptune* appeared upriver, conveying troops of the 8th USCT to Yellow Bluff in relief of the 55th's contingent. The USCT men disembarked, and Smith filed on board with his comrades for their voyage to Folly.[23]

The 55th was among the regiments redeployed from Florida to maintain the siege at Charleston as other troops transferred to Virginia with Major General Gillmore. The *Neptune* docked at Pawnee Landing in pouring rain, two days in advance of the *Sentinel*. Fox, finding much of the island deserted, immediately detailed two-thirds of the men to picket duty. Smith, however, received orders to report to the adjutant at headquarters, a summons pertaining to provost guard duties. All was not well within either the 55th or the 54th Massachusetts.[24]

The previous August, during the Siege of Battery Wagner, black troops discovered the federal government had set their pay at ten dollars per month from which three dollars was deductible as a clothing allowance. This was the same pay set for the army's black laborers, well below the thirteen dollars per month pay received by white troops.

The pay reduction had been unintentional. In May 1863, needing a legal ruling to set the pay for soldiers in the newly established United States Colored Troops, Secretary Stanton requested War Department Solicitor William Whiting to clarify the law. Although the Militia Act had focused on employing the thousands of escaped slaves surrounding Union army camps in military or civilian capacities, the language incorporated the phrase "persons of African descent" to identify these individuals and set their pay. Whiting ruled the act governed the enlistment and pay of all black troops.[25]

None of this was understood by the Massachusetts troops. Their regiments, having enlisted with the promise of pay equal to that of whites, felt betrayed, believing the government had broken its promise to them and was treating black troops as if they were laborers, not soldiers.

In protest, the soldiers of the 54th and 55th Massachusetts (with only a few exceptions) refused to accept the lower pay, but they continued to serve, trusting in their supporters and Congress to rectify the matter. By April the issue still loomed unresolved (due in part to Congress not having been in session for months), exhausting the patience of many, in particular those with families in want of food, clothing, and shelter.

Dissenting troops claimed the government had violated its contract with them, and, therefore, they were no longer legally required to obey orders. Discord had worsened among those at Palatka and escalated with the return to Folly in the spring. Individually, in small numbers, and then increasingly in larger groups, enlisted men disobeyed orders and refused to perform their duties; some even fought with their officers.[26]

Admittedly, with his own family living in slavery and beyond his financial assistance, Smith likely empathized with the anguish of his fellow soldiers, but he could not support their actions. As did perhaps the majority of the regiment, Smith knew military enlistment did not equate with civilian contractual obligations, a realization reinforced by his service in the provost guard. Those refusing to obey orders were engaging in acts of mutiny, punishable by imprisonment or death.

It was not just the threat to enlisted men that worried officers and like-minded soldiers such as Smith, but also the threat to the 54th's and 55th's very existence should the discord spread. In the midst of such fears, on June 14, Hartwell and Fox revealed their trust and confidence in Smith with his promotion to corporal.[27]

Colonel Hartwell exercised considerable restraint, resorting to reason, frequent personal intervention, and close supervision of the troops by his officers. Courts-martial imposed penalties in the more serious instances, but even Hartwell could not prevent the execution by firing squad of Private Wallace Baker, who had struck Lieutenant Ellsworth with the lieutenant's sword. All the regiments on Folly Island were assembled on the morning of June 18, ensuring the enlisted men witnessed Baker's execution, the third Smith had been forced to endure.[28]

Congress passed the pay bill in late June, but the enlisted men did not trust the report, believing it to be a rumor. Official notification arrived on August 22, but Congress's resolution of the matter was not clear-cut and raised a new controversy.[29]

Black troops who were free on April 19, 1861, the date the Union officially recognized a state of war with the Confederacy, received pay, equipage, and clothing equal to white troops of the same rank retroactively to their dates of enlistment. They were also to receive their bonus pay. Those who were not free on that date would also receive equal pay and allowances retroactively to January 1, 1864, but their retroactive pay for previous service would remain unchanged. The provision, a compromise required for passage of the bill, was needed to appease congressional opposition to retroactive pay.[30]

The enlisted men were apprehensive about the administration of an oath to determine their status, possibly establishing a record that they had been slaves. "[T]hey feared some deception," Fox noted in the regimental history, "some few going so far even as to consider the whole thing a trap to ascertain who had been held as slaves, in order to return them to their masters at the close of the war." The apprehension was all the more daunting for soldiers such as Smith who had escaped from slavery in a loyal state.[31]

In response, the 54th's Colonel Edward N. Hallowell (brother of Colonel Norwood P. Hallowell) devised the "Quaker Oath" allowing men to conceal their status as escaped slaves: "You do solemnly swear that you owed no man unrequited labor on or before the 19th day of April, 1861. So help you God." As Captain Luis F. Emilio of the 54th Massachusetts explained, "Some of our men were held as slaves April 19, 1861, but they took the oath as freemen, by God's higher law, if not by their country's." In late August, Smith took the oath along with all but a few members of the 55th; his status as "Free" was entered upon the regiment's muster roll, and on September 30, he received his full pay.[32]

CHAPTER 5

RIVERS' CAUSEWAY TO HONEY HILL

July–November 1864

O N THE NIGHT OF JUNE 30–JULY 1, 1864, Corporal Andy Smith stood picket duty on Long Island, watching his regiment cross the water from Pawnee Landing en route to James Island. He was exasperated. The troops believed they were about to attack Charleston, and Smith, who had yet to fire his musket in battle, did not want to be left out of the action. Then, suddenly, the mission was delayed. The regiment returned to Pawnee Landing to spend the next day in the sun, the men attacked by mosquitoes while clinging to the ground to conceal themselves from Confederate view.[1]

The next night Smith watched again as the 55th Massachusetts crossed the water from Pawnee Landing. Wanting to join his regiment, he attempted to obtain release from picket duty, but his initial requests went unheeded: "I was on Long Island on picket duty under Captain [Robert J.] Hamilton . . . during the time the expedition was passed to go to James Island and they got there about 2 o'clock at night," but Captain Hamilton "refused to relieve me until relieved by Colonel [Alfred] Hartwell." Smith then asked Captain Charles E. Grant of his own Company B: "I went to Captain [Charles] Grant to get released. But he said he could not because Captain Hamilton outranked him. Then I went to Col. Hartwell and he released me." Hartwell allowed Smith to join the regiment, serving as his orderly.[2]

Colonel Hartwell commanded a brigade of three regiments, the 33rd USCT, 55th Massachusetts, and 103rd New York Infantry. Lieutenant Colonel Charles Fox commanded the 55th. The brigade quietly moved to the west end of Long Island, where Smith entered a pontoon boat to cross the water to Tiger (modern-day Peas) Island.[3] Smith disembarked with his fellow troops into water and soft mud, some of the men sinking nearly to their waists. Reaching land, he took the advantage afforded by dry ground and lay down with the other troops for a few hours of rest.

Meanwhile, a half-mile to the west, opposite Grimball's Causeway, Colonel William Heine's brigade waited to attack James Island at daylight in concert with Hartwell's troops. The two brigades, each one thousand strong, would conduct demonstrations, displays of force to convince Confederate leaders the city's defenses were seriously threatened. In the morning, Hartwell's regiments were to cross onto James Island via Rivers' Causeway and press the defenses of Fort Lamar, thereby forcing the Confederates to transfer soldiers from Fort Johnson to Fort Lamar. With its garrison thus weakened, Fort Johnson would come under attack by another one thousand Union troops who were to depart by boats from Morris Island the following night.[4]

If Fort Johnson were captured, the Union demonstrations threatened to morph into something more, possibly the capture of Charleston. Strategically positioned, Fort Johnson's artillery commanded the harbor and the city. Confederate leaders would either have to recall frontline troops to fight for Charleston (thus weakening their operations in Georgia and Virginia) or risk the city's capture.[5]

Before daybreak, keeping close to Colonel Hartwell, Smith joined the brigade's long, thin line as he stepped off from Tiger Island into shallow water to follow a path through more than 650 yards of tidal marsh to Sol Legare Island.[6] He came ashore to the sounds of scattering fire exchanged between Confederate pickets and Hartwell's skirmishers. Ahead Smith could see the 33rd USCT and 103rd New York, already in column along a road. The 55th formed at the rear, and the brigade began advancing to the far side of the island, a distance of less than three-tenths of a mile, intending to cross to James Island by means of Rivers' Causeway, an elevated road spanning two hundred yards of high marsh.[7]

Upon reaching the base of Rivers' Causeway, the head of Hartwell's column came under converging artillery fire from Fort Lamar, a mile to its right, and from two 12-pound Napoleons to its front, situated behind earthworks at the causeway's head on James Island. Smith saw the 33rd USCT deploy into the savannah left of the causeway and the 103rd New

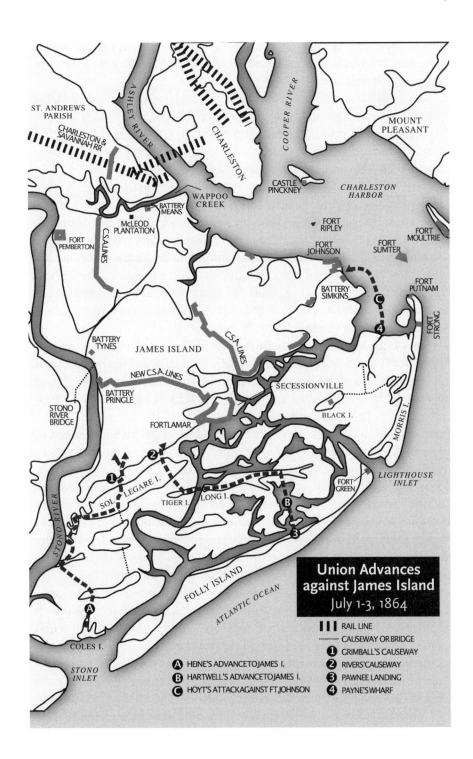

ST. ANDREWS
PARISH

CHARLESTON &
SAVANNAH RR

ASHLEY RIVER

CHARLESTON

COOPER RIVER

MOUNT
PLEASANT

WAPPOO
CREEK

CASTLE
PINCKNEY

CHARLESTON
HARBOR

BATTERY
MEANS

McLEOD
PLANTATION

C.S.A. LINES

FORT
PEMBERTON

FORT
RIPLEY

FORT
JOHNSON

FORT
SUMTER

FORT
MOULTRIE

BATTERY
SIMKINS

FORT
PUTNAM

C

4

FORT
STRONG

BATTERY
TYNES

JAMES ISLAND

C.S.A. LINES

NEW C.S.A. LINES

BATTERY
PRINGLE

SECESSIONVILLE

STONO
RIVER
BRIDGE

FORT LAMAR

BLACK I.

MORRIS I.

2

1

SOL LEGARE I.

TIGER I.

LONG I.

FORT
GREEN

LIGHTHOUSE
INLET

STONO RIVER

B

3

A

FOLLY ISLAND

ATLANTIC OCEAN

COLES I.

STONO
INLET

**Union Advances
against James Island**
July 1-3, 1864

| | RAIL LINE
·········· CAUSEWAY OR BRIDGE
1 GRIMBALL'S CAUSEWAY
2 RIVERS' CAUSEWAY
3 PAWNEE LANDING
4 PAYNE'S WHARF

A HEINE'S ADVANCE TO JAMES I.
B HARTWELL'S ADVANCE TO JAMES I.
C HOYT'S ATTACK AGAINST FT. JOHNSON

York to the right. Meanwhile, the 55th Massachusetts, serving as the reserve, remained on Sol Legare Island and deployed into line across the road leading to Rivers' Causeway.[8]

Alongside Hartwell, Smith also watched as the 33rd USCT and 103rd New York went to ground in search of cover instead of charging the two Napoleons, but Hartwell, woefully lacking battle experience, did not order an attack. Instead, he conferred with the regiments' commanders, who insisted a successful attack on the Napoleons would be impossible.[9]

Hartwell initially ordered Lieutenant Colonel Fox to face the 55th's line left to march away from the little battlefield (in the direction of Grimball's Causeway), but most of the company officers did not hear Fox's orders. With only three companies attempting to face left and the others facing forward, the regiment's line remained immobile under the incoming artillery fire. Hartwell finally realized the safest action was for the 55th to charge the guns. All the while, Andy Smith had been at Hartwell's side beseeching him to attack. Hartwell turned to Smith and gave him the attack orders to deliver to Captain Grant.[10]

Years later Smith wrote to Burt Wilder, "I carried orders from Col Hartwell to Capt Grant at the Battle of [Rivers'] Causeway to charge. I went a 1/4 of a mile under a heavy fire." Grant did not understand Smith was arriving with orders and "remarked that he (Capt Grant) made $100.00 this morning before breakfast. He was alluding to the horse he had captured and was at that time riding." But men in the regiment had seen Smith running in from Hartwell and anticipated the command (some of them overheard him convey the order to Grant).[11] "Capt Grant's first order was 55 in line and before he could finish the Order . . . [to] the Regiment," Smith recalled, "[Private George] Buckner sprang from the line and said in a loud voice! Boys lets go to them guns. . . . Remember Fort Pillow." At that instant, without orders, the men charged the Confederate guns. Sergeant Major James M. Trotter recorded they were "cheering, shouting, and the battle cry 'Fort Pillow' came forth from many a throat."[12]

The men of the 55th arrived in no discernible order to overrun the guns. Captain Charles Soule and the color company "scrambled over the marsh and tumbled into the redoubt, all together,—a hot, ragged, and excited crowd," and some of the men turned the cannons to fire on the retreating Confederates. The capture of the Confederate guns at Rivers' Causeway was the climax of Andy Smith's first infantry action, and it is not certain he ever had an opportunity to fire his musket.[13]

Upon crossing the causeway to James Island, Hartwell faced the brigade right to demonstrate against Fort Lamar, but he quickly received new or-

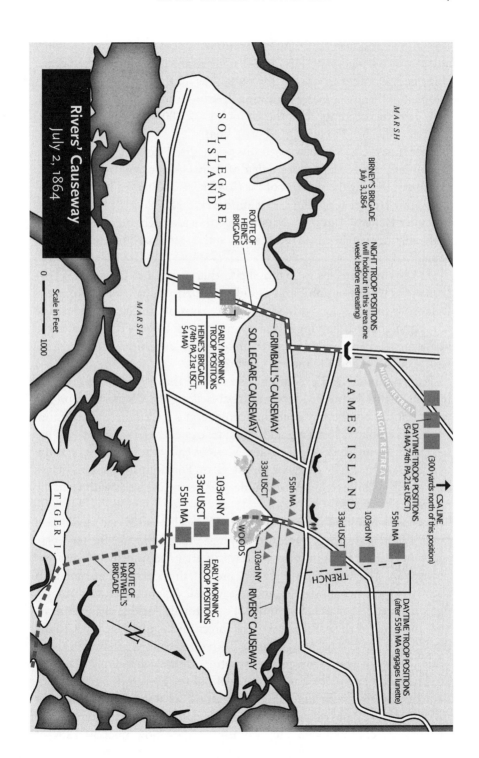

Rivers' Causeway
July 2, 1864

0 ———— 1000
Scale in Feet

MARSH

SOL LEGARE ISLAND

MARSH

TIGER I.

ROUTE OF HEINE'S BRIGADE

EARLY MORNING TROOP POSITIONS
HEINE'S BRIGADE
(74th PA,21st USCT, 54 MA)

SOL LEGARE CAUSEWAY

GRIMBALL'S CAUSEWAY

BIRNEY'S BRIGADE
July 3, 1864

MARSH

NIGHT TROOP POSITIONS
(will holdout in this area one
week before retreating)

DAYTIME TROOP POSITIONS
(54 MA/74th PA,21st USCT)

JAMES ISLAND

NIGHT RETREAT

NIGHT RETREAT

CSA LINE
(300 yards north of this position)

33rd USCT

55th MA

103rd NY

55th MA

DAYTIME TROOP POSITIONS
(after 55th MA engages lunette)

TRENCH

33rd USCT
33rd USCT
103rd NY
55th MA

EARLY MORNING TROOP POSITIONS

WOODS

RIVERS' CAUSEWAY

ROUTE OF HARTWELL'S BRIGADE

N

ders to halt and take cover. Ahead Smith could see a long drainage ditch adjacent to a hedge, only 333 yards distant, into which he crouched down alongside the other troops for the remainder of the day.[14] As the soldiers huddled in the ditch, many becoming ill without protection from the sun, their presence accomplished the Union's goal: 100 of Fort Johnson's 230 defenders departed to reinforce Fort Lamar.[15]

Late that night, Smith crawled out of the ditch with his fellow soldiers and quietly moved along the edge of James Island toward Grimball's Causeway. Passing the remains of the Confederate battery at Rivers' Causeway, 55th troops took the two Confederate Napoleons in tow. Later, Brigadier General Alexander Schimmelfennig awarded the captured guns to the regiment, to be displayed proudly at the 55th's headquarters on Folly Island.[16]

As Hartwell's troops were moving farther away from the guns of Fort Lamar, the Union's amphibious assault commenced against Fort Johnson. Delayed by a low tide and inadequate preparation, the attackers lost the cover of night and, arriving at dawn, came under artillery fire. Most of the boats turned back, abandoning their commander, Colonel Henry Hoyt, with six officers and 135 men to capture.[17]

Poor planning and execution also caused the failure of two Union movements to destroy bridges and trestles along the Charleston and Savannah Railroad, thereby enabling Confederates to reinforce Charleston. With his opponent receiving additional troops each day, Foster spent the next week trying to decide if his forces could carry the earthworks of the Confederate New Line to renew the attack on Fort Johnson. But his delays only ensured Union regiments would incur heavy casualties with virtually no chance of success.[18]

As Foster agonized over the decision, Hartwell's and Heine's troops on James Island endured periodic artillery and musket fire and the far worse agony of lying in full sun for seven days, interrupted only by intermittent downpours. The mosquitoes were ever present, the heat merciless, and men began to experience sunstroke. Smith, serving as Colonel Hartwell's orderly, likely suffered less than his comrades. Foster finally decided against the attack and ordered the withdrawal of his forces for the night of July 9. In the dark, Smith crossed bridging leading from Grimball's Causeway to Coles Island, from where an army transport returned the 55th to Folly Island.[19]

The men of the 55th learned much about the hardships of the battlefield during the week following their attack at Rivers' Causeway, but Colonel Hartwell and other Union leaders had little opportunity to mature as battlefield commanders. A few months later, on November 30, 1864, at

Honey Hill, South Carolina, Union troops would again engage in battle, and men of the 55th Massachusetts—in particular, Color Sergeant Robert King and Corporal Andrew Smith—would face extraordinary danger.

ON NOVEMBER 25, 1864, Lieutenant Colonel Fox detailed Andy Smith to the color guard for a combined army-navy operation in support of Major General William T. Sherman's March to the Sea. Major General Foster had organized the Coast Division, a force of 5,500 soldiers and sailors commanded by Brigadier General John P. Hatch. The army's component was divided into two brigades, the first led by Brigadier General Edward E. Potter, a competent but tactically inexperienced staff officer, and the second by Colonel Hartwell. Assigned to Hartwell's command, the 54th and 55th Massachusetts were brigaded together for the first and only time.[20]

At Sherman's request, the Coast Division was to break the line of the Charleston and Savannah Railroad about Pocotaligo. If successful, the mission would inhibit the escape of Confederate Lieutenant General William J. Hardee's army of more than nine thousand men from Savannah. The Union chief of staff, Major General Henry W. Halleck, who had little faith in the military prowess of the forces at Charleston, also allowed that a demonstration to draw Confederate troops from Sherman's path would constitute a successful mission.[21]

Late on Sunday afternoon, November 27, Smith departed Folly Island aboard the steamer *Mary Boardman* with six companies of the 55th. Traveling with an escort of gunboats and heading south along the coast, it would have been evident to Smith they were on course for Hilton Head, where they arrived at 2:00 AM to wait for hours in the harbor. Finally, late that morning, the *Mary Boardman* took on the 55th's two additional companies assigned to the Coast Division and proceeded to Parris Island for a twelve-hour coaling stop.[22]

There Smith and his comrades, with their rifles stacked nearby, were able to enjoy an afternoon of swimming and being in the open air onshore. The coaling was not completed until midnight, by which time the *Mary Boardman* was engulfed in fog and thus remained at the coaling station wharf until sunrise. Isolated and without orders, those on board were unaware the expedition had already set out in fog at 2:00 AM.[23]

The *Mary Boardman* departed for Hilton Head at sunrise but received instructions en route and turned upstream for Boyd's Landing. The fog slowly began to dissipate, allowing Smith to enjoy expansive views of the Broad River—its width, in excess of two miles at its mouth, tapered to a

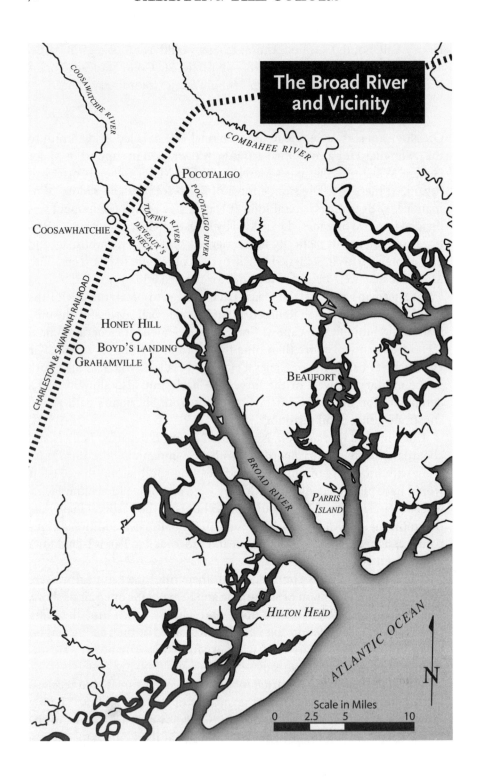

The Broad River
and Vicinity

COOSAWATCHIE RIVER

COMBAHEE RIVER

POCOTALIGO

COOSAWHATCHIE

TULIFINY RIVER

POCOTALIGO RIVER

DEVEAUX'S NECK

CHARLESTON & SAVANNAH RAILROAD

HONEY HILL

BOYD'S LANDING

GRAHAMVILLE

BEAUFORT

BROAD RIVER

PARRIS ISLAND

HILTON HEAD

ATLANTIC OCEAN

N

Scale in Miles

0   2.5   5   10

still-impressive mile and a quarter upstream. Carefully adhering to the channel, the *Mary Boardman* passed three grounded army transports and then, after turning into Boyd's Creek about 3:15 PM, finally ran aground several hundred yards from its destination. The regiment disembarked by relays into tugboats ferrying soldiers to a muddy bank, requiring Smith and his comrades to scurry inelegantly up to dry land on the grounds of the deserted Boyd plantation house.[24]

Smith found the landing of troops, equipment, and stores to be hours behind schedule. The Coast Division was to have reached Boyd's Landing at dawn, but many of the army's transports departing from Hilton Head in the fog had run aground or lost their way. By 8:00 AM, only the naval squadron had arrived and, unfortunately, alerted the Confederate pickets.[25]

The Confederate early warning system—designed to enable local forces to delay Union incursions until reinforcements arrived by railroad—went into high alert as the picket from Boyd's Landing reported the arrival of Union gunboats to his sergeant at Grahamville's telegraph office.[26] The Union thus lost the element of surprise as the landing of troops, horses, artillery, and supplies continued throughout the afternoon into the night and the next day.

Both of Hatch's brigades should have been advancing toward the railroad in the morning, but, until late in the day, the only troops sent forward were to guard the landing. Smith had arrived in time to see Hatch and Potter set out at 4:00 PM for Grahamville with the cavalry and the four regiments of Potter's brigade that had landed. Hatch's column reached only as far as Bolan's Church, three and a half miles from Boyd's Landing, at 2:00 AM to bivouac for the night, after marching and countermarching for fifteen miles.[27]

At dawn, Smith waited as the artillery and Potter's late arriving regiments moved out to join Hatch's column. Then, at sunrise, 7:06 AM, he departed Boyd's Landing with Hartwell's brigade, reduced in strength to the 54th and 55th Massachusetts. The remaining regiments, the 26th USCT and the 120th USCT, were still missing on the Broad River.[28]

The 54th Massachusetts, like the 55th, had only eight of its companies for the campaign. Already vastly understrength, Hartwell received orders on the march to detach four of the 54th's companies to guard the intersection of the Boyd's Landing Road and the River Road. He was also to leave two other companies to guard the River Road near Bolan's Church. Thus, before reaching the battlefield, Smith found himself in a "brigade," which should have been four regiments strong, reduced to ten companies, the strength of a single regiment.[29]

Hartwell's command reached the intersection at Bolan's Church and halted by a brook where Smith could hear distant skirmishing and cannon fire. Receiving orders, Hartwell detailed the two companies of the 54th Massachusetts to guard duty near the church and led his little force up the Grahamville Road. About halfway down the length of the column, Smith marched near Color Sergeant Robert King, who was carrying the national colors. Reaching the cotton field below Euhaw Swamp, the troops deployed into line and passed over ground where the first Union dead of the battle lay.

After crossing the cotton field, Hartwell's brigade reformed into column (the weakest attack formation) on the road to pass over the causeway through Euhaw Swamp. Beyond the swamp, Smith saw a burning field on the right of the road. (He later learned the Confederates had set the fire to repel a Union flanking movement.) Forming a two-company-wide front, the 55th helped to extinguish the fire while crossing uphill to the far end of the field. At the brow of the hill, Hartwell "received orders to halt and hold my command compact and ready."

Smith could hear distant sounds of artillery and skirmishing fire, revealing Potter's brigade to be advancing against light resistance. Meanwhile, Hartwell's command "rested for half an hour," Captain Soule related. "There was nothing in sight except a battery of artillery in the road at the left. The sound of skirmishing had ceased and the fields and woods wore a Sabbath quiet, when suddenly and violently firing by volley began at the front and the artillery opened again."

Their brigade was still waiting, now clearly hearing the sounds of battle, when orders arrived calling them forward. Smith moved out quickly in march column with the color guard and, turning up the Grahamville Road, soon saw their path blocked by wagons, artillery carriages, caissons, and crews. Maintaining their column formation soon became unfeasible, and Smith joined his fellow troops to move around obstacles in single file until they neared the front and could reform the column as they entered the woods. En route, they learned the head of Potter's column had marched around the sharp left turn in the Grahamville Road and into the fire of six cannon blocking the path before them.[30]

Smith could hear exchanges of musket fire between the Confederates and Potter's regiments that had deployed into the woods on both sides of the road to establish a defensive line. Ahead the sharp left turn in the Grahamville Road came into view, near which Union artillery pieces were positioned. Below the left curve, to the right of the road, was a straight path into the forest, called the wood road by the troops, down which Smith en-

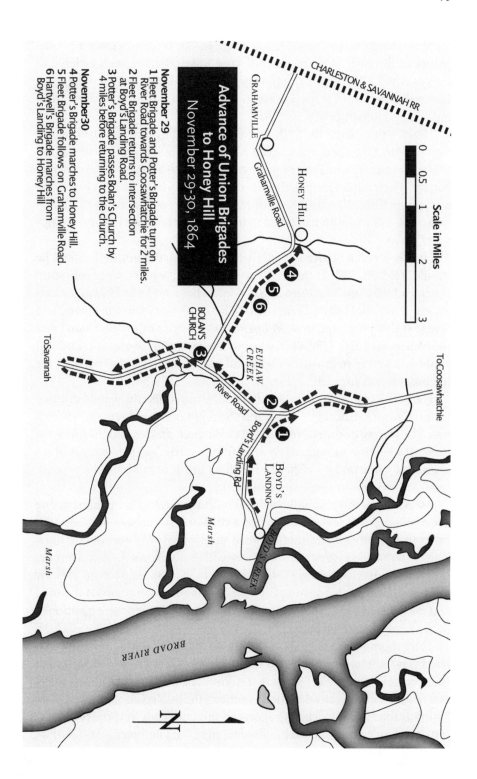

Advance of Union Brigades to Honey Hill
November 29-30, 1864

November 29

1 Fleet Brigade and Potter's Brigade turn on River Road towards Coosawhatchie for 2 miles.

2 Fleet Brigade returns to intersection at Boyd's Landing Road.

3 Potter's Brigade passes Bolan's Church by 4 miles before returning to the church.

November 30

4 Potter's Brigade marches to Honey Hill.

5 Fleet Brigade follows on Grahamville Road.

6 Hartwell's Brigade marches from Boyd's Landing to Honey Hill.

CHARLESTON & SAVANNAH RR

GRAHAMVILLE

Grahamville Road

HONEY HILL

BOLAN'S CHURCH

To Savannah

River Road

EUHAW CREEK

Boyd's Landing Rd

BOYD'S LANDING

BOYD'S CREEK

To Coosawhatchie

Marsh

Marsh

BROAD RIVER

N

Scale in Miles
0   0.5   1   2   3

tered in a single line with his fellow soldiers. But the two remaining companies of the 54th Massachusetts did not follow, having been ordered to support the 127th New York Infantry in the woods on the left of the road. Hartwell's "brigade" arrived at the front lines reduced to the strength of only eight companies of the 55th.[31]

Hatch had ordered the 55th to the wood road to provide covering fire for the 35th USCT, engaged ahead across the Grahamville Road and attempting to carry out Potter's impossible order to attack the Confederate battery. Their situation quickly degenerated into chaos, and, as described by Captain Soule, "Before the 55th Massachusetts could be closed up and formed the Thirty-fifth had fallen to the rear and there was nothing to support."

Hartwell, still a novice at battlefield command, did not understand he should hold the 55th at the wood road and await orders, especially since Hatch had told him "not to go into action, if [he] could help it, until further orders." Instead, Hartwell reasoned, "The musketry from the enemy was severe at this point; the men whom we had in front of my line along and near the road [35th USCT] had come to the rear in confusion, and as I could not well remain where I was, and had no orders to fall back, I gave the order to advance."[32]

Hartwell's explanation is difficult to fathom because the woods shielded his men from Confederate view, and the regiment could remain where it was. The troops, of course, responded to Hartwell's order, and the line went forward with the color guard. Within fifteen yards Smith, like most of his comrades, came under musket and artillery fire as he passed into the open, finally allowing him to see what awaited.

A line of earthworks followed the military crest of a ridgeline rising about twenty-five feet above and at a distance of perhaps one hundred yards from a stream running between the Union and Confederate lines. The center of the earthworks, a battery with embrasures for four cannon, sat on the north side of the Grahamville Road. Concealed from view by the woods and the left turn in the road, the battery commanded the road and the causeway over the stream. Two additional cannon were positioned in the road next to the battery.[33]

Long unknown to the Union command, the earthworks on Honey Hill had been built to block the road leading to the Charleston and Savannah Railroad at Grahamville. Dating to the winter of 1861–1862, they were part of a network of defenses designed to protect the South Carolina coast from Union infiltration by delaying access to the few roads and rivers leading into the state's interior, thereby allowing time for reinforcements to arrive by railroad. The failure of Foster's Coast Division to advance as planned had allowed the Confederates more than twenty-four hours to prepare their ambush of Hatch's column.[34]

Quickly receiving the order to retreat, Smith returned with the color guard and five of the 55th's companies to the relative safety of the wood road, but Companies E, I, and K on the regiment's right wing, with Colonel Fox and Captain Soule, did not hear the orders. Protected by the cover of forest, they continued forward and to their right to come upon the left flank of the 25th Ohio Volunteer Infantry. There the three companies remained separated from the remainder of the regiment for several hours.

Hartwell issued new orders, and Smith faced left with his comrades to return to the Grahamville Road. Below the road's left turn and sheltered from enemy fire, Hartwell formed the remaining five companies of the 55th, about three hundred men, into column by companies, its width restricted by the narrow path to a four-man front.[35] Smith and the remainder of the color guard took their position with Company C near the middle of the column.

It was evident to all they were being organized into column to charge the battery, but Hartwell knew what the troops did not: the 55th's attack was intended to draw the fire of Confederate guns, in sacrifice of their lives, to enable the 127th New York to cross the stream and charge the battery obliquely on its right.[36]

The idea to attack the fortified center of the Confederate line, which had been proposed by Lieutenant Colonel Stewart L. Woodford and Colonel William Gurney of the 127th New York and approved by the inexperienced Potter, was preposterous and should have never been attempted. The New York regiment contained only about 450 men, but even if it and the 55th had been at full strength, there would have been little or no chance of success. Perhaps Hartwell was too naive to appreciate the futility of the 55th's effort because he would order the regiment to charge not once, but twice.

At the center of the Confederate works, Captain Henry Middleton Stuart loaded his guns with double canister and fired when the first two companies cleared the turn in the road. Confederate artillerist Charles Alfred de Saussure saw "the full charge of [canister] from all 3 guns [go] into their ranks. I've seen wheat and oats go down before the scythe or mowing machine and that is the way the ranks, both first and second, fell beneath the hail of bullets." Smith's position in the center of the column did not come under Stuart's fire, and he fell back behind the turn in the road with the other survivors.[37]

Meanwhile, the 127th New York had crossed the creek on an oblique angle to the left of the 55th's charge, but only managed to advance as far as the marsh on the creek's opposite bank. The New York troops remained for about ten minutes, standing in water and trying to conceal themselves behind brushwood, before retreating into Union lines.[38]

Hartwell, inexplicably, resolved to attempt another charge, but he first ordered the color guard to the front ranks. With Color Sergeant King and the seven other corporals, Smith moved forward from the guard's regular position near the middle of the column. The front rank, only four men wide, reformed with Smith on the left flank, Corporal John H. Patterson carrying the regimental flag, King carrying the national flag, and Mathew McFarlan, the next ranking corporal (by date of promotion), on the right flank. The remaining color corporals entered the second and third ranks with the men from Company C. They were to lead the regiment against the battery. Color Sergeant King turned to Corporal Smith and said, "Will you come with me? I am going to carry the flag into the fort or die."[39]

From his horse, with his hat in one hand and his sword in the other, Colonel Hartwell yelled, "Follow your colors, my men!" The column moved forward. "It was like rushing into the very mouth of death going up this road facing [6] pieces of death dealing cannon," Sergeant Major Trotter recounted. "Colonel Hartwell and all of us knew this. But when commanded to charge, 'twas not his to refuse.'" The color guard marched up the road, moved beyond the turn, and crossed the creek. Inside the Confederate battery, Sergeant John A. Moore watched as "a Yankee officer dashed around the bend, waving his sword and encouraging his men." Captain Stuart fired.[40]

But the color guard was unharmed, and Color Sergeant King led Smith, Patterson, and McFarlan up the hill. The artillery had fired over the front ranks to hit closer to the center of the column, about where the color guard would normally have been. Captain William Crane, riding next to the colonel, shouted, "Come on boys, they are only Georgia militia!" just before he "was struck in the forehead by a canister ball and instantly killed. Lieut. [Winthrop] Boynton, his college friend and classmate, was struck in the leg by a bullet, fell forward, rose again, was again struck, and sank dead in the road-side stream." A round of canister killed Colonel Hartwell's horse, which collapsed to pin Hartwell under the weight of its body.[41]

During the seconds it took for the Confederate gunners to reload, the color guard charged forward with the more than two hundred other survivors still in the attack. As Smith, Patterson, King, and McFarlan continued their uphill rush, Patterson briefly fell behind, this probably being the mo-

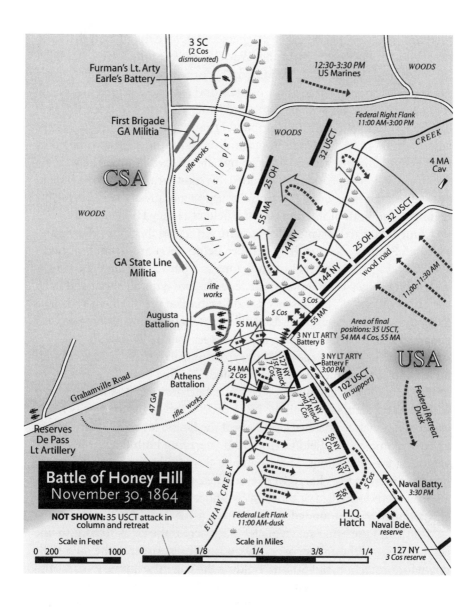

ment a musket ball hit his right arm, and Smith moved into the gap on King's immediate left. Smith recounted, "we had nearly reached the muzzles of the guns," within fewer than twenty yards of the cannon, when a tremendous blast staggered the color guard. King was hit in the chest by an unexpanded shell of canister. McFarlan, "touching elbows" that moment with Sergeant King, was hit with three bullets as he reached for the flag. Smith instantly reached out to King and "caught him with one hand and the flag with the other when he staggered back." He then heard the voice of Lieutenant Ellsworth screaming, "For God's sake Smith, save our flag!"[42]

Smith held the flag aloft and joined Corporal Patterson to unify the colors, but with so many dead and wounded and with no reinforcements, the regiment could go no farther. Smith and Patterson began to guide the 55th off the field. A soldier from Company D ran over to pick up McFarlan, who had fallen across King's body, and carry him to safety as the color bearers found themselves moving through air alive with musket balls. Then Smith saw Patterson had been wounded, his right arm "broken by a bullet." Smith took the regimental flag from Patterson and proceeded to bring his regiment and both of its colors off the field at Honey Hill.[43]

Confederate artilleryman de Saussure witnessed the 55th's charge and affirmed Smith's account. "I remember being on guard detail that night and pacing my beat, 60 feet or so before and parallel to the breastworks and having to step over and around dead negroes lying all about and in all sorts of postures."[44] The presence of bodies marked the regiment's advance to within less than twenty yards of the Confederate guns. Color Sergeant King had nearly carried the flag into the "fort" before he died.[45]

As color bearers, Sergeant King, Corporal Patterson, and Corporal Smith had been prime targets for the enemy. Saving both flags in the face of the enemy would have been especially dangerous even if Smith had been white, but his actions were all the more perilous given the animosity many Confederates felt for the black soldiers of the Union army. That Smith survived to come off the field at Honey Hill carrying both flags, unharmed, verged on the miraculous. More than one-third of the approximately three hundred men in the charge were casualties: two officers and thirty-nine enlisted men were killed or mortally wounded, three officers and sixty-five enlisted men were wounded.[46]

Smith and the other survivors fell back across the creek to go into line on the Union right under cover of woods. Officers ordered the men to lie down for protection, but Smith, "holding the flag up gripping it with [my] arm," was partially exposed. He drew more than his share of Confederate fire until "Captain Soule ordered me to get up and stick the flag in the ground and get away from it. Then he saw [two] bullets go into the ground close up to my head."[47]

Hatch ordered the withdrawal to commence at nightfall protected by infantry and artillery. Determined no one alive would be left behind, Smith and his fellow troops searched the ground. As the Coast Division began its retreat over the route they had taken that morning, the 54th and 55th Massachusetts broke "into squads to carry the wounded back on stretchers extemporized from muskets and blankets." Bolan's Church became a field hospital.[48]

The charge of the 55th was missing from both Hatch's and Potter's reports of the battle. No mention was made of the bravery of Robert King or Andy Smith. It was as if the charge of the 55th had never happened. Instead, Hatch reported his command to have made a determined effort, a hard-fought, offensive battle to draw Confederate troops from Sherman's path. He then supposedly withdrew his command in the face of a superior force shielded by impenetrable terrain. Foster, in turn, reported to Chief of Staff Halleck that enemy infantry in excess of four thousand troops supported the Confederate artillery at Honey Hill, more than doubling the number of enemy defenders and claiming a far more effective demonstration than in fact had occurred.[49]

The 55th's terrible sacrifice at Honey Hill was wasted during the battle and ignored by the army's high command thereafter, but the soldiers of the regiment could take some solace in the fact they had proved their courage as fighting men. Symbolically, Honey Hill had similar meaning for the men of the 55th Massachusetts as "Fort" Wagner had for the men of the 54th Massachusetts. At Honey Hill, the men of the 55th went the farthest of all, and the man who had come closest to the Confederate cannons would continue to lead them. Andy Smith now carried the colors. Indeed, the very next day, "the charge of the colors was given" by the commanding officers of the regiment "to Corp. Smith . . . and as soon as possible [February 1, 1865] he was promoted and appointed Color Serg. for good conduct."[50]

The simple truth was that ordered by inexperienced, subordinate officers instead of by their commanding general, men of the 55th Massachusetts twice in column charged the enemy against impossible odds, and common soldiers such as Color Sergeant Robert King and Corporal Andrew Smith responded with exceptional initiative, determination, and courage.

CHAPTER 6

BOYD'S LANDING TO CHARLESTON

December 1864–February 1865

EXHAUSTED, ANDY SMITH fell in for roll call at dawn with the 55th Massachusetts absent half of its officers, including Colonel Hartwell, and a third of the enlisted men. Smith had worked into the early morning carrying wounded onto hospital ships; thereafter, cold temperatures inhibited sleep during the night's few remaining hours.[1]

After roll call, Smith departed with his brigade to establish a defense perimeter encompassing the intersection of the River Road and Boyd's Landing Road two miles from Boyd's Neck. The 55th held the left flank of the infantry line, the 102nd and 26th USCT the center, and the 54th Massachusetts the right flank.[2]

These defensive preparations, combined with artillery fire and infantry probes beyond the line, were intended to divert Confederate attention from preparations to transfer the Coast Division to its new base at Deveaux's Neck on the Tulifinny River. From there Hatch was to make a second move against the Charleston and Savannah Railroad, but without the 54th and 55th Massachusetts. They would be left behind to cover the retreating regiments and defend Boyd's Neck.[3]

About midnight on December 5-6, Andy Smith stood at the defense perimeter in the cold and rain, alert to the danger of Confederate attack from the woods to his front. Behind his back, the change of base to Deveaux's Neck was quietly underway. Then, the two USCT regiments in the center of the defense perimeter withdrew toward their transports.[4] The 54th and 55th should have formed as skirmishers withdrawing on the rear of the USCT regiments, protecting them from attack while also falling back to their new entrenchments closer to Boyd's Neck.

Instead, both regiments remained at the perimeter, the 55th under orders to extend its line toward the center over the ground relinquished by the USCT troops. Smith shifted his position as the intervals between soldiers in the line expanded to more than six feet. The regiment was in a loose skirmish order extending more than a half-mile through woods, in the dark, where at any moment they might be under attack by an enemy they could not see. The 54th also extended its line from the right flank, but the 55th covered a greater distance.[5]

The 55th's position was utterly defenseless, yet Hatch's headquarters rebuffed an appeal to withdraw. Compounding the error, Hatch and his staff soon departed for Deveaux's Neck, leaving the 54th and 55th without orders to fall back. Smith spent tension-filled hours with his comrades staring into the dark, listening for the sounds of enemy movement, and waiting. In the hour before dawn, Colonel William Silliman (temporarily commanding the 2nd Brigade in Hartwell's absence) issued orders on his own authority to withdraw the regiments.[6] The 54th and 55th owed far more to the inattentiveness of the Confederates in the cold and rain than to the leadership of the Coast Division.

The 54th transferred to Deveaux's Neck the next evening, December 6, and Smith spent the next five weeks isolated with his regiment in enemy territory at Boyd's Landing. Without the strength of the 54th, the 55th's situation was potentially perilous. Confederate pickets continually monitored the regiment's movements, accompanied by exchanges of fire, but the purpose of this—whether to annoy or prepare to attack—was not evident to the defenders. Certainly, Boyd's Landing was a desirous position for the Confederates to take, one from where their artillery could disrupt the Broad River supply line to Hatch's command.[7]

The problems of coping with cold, rainy weather now consumed Smith's daily life, a situation made more trying by the absence of winter clothing and shelter. As were his comrades, Smith was in the same clothes he wore when departing Folly Island and carried only his rubber blanket for protection and warmth. Without tents, the men improvised shelters, described by Dr. Wilder as "'wigwams' of the long grass and branches of the trees; some of them have been covered lightly with earth. In front of each hut is a semicircular wall about two feet high for a fireplace."[8]

Meanwhile, Smith again listened to the sounds of battle he could not see, allowing him to follow the course of the war as it carried on beyond Boyd's Landing. At night, reverberations from trains running the Coast Division's guns reached the landing, affirming Hatch's continuing failure to cut the Charleston and Savannah Railroad. Meanwhile, sounds of cannon emanating from Georgia, thirty miles to the south, revealed the arrival of Sherman's columns marching toward the sea and investing Savannah. The thunderous explosions climaxed on December 20 when, just hours before Sherman's army entered the city, the Confederates evacuated Savannah with the aid of the Charleston and Savannah Railroad, and Lieutenant General Hardee's army of nine thousand soldiers crossed into South Carolina en route to reinforce Charleston's garrison.[9]

Smith and his comrades endured the cold and isolation at Boyd's Landing for another three weeks until orders to withdraw arrived on January 11.[10] Under the cover of darkness, Smith embarked on the *Fountain* to find himself and his regiment aboard an unseaworthy army transport. The troops carefully distributed their load and remained still to balance the *Fountain* as it made its way to Hilton Head. Arriving in the harbor without capsizing, the craft fortunately incurred mechanical failure, requiring the 55th to transfer to a seaworthy vessel, the *Sylph,* for the remainder of its journey. On January 13, the regiment arrived safely at Fort Thunderbolt near Savannah.[11]

Smith departed the *Sylph* with the other enlisted men to begin a stay of a few weeks on Savannah's Sea Islands. There the regiment received new uniforms, and at Fort Burton on January 31, 1865, Smith was promoted to color sergeant of the 55th Massachusetts by order of Lieutenant Colonel Fox: "Sergt. Andrew Smith having as Corporal of the Color Guard taken the Colors after the fall of Sergt. King and carried them through the rest of the action, is hereby detailed as Color Sergt. in recognition of his conduct on that occasion." On February 1, the men boarded the *Cosmopolitan* to rejoin Foster's command in support of Sherman's Carolinas Campaign.[12]

After a delay of several weeks caused by heavy rains and flooding, Sherman's columns began their advance into South Carolina with the intent of moving on Columbia, the state capital. The 55th was to participate in coastal demonstrations to convince Confederate leaders that Sherman's objective was Charleston, causing them to hold General Hardee's army within the city and direct other forces toward the coast, away from Sherman's front.

Arriving at Hilton Head on the night of February 1, the 55th received orders to join General Potter's command near Adam's Run in demonstra-

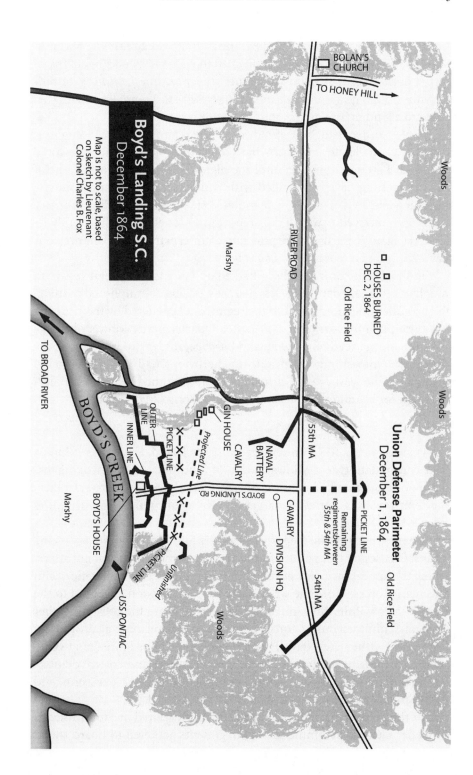

Boyd's Landing S.C.
December 1864

Map is not to scale, based
on sketch by Lieutenant
Colonel Charles B. Fox

BOLAN'S
CHURCH

TO HONEY HILL →

Woods

Marshy

RIVER ROAD

HOUSES BURNED
DEC. 2, 1864

Old Rice Field

Woods

TO BROAD RIVER

BOYD'S CREEK

Marshy

BOYD'S HOUSE

USS PONTIAC

OUTER
LINE

INNER LINE

PICKET LINE

Projected Line

GIN HOUSE

CAVALRY

NAVAL
BATTERY

BOYD'S LANDING RD.

PICKET LINE

Unfinished

CAVALRY

DIVISION HQ

55th MA

Union Defense Parimeter
December 1, 1864

Remaining
regiments between
55th & 54th MA

PICKET LINE

54th MA

Old Rice Field

Woods

tions against the Charleston and Savannah Railroad. Smith was about to participate in an especially poorly planned movement. The regiment transferred over water that night to another transport, the *Louisburg*, to rendezvous on inland rivers with the 144th New York Volunteer Infantry en route to a landing site on the South Edisto River.

Careless orders had, however, directed the regiments to a landing protected by Confederate artillery. With its direct path blocked, the 55th would not reach Potter's command until the night of February 5, with most of the intervening days being filled with fruitless marching and countermarching in search of an alternate route. Then, the next morning, February 6, the 55th received new orders to report to Colonel Hartwell on Folly Island, yet again requiring the regiment to countermarch over their previous day's ground and reboard the *Louisburg*.[13]

Smith and his comrades disembarked on Folly Island after a voyage in rough weather and days of useless marches, having accomplished nothing, to encounter one more insult to the regiment engendered by their superiors' poor planning. Just two days earlier, Quartermaster Mowery had departed with the regiment's tents and baggage, under orders to move the equipment into storage at Beaufort. The troops had no choice but to bivouac on the seashore in February, and Smith joined his fellow soldiers to search for abandoned tents and lumber among old campsites.[14]

ON FEBRUARY 7, as the 55th returned to Folly Island, Sherman's columns were consolidating near Midway, south of Columbia. Within striking distance of Augusta and Charleston, Sherman conducted feints toward each, the feint toward Charleston targeting Orangeburg, only seventy miles away.[15]

Foster's troops in the Department of the South now began advancing against Charleston from multiple directions to demonstrate, but not attack, giving the appearance they were surrounding the city in cooperation with Sherman's forces. From the west, Hatch's Coast Division advanced to the Edisto River, within thirty miles of Charleston. From the coast, Brigadier General Schimmelfennig's forces prepared to demonstrate against James Island, and within a few days, Potter would land troops more than twenty miles to the northeast at Bulls Bay. Schimmelfennig's and Potter's demonstrations were to be the last Union movements against Charleston, and Andy Smith would participate in each.[16]

On the cold night of February 9–10, Smith waited at Stono Inlet as Brigadier General Schimmelfennig's regiments gathered to board trans-

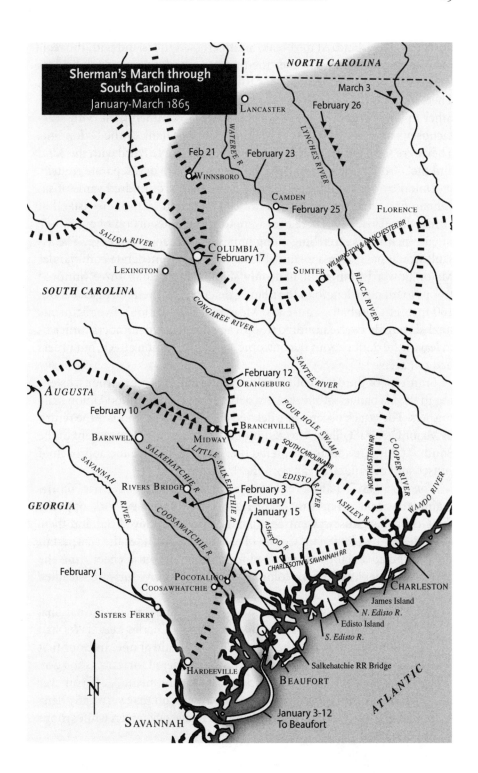

Sherman's March through
South Carolina
January-March 1865

NORTH CAROLINA

March 3
February 26

LANCASTER

WATEREE R.

LYNCHES RIVER

Feb 21   February 23

WINNSBORO

CAMDEN
February 25

FLORENCE

SALUDA RIVER

COLUMBIA
February 17

LEXINGTON

SUMTER

WILMINGTON & MANCHESTER RR

BLACK RIVER

SOUTH CAROLINA

CONGAREE RIVER

SANTEE RIVER

February 12
ORANGEBURG

FOUR HOLE SWAMP

AUGUSTA

February 10

BARNWELL

MIDWAY

BRANCHVILLE

SOUTH CAROLINA RR

NORTHEASTERN RR

COOPER RIVER

SALKEHATCHIE R.

LITTLE SALKEHATCHIE R.

EDISTO RIVER

WANDO RIVER

SAVANNAH RIVER

RIVERS BRIDGE

February 3
February 1
January 15

ASHLEY R.

GEORGIA

COOSAWATCHIE R.

ASHEPOO R.

February 1

POCOTALIGO
COOSAWHATCHIE

CHARLESTON & SAVANNAH RR

CHARLESTON

James Island
N. Edisto R.
Edisto Island
S. Edisto R.

SISTERS FERRY

N

HARDEEVILLE

Salkehatchie RR Bridge

BEAUFORT

ATLANTIC

SAVANNAH

January 3-12
To Beaufort

ports to Coles Island. At daybreak, Smith crossed the island with the regiment to negotiate his way over the first of several narrow plank bridges connecting the intermediate isles to Sol Legare Island's southern edge. There, roughly opposite Grimball's Causeway, the 55th halted with the two other infantry regiments of Colonel Hartwell's command, the 54th Massachusetts and 144th New York, to form the right flank of the Union line. They were soon joined on their left by Colonel George Baird with the 32nd and the 33rd USCT, who reached Sol Legare's shore by a separate route.[17]

Union troops would have to cross more than six hundred yards of savannah grassland that separated Sol Legare Island from James Island at Grimball's Causeway. There they were to strike one portion of a new line of entrenchments stretching along James Island's southern edge. The assault would have been a formidable task, except Confederate commander Major Edward Manigault had only slightly more than three hundred troops to man the length of the island's defenses. Of these, he placed about 160 men at Grimball's Causeway. Meanwhile, the Union's five regiments totaled roughly twelve hundred troops, an advantage in numbers sufficient to leave little doubt about the outcome should the Union attack, but orders had not arrived.[18]

Smith spent the day in bitter cold, waiting with the other troops, listening to the exchanges of musket fire between Confederate and Union skirmishers. The attack orders were delayed all day to accommodate the return of Major General Gillmore to resume command of the Department of the South.[19] Gillmore's steamer entered the Stono River with the approach of sunset, and the attack began with the 55th in reserve.

The 33rd USCT had never before advanced in line under fire. Yet the regiment was placed in front to the right of the 144th New York, opposite the Grimball's Causeway entrenchments. The 33rd moved out and then, as witnessed by Lieutenant Colonel Fox, coming "[u]nder the sharpest of the fire the advancing line wavered for a moment; but a cheer from the 55th as they deployed [from column] into line, to move forward, steadied it at once."[20]

Color Sergeant Andy Smith advanced with the line carrying the national flag in an attack described by Second Lieutenant Charles Lee: "[We] had to charge some earthworks; the Rebs held out . . . and at one time our first line came so near breaking that the 55th were ordered forward as the gen. said 'to save the day;' we coming up at just that moment. . . . If you ever hear anyone say the colored troops will not fight you may very flatly deny it; they are perfectly magnificent under fire. I have never seen white troops go into it with any more if as much spirit."[21]

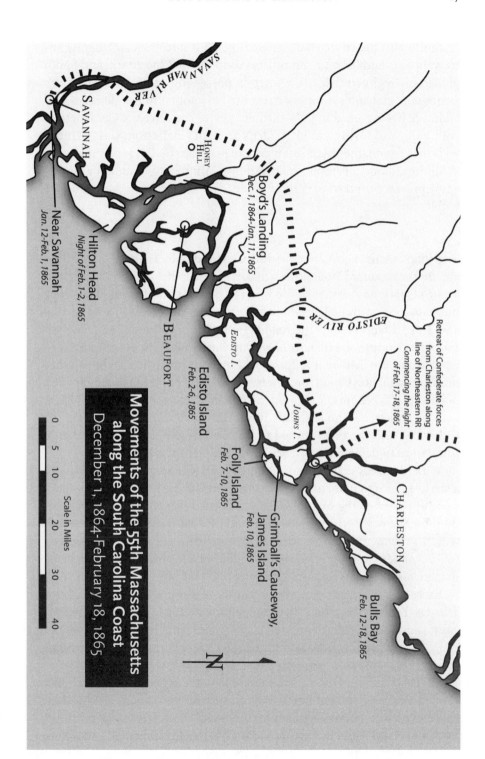

Movements of the 55th Massachusetts
along the South Carolina Coast
December 7, 1864–February 18, 1865

Scale in Miles

0   5   10   20   30   40

N

SAVANNAH RIVER

SAVANNAH

HONEY HILL

Boyd's Landing
Dec. 1, 1864–Jan. 11, 1865

Near Savannah
Jan. 12–Feb. 1, 1865

Hilton Head
Night of Feb. 1–2, 1865

BEAUFORT

EDISTO I.

Edisto Island
Feb. 2–6, 1865

EDISTO RIVER

Retreat of Confederate forces
from Charleston along
line of Northeastern RR
Commencing the night
of Feb. 17–18, 1865

JOHNS I.

Folly Island
Feb. 7–10, 1865

Grimball's Causeway,
James Island
Feb. 10, 1865

CHARLESTON

Bulls Bay
Feb. 12–18, 1865

Smith and the color guard guided the 55th into the Confederate entrenchments and beyond, but officers soon recalled the attack, and Smith guided his regiment back to reform in possession of Major Manigault's trenches. Manigault's troops had retreated to another line of defenses, and Gillmore had no need to fight further, only to convince the Confederates with a show of force to hold Hardee's army in Charleston. Union troops withdrew from James Island after dark to positions on the adjacent islands. With the support of naval artillery, they continued to maintain a threatening presence for days to come, but the 55th Massachusetts would not be with them.[22]

THE NEXT NIGHT, February 11, Smith departed Folly Island with the 55th aboard the steamer *Cosmopolitan* to participate in the Union's final action against Charleston. Potter's expedition of thirteen hundred men was supposed to land at Bulls Bay, about twenty miles northeast of Charleston, and move inland to seize the road between Mount Pleasant and Georgetown. His troops were then to "throw up works, and give the affair the appearance of a permanent lodgment." This movement was to be another diversion signaling Union forces were encircling Charleston in anticipation of Sherman's columns closing on the city from the state's interior.[23] Sherman, of course, had no such intention. His forces were presently nearing Columbia, and the threat posed to him by Hardee's army, embedded in Charleston to defend the city, was diminishing by the hour.

With its waters shallow and its shores lined with marshes, Bulls Bay was a terrible place to maneuver ships or land troops, problems that soon became apparent to the men of the 55th. The *Cosmopolitan*'s draft was too deep for the bay, and Andy Smith found himself transferring over water with his regiment to board another unseaworthy transport. The *Augusta* was a steamer with two engines that could not coordinate the movements of its two side wheels and rudders.[24]

Except for a brief respite allowed onshore at Bulls Island the night of Tuesday, February 14, the 55th spent February 12–18 confined to the *Augusta*, a period of tedium and inactivity punctuated by two gales, one of which developed into a powerful storm Smith had to endure belowdecks on the precarious craft with more than seven hundred other men.[25]

On February 16, Potter abandoned his initial attempt to land against Confederate defenders at Sewee Bay, on the southern shore of Bulls Bay, and moved his operations north to Owendaw Creek. He temporarily left the 55th behind with the *Augusta* and one gunboat to hold the Confederate

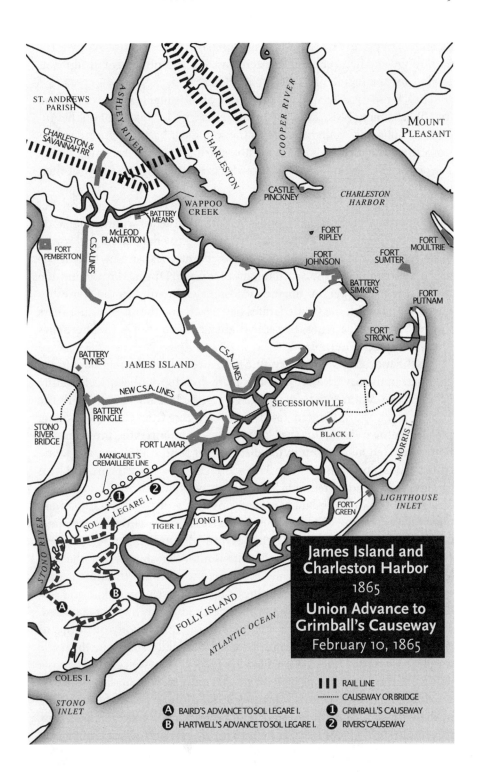

ST. ANDREWS PARISH

ASHLEY RIVER

CHARLESTON & SAVANNAH RR

CHARLESTON

COOPER RIVER

MOUNT PLEASANT

WAPPOO CREEK

BATTERY MEANS

McLEOD PLANTATION

CASTLE PINCKNEY

CHARLESTON HARBOR

FORT PEMBERTON

C.S.A. LINES

FORT RIPLEY

FORT JOHNSON

FORT SUMTER

FORT MOULTRIE

BATTERY SIMKINS

FORT PUTNAM

FORT STRONG

BATTERY TYNES

JAMES ISLAND

C.S.A. LINES

SECESSIONVILLE

NEW C.S.A. LINES

BATTERY PRINGLE

BLACK I.

STONO RIVER BRIDGE

FORT LAMAR

MANIGAULT'S CREMAILLERE LINE

MORRIS I.

SOL LEGARE I.

TIGER I.

LONG I.

FORT GREEN

LIGHTHOUSE INLET

STONO RIVER

FOLLY ISLAND

ATLANTIC OCEAN

**James Island and
Charleston Harbor**
1865
**Union Advance to
Grimball's Causeway**
February 10, 1865

COLES I.

STONO INLET

RAIL LINE
CAUSEWAY OR BRIDGE

Ⓐ BAIRD'S ADVANCE TO SOL LEGARE I.
Ⓑ HARTWELL'S ADVANCE TO SOL LEGARE I.

❶ GRIMBALL'S CAUSEWAY
❷ RIVERS' CAUSEWAY

defenders in place. The following morning, the *Augusta* was to convey the 55th to Owendaw Creek but ran aground and did not arrive until it was too late for the regiment to disembark.[26]

Thus, Smith was destined to spend one of the notable nights of the war, that of February 17–18, crowded belowdecks with his regiment on the *Augusta* in Bulls Bay, again listening to the sounds of battle. He heard explosions from the direction of Charleston during the early morning hours, but neither he nor anyone else belowdecks on the *Augusta* knew of their importance.[27]

On February 18, Potter was anxious to advance toward Charleston, but with only thirteen hundred troops, he dared not leave without the 55th. The regiment was finally taken off the *Augusta* in small boats and rowed to shore, but the landing was not completed until near sunset, forcing the brigade to bivouac on the beach for another night. During the evening, the troops learned the reason for the explosions emanating from Charleston the previous night: the Confederates had evacuated the city.[28] Other news was still to arrive: during the same night of February 17–18, Sherman's forces occupied Columbia.

On the morning of February 19, Smith awoke with the regiment to see gunboats in the bay "dressed in colors from deck to masthead," celebrating Charleston's capture. Potter departed with the brigade at sunrise in the hope of intercepting Confederate troops retreating from Charleston along the Georgetown Road, but the Confederates had passed the previous day. Potter then led his column in the direction of Mount Pleasant, attracting contrabands along the way. The 55th was charged with their care and with foraging, as Fox admitted: "On a small scale we followed Sherman's example, and cattle in abundance, horses, poultry, and sweet potatoes were plenty in our camp." That evening, Smith slept by the Christ Church line, Charleston's abandoned outer defenses near Mount Pleasant.[29]

The next morning, February 20, with Smith carrying the flag, the 55th led the Union column down the main road to Mount Pleasant to commence a memorable day. A scattering of individual Union sailors and soldiers had recently entered the town, but the Union army had not appeared. Thus, Fox observed, "the 55th was the first organized body of troops to enter the town after its evacuation. Words would fail to describe the scene which those who witnessed it will never forget,—the welcome given to a regiment of colored troops by their people redeemed from slavery."[30]

Mount Pleasant's white residents were out of sight, probably remaining in their houses, "but the colored population turned out *en masse*," Fox recorded, "and welcomed the Regt. with cheers and shouts, tears and

"'Marching on!'—The Fifty-fifth Massachusetts Colored Regiment singing John Brown's March in the streets of Charleston, February 21, 1865," *Harper's Weekly*, March 18, 1865. (*Library of Congress*)

prayers, dancing and singing. The blessing showered upon the men, in truthful though broken words from aged lips, the frequent grasp of the hand, the tearful eyes, and the smiling faces of that day will long be remembered by the soldiers of the 55th as their first experience & perhaps their brightest and truest, in bearing the tidings of freedom to their kindred by race in the land of slavery." Fox wrote to his wife, "If I were to live to the extreme of the usual age of men, the memory of this day would remain bright and distinct to the end."[31]

In the evening, Smith enjoyed the amenities of the 55th's fine campsite, a flat field between Mount Pleasant "and Sullivan's Island, where air and water were good, and there was a fine place for salt-water bathing, of which the men soon availed themselves," even in the cold of winter. They enjoyed one restful night. In the morning, orders arrived to move to Charleston Neck, on the peninsula above the city.

Late in the afternoon, the 55th boarded another steamer to cross the harbor, arriving shortly before sunset. In fading daylight, the regiment fell in along the street by the wharf. Smith took his place with the Color Guard in the column, just ahead of its center, and unfurled the flag. The men were ordered to give "three rousing cheers . . . and they were given with a will."[32]

When the 32nd USCT arrived from Mount Pleasant, the regiments began to march through Charleston. Initially, Smith saw devastation wrought by bombing and fire as the column traversed the ruins of the lower city. Then, upon reaching the neighborhoods laying beyond the destruction, Smith could see people in the streets ahead, celebrating their freedom as they awaited the arrival of black Union regiments: "The men were told that keeping in their ranks they were at liberty to cheer, shout and sing as much as they chose—and they availed themselves of the privilege in its fullest extent. . . . The white inhabitants kept mostly in their houses, only some of the poorer class appearing in the street, but at almost every window either openly or behind blind or curtain curiosity proved stronger than sentiment."[33]

Charleston's black and white residents watched as a black man carried the national colors through the city, and Fox opined, "The 55th was the first full Regt. I think, that marched through the city of Charleston; the first colored Regt. I am quite sure."[34] If he was correct, then Color Sergeant Smith could have been the first person to return the flag of the United States on parade to the streets of Charleston.

Fox recorded the scene for posterity:

[T]he colored population were in their glory—Prayers and thanks—giving cheers and shouts of welcome were heard on every side. Men and women crowded to shake hands with men and officers at every opportunity, and to talk with them earnestly and understandingly about the past, present, and future. . . . On through the rebel city the column passed, the walls ringing to the echo of manly voices singing in chorus, 'John Brown,' 'Babylon is Falling,' 'The Battle Cry of Freedom,' and other similar songs.

After a march of more than four miles, the 55th reached its destination on Charleston Neck, joining the other regiments in Potter's new brigade.[35]

For the second consecutive night, Andy Smith slept by the earthworks of Charleston's Confederate defenses.

PART 2

DUTY

CHAPTER 7

WAR'S END

February–September 1865

THE 55TH MASSACHUSETTS DEPARTED Charleston Neck on the morning of February 22, with Brigadier General Potter's command to monitor the withdrawal of Charleston's Confederate garrison toward the Santee River. Andy Smith would spend more than two weeks of hard marching in winter rain and witness slavery's end on low country plantations north of Charleston.[1]

Marching in rain, the Union column came under skirmishing fire on February 24 as it encountered the Confederates' rear guard. Throughout the following day, Confederates engaged Potter in a successful delaying action northeast of Moncks Corner. He took up the chase the next morning, February 26, and Smith marched with the column through ankle-deep water for much of the day. Approaching sundown, they arrived at St. Stephens Depot to learn the Confederates had escaped across the Santee River by train, ensuring their safe departure by burning the Northeastern Railroad bridge.[2]

Potter's expedition now reverted to its secondary purpose: to raid plantations. Under orders, quartermasters had not provided Potter's regiments with full rations, forcing his troops to forage for provisions on local farms and plantations. The process was already well underway before reaching St. Stephens Depot. Camping at night, officers deployed foraging details to nearby plantations with orders "to take . . . whatever was needed for the use of the command or whatever could be made serviceable by the enemy, especially horses and teams." Soon foragers deposited "piles of chickens, turkeys, ducks, geese, sweet potatoes, bags of flour and meal, hens, eggs" for the quartermaster to divide among the troops. With Smith already serving as color sergeant, there is no indication he was detailed to or participated in foraging activities, though he certainly shared in the meals provided.[3]

Departing from St. Stephens on March 2, Smith entered pristine plantation country, untouched by the devastations of war, to witness a world of privilege and wealth built on the foundation of slavery. He would also see slaves hearing the words they were free, the good news received as soon as they encountered soldiers, either on the march passing through fields or upon arrival at plantation houses. Potter attempted to render planters near destitute by burning, pillaging, confiscating weapons and food, and, of course, depriving them of their now former slaves. But freedom did not come easy amid such chaos, as Smith learned on a subsequent low country expedition in April.

After a march of several hours, Smith found himself in a place of planter privilege, the village of Pineville, where the column halted for its midday meal. All around, he saw summer houses belonging to planter families who annually escaped to Pineville's cooler and healthier high ground. These fortunate few thereby abandoned the heat and summer sickness prevalent on low country plantations to the overseers and slaves who remained to work the fields. The soldiers did little damage in the village, other than appropriating fence rails for firewood to cook their meals, until departure. Then Potter directed his mounted troops to burn unoccupied houses (those without a staff of resident slaves), about eight to ten in number.[4]

For several days, Potter had used confiscated horses to send mounted infantry in advance of his column's route to burn vacant houses and loot plantations. Some of Potter's infantry also stole away from the column to loot and burn, especially those in the 21st USCT who had escaped from slavery on local plantations. Potter's troops, including the looters, not only carried the message of freedom, but they also told former slaves they might either remain on the plantations or accompany Union troops to Charleston.[5]

That evening Potter's column arrived at Pooshee, a plantation belonging to the Ravenel family, only to learn looters had come the previous evening. He evidenced little concern and instructed his troops to settle for the night near the southern boundary of Pooshee land. From his bivouac, Smith

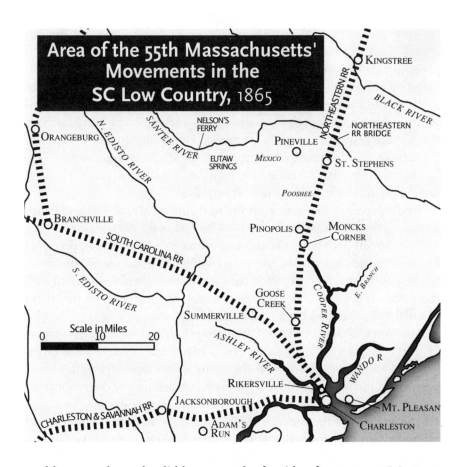

Area of the 55th Massachusetts' Movements in the SC Low Country, 1865

could see another splendid house on the far side of a stream at Wantoot, the neighboring plantation of Charleston mayor Charles MacBeth, presently in the city with his family. The next morning, some of Potter's troops took the opportunity to loot whatever might still be carried away from Pooshee, and when the Union column departed, the vacant plantation house at Wantoot was in flames.[6]

Smith now carried the flag in a column that had increased considerably in length, augmented by numerous former slaves seeking a new life in Charleston. After a day's march over muddy roads, the troops returned to the area of Moncks Corner, where the column divided. The refugees, escorted by one brigade, departed for Charleston. Smith was among the remaining troops who were to sweep "the whole country on both banks of the Cooper River," destroying rice mills, seeking stores of rice and cotton, confiscating horses and mules. The 55th would advance down the Cooper's east bank.[7]

Smith moved through more beautiful countryside to see many fine but vacant houses and numerous former slaves seeking to depart from their plantations. The brigade's work completed by March 6, Potter led his command inland on the return march to Charleston, an often difficult march in the rain to Daniel Island, where, ironically, the troops faced food shortages because Union foragers had already scavenged the area. On March 10, the *Augusta* arrived to ferry the command slowly and awkwardly back to Charleston. Smith moved out once again on Meeting Street to carry the flag through the city as the 55th returned to Charleston Neck. The next day the regiment made camp near Rikersville.[8]

Smith departed Rikersville on the morning of March 17 amid much fanfare as the 55th marched through Charleston on parade "down King and Bay Streets with band playing and colors flying, every man doing his best to give the regiment a regular and soldierly appearance." Fox noted, "[t]he band or drum corps played constantly," and "arms were carried with great attention. . . . The desire [was] to make a good show in this [city] where they had so long been held in derision."[9]

The 55th was en route to the South Atlantic Wharf to board a transport for conveyance to its new base on James Island. Headquarters was established at McLeod plantation on the island's northern edge with several companies, including Smith's Company B, camped nearby. The regiment's arrival on James Island was interrupted by a gruesome discovery on March 19: the remains of their soldiers killed in the attack at Rivers' Causeway had been lying exposed to the elements since the previous July. As the color sergeant, Smith participated in the escort to recover and convey the remains (the bones of seven 55th men and two soldiers from the 33rd USCT comingled into one coffin) to headquarters at McLeod plantation. Then, on March 26, again as the color sergeant, Smith participated in the solemn military funeral the regiment accorded these soldiers, interring them in a beautiful, wooded location within the remnants of an old earthwork, Battery Means. Today, the remains of Battery Means lie beneath the golf course of the Country Club of Charleston, encompassed by the eleventh tee.[10]

A FEW DAYS LATER, on March 30, the 55th's tranquil duty at Charleston was disturbed by the shooting of Private Alfred E. Pelette, whom Burt Wilder described as "one of the greatest rascals in the regiment." Pelette had slipped away from the camp at Rikersville, remaining at large for nearly two weeks until officers sighted him and another deserter in Charleston, each dressed in civilian clothes. Fox assigned Captain Grant to lead the arresting party.

The ranking noncommissioned officer was Senior Musician and Drum Major Sergeant Eli Lett, under whom Pelette had served in the band. Fox also selected Smith, who was experienced in provost guard duty and had intervened against Pelette the previous November to protect the regiments' laundress from Pelette's drunken antics.[11]

Captain Grant's party located Pelette in Charleston, but he managed to elude his captors, among whom was Smith. Sergeant Lett then sent "Sergeant Smith to arrest him again. I gave orders [to Smith] such as had been given me, that if he [Pelette] would not go any other way, to Shoot him down." From soldiers of the 54th Massachusetts, Smith learned Pelette had gone to East Bay Street, where five companies of the regiment were temporarily camped. Pelette later testified he had joined the 54th troops to eat a meal, but he had a more important reason for intermingling with them. The men of the 54th were waiting to be conveyed by a steamer to Georgetown, providing Pelette with a means to escape from the city. Thus, Pelette was actively deserting when Smith, working alone, found him.[12]

Pelette would not go with Smith, even after several requests and Smith's warning he would shoot him. Finally, "on his repeated refusal to give himself up [Smith] fired and inflicted a severe though not fatal wound." The round entered Pelette's right breast and carried through to his back, and Smith obtained assistance to transport Pelette to a hospital in Charleston. Fox concluded Smith's "action was proper and justifiable and likely to have a beneficial result in the Regt." Indeed, if Smith had not fired, he would have violated his orders.[13]

Wilder shared Fox's confidence in Smith, recording in his diary, "Col. Fox told Smith that he could not have acted otherwise; that, hard as it was for him, his prompt action might be the means of saving the lives of others who might be tempted to follow Pelette's example & be shot for disobedience. Smith's story was manly, simple, and straightforward, with no sign of boasting or mock regret; for he knew he had done his duty and obeyed his orders. From this incident our men will recognize the authority and power of the non-commissioned officers."[14]

Pelette remained in the hospital while the regiment was absent on another expedition in April. Late in the month, Fox discovered Pelette was recovering quite nicely and had been "allowed to go about the city without guard and to visit dances and other places of amusement." Fox quickly put an end to Pelette's participation in Charleston's nightlife and had him arrested again.[15]

On May 23, Pelette's case came before a court-martial. He pleaded guilty to the first charge, desertion, but not guilty to the specifications (the facts presented in support of the charge). He also pleaded not guilty to the second charge, disobedience of orders, and to its specifications. Pelette did not explain his objections to the specifications of desertion, attempting instead to present himself as a good soldier until he left the regiment at Rikersville. Sergeant Isaiah H. Welsh of Pelette's Company C testified in support of his character:

> Question by Defense: "What has been my general character as a soldier in the Company?"
> Answer [Sergeant Welsh]: "Very good indeed."
> Question by Defense: "Have I ever been backward in performing the duties allotted to me?"
> Answer: "No you have not."
> Question by Defense: "Have I ever been punished previous to this arrest?"
> Answer: "Once only."
> Question by Defense: "Was it for a grave offense or otherwise?"
> Answer: "It was for being drunk."
> Captain Grant being recalled for the defense was examined on his previous oath.
> Question by Defense: "Have I not performed my duties well during my service?"
> Answer: "To my knowledge you have."[16]

Pelette could have been arrested on more serious charges than drunkenness on the November night when Smith had subdued him, but Sergeant Welsh, who was apparently trying to help Pelette, did not elaborate on the charge; Captain Grant, who had been on furlough in November, was evidently unaware of the details of the arrest. As the regiment was not in Charleston during the court-martial, no one was available to comment on Pelette's character, except Smith and Lett, and neither was asked to do so by the court. Thus Pelette managed to introduce the suggestion of good service as a mitigating factor in his defense.

The testimonies of Sergeants Lett and Smith, however, presented far more significant obstacles for Pelette as he attempted to challenge the charge of disobedience of orders. Sergeant Lett's account was revealing about Pelette's disposition and the problems he presented for Smith, clearly establishing Smith had been ordered to do exactly as he did: shoot Pelette if he resisted arrest.

I went to the house where he [Pelette] was; Situated near King Street, Charleston, down an alley between King and Meeting. I called him out of doors, and told him I was sent to arrest him, and take him to the regiment then on James Island. I told him, after I arrested him that he would have to go with me, I told him it was no use getting excited as I had my orders and that he would have to obey them, for he swore "that he would be damned" if he would go with me. He said also that he wanted a guard with muskets to take him. I told him I had Sufficient arms. I told him again he had to go with me, when he repeated again "he would be *damned* if he would go;" I said I must take him one way or the other, he replied I might shoot him. "You can shoot me. I would rather be shot by you than the damn white Officers," I told him that as far as the shooting was concerned I did not want to shoot him, I wanted him, [to] go quietly. He then went down to Duncan Street to get his Soldier's Clothes. I was with him, and I left him there in charge of Sergeant Smith, until I went to the Citadel and back, we then took him up to the Citadel, and put him in the Guard house there until such time as we could get a boat to take him across, after the boat was ready at West Point Mill, I took him down by King Street to the dock, when waiting there for the boat's crew, he ran off. I then sent Sergeant Smith to arrest him again. I gave orders such as had been given me, to Shoot him down.[17]

Smith testified next, affirming Lett's account and describing the circumstances of Pelette's arrest:

Sergeant Lett first went into the house, where the accused was, he came out and went down the Street, I went with Pelette to his house where his wife was, to see her, and for him to change his clothes. I then took the accused to the Captain, and he ordered me to go to the Citadel with him. I put him in the Guardhouse there, and Captain Grant told me to wait there whilst he got a boat ready to take the accused over [to James Island]. Captain Grant then sent Eli Lett to me to say the boat was ready and to take the accused down, when we got there it was so rough, we could not cross. Whilst waiting there he slipped off. I found that he had gone up to the left wing of the 54th Mass Volunteers, somewhere in East Bay Street. I arrested him again by orders from Eli Lett. I asked him if he had not acted mean towards me, getting off as he had done. He replied "do you think I have treated you mean[?]" I told him yes. I then told him to get his cap and go with me, he refused to go with me, and said he would go pretty soon. I then drew my revolver, I cocked it, and told him that I gave him two minutes to either go or not, for I would kill him if he did not go with me. I then asked him three times to go, which he refused. I then shot him. After I shot him, he said he would go. I cocked my pistol again, then he started to go, and went as far as he said he could. I then told him to lay down. I went to the dock and reported to an officer of the 54th Mass. Vols. and asked him to take charge of the accused until I could let Captain Grant know. Captain Grant ordered him to be sent to the General Hospital and for me to return to the Regiment.[18]

Pelette then testified, attempting to discredit Smith's testimony, arguing Smith, by his own statement, had no authority over him, had acted unreasonably, and had shot him unnecessarily:

When I was arrested we could not get over to James Island on account of wind and tide. The Sergeant that had arrested me [Sergeant Lett] had left the dock, and I asked the Color Sergeant, who had charge of me? He said Sergeant Lett the Drum Major, but that he had gone away. I told the Color Sergeant that I would like someone to go with me as I wanted something to eat. He replied he could not go, so I said I would go by myself. I then went to the 54th Mass Vols and got my dinner, when there Sergeant Smith came down, and asked if I had not treated him meanly. I said no, for you told me you had no charge of me. He then told me to get my cap and go with him. I told him I would go in a moment, just to wait, he replied that that is all I want to hear, he stepped back a few paces, and I laughed at him, when he fired his revolver, and the ball struck me in the right breast. After he had shot me, he told me to go with him. I replied I could not do so. He said if I did not do so, he would shoot me like a dog. I started on down the dock, when Lieutenant Swales met me. He told me to stop and lay down, that I had no business walking, and he wanted the doctor to see me. Dr. Baker came and took the ball out of my back, and sent me to the Post Hospital where I stayed five weeks.

In the hope it would lessen his sentence, Pelette concluded his statement emphasizing he had been shot: "I have nothing further to say but throw myself on the mercy of the Court. I have suffered a great deal from the effects of this shot."[19]

Private Pelette was found guilty of all charges and specifications and sentenced to "hard labor for One Year . . . and to forfeit to the United States

Treasury all his pay during the period of his confinement." It is difficult to know if Pelette's protestations had any impact on the length of his sentence, which easily could have been longer. If anything mitigated the severity of his punishment, it was likely the war's end. Pelette endured his imprisonment at Fort Marion in Florida, and the regimental history listed him as living in Charleston after the war.[20]

AT SUNRISE ON APRIL 6, Smith departed Charleston Neck, his regiment's duty on James Island having been abruptly terminated. Colonel Hartwell commanded a brigade of two infantry regiments, the 55th Massachusetts and the 54th New York, on a return mission to the low country plantations south of the Santee River. The pilfering committed during Potter's previous expedition precluded any hope of living off the land, so Smith and the other troops carried eight days of rations.[21]

Hartwell's small command was to deter local mounted vigilantes and Confederate cavalry—in particular, a band commanded by Lieutenant Edward Pettus—from disrupting another Union raid led by Potter in progress north of the Santee River. These groups, called "scouts" by the planters, often intermingled, operating to safeguard local planters and control freedmen in the wake of Potter's previous raid into the low country.[22]

Hartwell's assignment bordered on the ludicrous as he was to search out and apprehend enemy cavalry using only his infantry, all available Union cavalry having been assigned to Potter. Smith and his comrades had little to do for the next two days except engage in hard marching as they chased Pettus's cavalry, said to have been murdering freedmen along the Cooper River. On April 7, as Hartwell advanced toward Pinopolis and the low country plantations, Pettus's troops closed around his column. They did not attack during the day but engaged in skirmishing that night. The next morning, in the rain and still under observation by Pettus, Hartwell led the brigade north to Pineville, and the mission suddenly took on new purpose.[23]

Smith entered the village to witness white residents descending on Hartwell while freedmen sought out enlisted men to covey terrifying accounts of scouts riding in to shoot some of them and hang others from trees. Whites, fearing for their lives, pleaded with Hartwell for protection. Meanwhile, Fox took testimony from numerous individuals and concluded the perpetrators "proved . . . to be a party of [Pettus's] Cavalry aided by some of the neighboring planters." The "indignation of the men" was raised "to the highest pitch," Fox recorded, "and but for the strict discipline to which this Regt. had been always accustomed, the village would have been in great danger of being burned."[24]

Smith saw local freedmen, fearful for their lives, gravitate to Union soldiers for safety. "[A]n exodus of the freed people commenced at this point," Fox recorded, "which continued during the remainder of the expedition, until the refugee-train was far larger than the rest of the column." Hartwell departed late in the afternoon leading his troops and the refugees on a five-mile march to Mexico, the plantation of Mazyck Porcher, a strong supporter of the perpetrators at Pineville. The expedition now assumed the responsibility for protecting families of freedmen escaping from Pettus's cavalry. [25]

As Smith entered Mexico, he was able to comprehend, as never before, the accumulation of wealth and luxury a slave plantation could afford its owner. Porcher's house was "the most elegant which the expedition had seen. . . . situated in a large park, shaded by magnificent trees," and, Hartwell believed, had become the place for "the headquarters of the Rebels in the vicinity." Porcher was the only person Hartwell could tie to the killings at Pineville, for which he soon began to experience the Union's wrath. Hartwell placed him under arrest to be conveyed to Charleston, and in the evening considerable looting of Porcher's house occurred.[26]

That night Smith bivouacked in the splendor and elegance of Porcher's estate. At daylight, April 9, the brigade departed Mexico with Porcher condemned to walk the distance to Charleston behind the headquarters wagon. As the column departed the plantation grounds, Smith looked back to see the plantation house in flames. Hartwell was careful to deflect responsibility from the regiment, but the fire appears to have been set by officers and troops from both regiments who, serving as the guard for the previous night, were the last to quit the grounds at Mexico.[27]

Under close observation by Pettus's cavalry, Hartwell led his column southwest toward Eutaw Springs, where they arrived midday. He had prohibited the burning of houses along the line of march except for one used by Pettus's men to fire on Hartwell's troops. Otherwise looting had been underway throughout the morning and continued after the column arrived at Eutaw Springs. Hartwell appears to have ignored these excesses of foraging, at least in part due to the need for food for the rapidly growing numbers of freedmen wanting to escape to Charleston.[28]

On April 10, the brigade formed in line across the Revolutionary War battlefield at Eutaw Springs to shelter the gathering freedmen from attack by Pettus. Smith watched the numbers of refugees grow as virtually all former slaves from area plantations arrived to join Hartwell's column for the trip to Charleston. The refugees totaled perhaps 1,500 individuals, many carrying their meager possessions, others using carriages, wagons, or pack animals "loaded [with] feather-beds and tinware, looking-glasses and iron pots, earthenware, damask curtains, silk dresses, frying-pans, churns,—in short, almost every article of dress and household furniture one can imagine in addition to food and forage."[29]

The column, more than a mile in length, departed late in the afternoon to avoid traveling in the heat of the day. The refugees were in the center, protected in the front and rear by the soldiers. They made camp about midnight at the edge of a swamp, surrounded by a semicircle of troops, and in the morning continued through the swamp. With the 55th now serving as the rear guard, Smith could see the trail of belongings discarded along the side of their path as the difficult route exhausted pack animals and broke down wagons. Worse yet, their progress was slow, and Pettus's cavalry was able to close on the column and began to kill stragglers.[30]

The column exited the swamp onto the state road under fire from Pettus's cavalry. Hartwell used artillery to disperse Pettus's troops and forestalled further attacks by threatening to set fire to houses along their path should any new incidents occur. Pettus continued to shadow the line of Union troops and refugees as they proceeded toward Charleston, leaving a path marked by more discarded possessions. Pettus's cavalry hovered in the distance when the column reached Goose Creek midday on April 12. There a temporary camp was established under protective guard, and most of the 55th, including Smith, returned to Rikersville.[31]

Late that night at Rikersville, Smith awoke to loud band music, "Hail Columbia, The Star Spangled Banner, Yankee Doodle, John Brown, Babylon is Falling &c." Colonel Fox had "turned out the band" to wake the camp upon receipt of the news Richmond had fallen to Union forces and General Robert E. Lee's Army of Northern Virginia had surrendered: "Cheer after cheer arose from the men as the news circulated, the officers appeared in anything but the regulation dress, and it was more than an hour before the camp was again quiet."[32]

ANDY SMITH DID NOT WITNESS the ceremonial flag raising over Fort Sumter on April 14, 1865, four years to the day after the fort's colors had been struck. Among the several thousand dignitaries, both civilian and military, only soldiers of the 35th USCT were present because their commander, Colonel Beecher, was the brother of Henry Ward Beecher, who was to give the oration. Instead, the 55th continued to shield the refugees at Goose

Creek from Pettus's cavalry and provide for their transfer first to Rikersville and then to the Sea Islands.[33]

On April 17, the regiment received orders to move its campsite from Rikersville to St. Andrews Parish, a pleasant location on the north bank of Wappoo Creek opposite their former James Island encampment at McLeod's plantation. On April 19, the men were busily preparing their new campsite and moving the regiment's equipment and baggage by way of the Ashley River and Wappoo Creek. Some were even in midstream when they learned of President Lincoln's assassination.[34]

"[T]he sad news," Fox related, turned "rejoicing to sorrow, gladness to mourning," and caused "intense excitement among the troops and the freed people." Lieutenant Lee expressed the feelings of anger, "We received the sad news today of President Lincoln's assassination. All I can say is that I hope this war will continue till every man, woman, and child of secession proclivities are either banished or exterminated. This may not be the right feeling but I cannot help it. Can anyone tell me what will be the satisfaction of simply hanging the perpetrators?"[35]

On April 20, Smith left Rikersville to carry the flag through Charleston as the 55th marched down Meeting Street en route to the wharves for transportation to their new camp. The regiment moved through a city in "mourning, flags at half-mast, minute-guns and tolling bells, the various headquarters draped in black, and the crape shrouding the colors and worn by the officers of the different commands, seemed feeble expressions of feeling, for so great a loss. Even the rebel population united in condemnation of so cowardly a murder; and scarcely a colored person could be met in the streets, who had not assumed, in some form or other, the badge of mourning." Fox overheard "a well-dressed old servant woman [say] to a crowd of her acquaintances, 'Pears like we all ought to put on black for him, for he was a mighty good father to us.'"[36]

The regiment's mood remained somber as it settled in at St. Andrews Parish. "I think every man in the Regt. felt it," Lieutenant Lee explained. "There was no noise, laughing, or singing, or anything of the kind; it certainly was a singular thing to see so many men who are usually perfectly careless about everything this sad, for sad they were." On May 2, news arrived in Charleston of the surrender of Joseph E. Johnston's and P. G. T. Beauregard's armies. The war had ended in South Carolina and the occupation begun.[37]

ON MAY 7, Smith once again took up the flag as the regiment marched inland to its final assignment, to assist the Freedmen's Bureau in protecting
the free standing of former slaves in the military Sub-District of Orangeburg and Barnwell. The column marched through what once had been bu-
colic plantation country bordering the Ashley River and passed by portions
of Charleston's crumbling earthworks, now sporting weeds. Nearing the
end of their journey, Smith carried the flag by the house of an old white
man who "threw up his hat and cheered, and actually cried when he saw
the flag."[38]

Before noon on May 8, the 55th arrived outside of Summerville to join
with Hartwell's new brigade, which he led into town on parade. The
brigade spent nearly two weeks there to participate in repairs to the railroad
before proceeding farther inland. Smith's duty, however, was with the
provost's guard, responsible for keeping the peace in Summerville and for
protecting residents from attacks by "lawless men" roaming the area. On
the whole, relations with local whites were peaceful.[39]

On May 10, while Smith was on duty in Summerville, slightly more
than two hundred miles to the southwest near Irwinville, Georgia, Union
troops captured Confederate president Jefferson Davis and his escort.
Among the members of Davis's guard was Private Harrison Smith, 2nd
Kentucky Cavalry, Andy Smith's seventeen-year-old white nephew with
whom he had been gathering corn on the winter morning of his escape
from slavery. Harrison Smith, with other members of the guard from Trigg
County, survived their time as prisoners of war and returned home.[40]

The 55th departed Summerville by train on May 19, but without Smith,
who returned to Charleston for Pelette's court-martial on May 23. Rejoin-
ing the regiment in Orangeburg, Smith found himself in a generally hostile
community, as described by Lieutenant Lee. "[Sherman's troops had] burnt
all the stores and public buildings and a few private residences. . . . [T]hey
are the most bitter I have yet met with; Charleston is nothing compared to
it; they especially dislike colored troops."[41]

As the brigade's officers carried out their responsibilities of holding
courts for civil and criminal trials and overseeing the writings of labor contracts, Smith was among those charged with keeping the peace in the
county's tension-filled atmosphere. Smith anticipated he might remain on
provost duty in South Carolina for another year, until the 55th's original
enlistments expired in May 1866.[42]

Then, in August, Major General Gillmore, succumbing to the demands
of South Carolina's planters and not wanting to deal with racial problems,

obtained approval to remove black regiments from the state's interior. The 54th and 55th Massachusetts were to be mustered out of the service; the USCT regiments were to be withdrawn for duty in coastal garrisons.[43]

The 55th departed Orangeburg by train on August 24. After arriving at the depot, Smith carried the flag through Charleston's streets for the final time as the regiment marched to the wharf near the place of its first entrance into the city on February 22. A transport conveyed the 55th across Charleston Harbor to Mount Pleasant, where, on August 29, 1865, Smith and his comrades mustered out of the service.[44]

The soldiers of the 55th Massachusetts still had to return to Massachusetts for the regiment to be formally discharged. Smith and the others arriving on the *Karnac* endured a wait of ten days at the army barracks on Gallops Island before the regiment could assemble, most of the delay being caused by the late arrival of the companies traveling with Hartwell on the *Ben Deford*. Part of the time was filled with processing the return of regimental equipment to the state, including the 55th's remaining battle flags, but what the men did to fill the additional hours is not known. After Hartwell's arrival, Smith and others had their photographs taken at the request of Hartwell. (See page ii of this volume.) Years later Hartwell donated these photographs to the State Library of Massachusetts, thereby preserving the only image of Andy Smith as a young man.[45]

On Saturday, September 23, the men received their pay and were "discharged from the service of the United States" but remained another two days on Gallops Island to participate in ceremonies the following Monday. The regiment left the island to land on Boston's Commercial Wharf at 9:00 AM to take its place in a long procession of bands, veterans, militia, and citizens moving through the streets of the city to Boston Common. There "the regiment was drilled in the manual of arms, the uniformity, spirit and accuracy with which the corps executed the orders of their commander, elicited merited applause—no Massachusetts regiment ever excelling the proficiency of the 55th," claimed the *Anglo-African*. "The dress parade and music by the Band attracted much attention."[46]

Upon completion of the Dress Parade, the regiment received its final orders: "The Parade is dismissed! Break ranks, march!" The men then partook of a meal, "a bountiful collation furnished by the friends of the regiment," and intermingled with guests from the crowd of observers. Finally, they shared "parting words with comrades" and "quietly disbanded, most of the men taking afternoon trains for their homes in the West." Among the 822 enlisted men who mustered out, Smith was one of 653 who "had left Readville in 1863, and had served with the regiment from its organization."[47]

They departed quickly. The *Weekly Anglo-African* (New York) reported, "by 5 o'clock p.m. two-thirds of the regiment were miles away, homeward bound." Smith left Boston by train for Chicago. He then transferred to the Chicago & Alton Railroad to cross the prairie to Bloomington. There he connected with the Illinois Central Railroad for the short, final leg of his journey to Clinton and the home of John Warner.[48]

CHAPTER 8

A WORLD TURNED UPSIDE DOWN: KENTUCKY AFTER THE WAR

September 1865–May 1866

A NDY SMITH WOULD SURELY HAVE PREFERRED to return home to his mother and sisters, but it was dangerous to do so. Union victory in the war did not erase the fact that slavery remained legal in Kentucky. There it had persisted in deteriorating conditions, embroiling the state in turmoil and violence as slavery's advocates struggled to defend their institution against federal encroachments that, by the end of the war, had legally freed more than 70 percent of Kentucky's 236,000 slaves.[1]

Whites in Kentucky tenaciously held onto the remnants of slavery, even more so than in Delaware, the only other state where the institution survived the war. It was only the ratification of the Thirteenth Amendment, on December 7, 1865, that forced Kentucky and Delaware to acquiesce in slavery's legal termination. Thereafter, federal involvement in Kentucky's affairs diminished, support for the Freedmen's Bureau lessened, and army regiments were either demobilized or transferred to duty in other states. Kentucky's free blacks and former slaves were left on their own to face a chaotic and uncertain future, and many chose either to leave the state or move to less-threatening urban areas. But Smith would return home. To understand why he did not pursue a promising future in Illinois, deciding instead to build his life Between the Rivers in Lyon County, it is necessary to gain insight into the world to which he would return.

TO ALL APPEARANCES, Smith's home county was not a land of opportunity for veterans, especially black veterans, returning from the war. The area had not been a battleground, but the land and its people suffered from a prolonged disruption of the labor force and proximity to the armies of both sides, subjecting civilians to seizures of their slaves as well as produce, livestock, and valuables by passing troops.

"Confederate soldiers left home proud and confident," Lyon County historian Odell Walker explained. "They left prosperous, well-kept farms, shops, stores and other businesses in the hands of family and slaves. They returned humiliated by defeat, the slaves that had carried the burden of labor had been set free. Horses and livestock had been confiscated by Union soldiers, other things moveable had been carried away by vandals. The corn, wheat and tobacco fields were grown up in weeds, bushes and briars, the well-kept houses, barns, and outbuildings were falling down. Many times the family was near starvation.... [C]onditions for returning Union veterans were very little, if any, better than that of the Confederates."[2]

The war had so disrupted agriculture that farmland, averaging ten dollars per acre in Lyon County in 1860, lost more than half its value to bring an average of only four dollars per acre in 1870, a percentage of loss greater than any other county in Kentucky during the 1860s.[3] The availability of inexpensive land likely enticed civilians and veterans of both races to remain or return to Lyon County, but the degree to which land prices might have influenced Smith's decision to return home is not known.

Among Livingston, Lyon, and Trigg, the three Kentucky counties with land between the Cumberland and Tennessee Rivers, Lyon was, at 256 square miles, the smallest, least developed, and, in 1860, had the smallest free population, 4,167 whites, 46 free blacks, and the fewest slaves, 1,094, of the three.[4] Lyon County would not go untouched by the social upheaval and turmoil following the war and the end of legalized slavery, but, as those forces swirled around it, there are indications its residents may have, with one possible exception, taken a less turbulent path.

A LABOR SHORTAGE, ensuing from the wartime and subsequent exodus of Kentucky's slaves, worked to the advantage of remaining freedmen. During April 1866, jobs were plentiful in Livingston County, the freedmen fully employed, and the county's bureau agent, J. Bond Thompson, reported more laborers were "eagerly sought." In May, Thompson could find only two freedmen to enter into a contract with a farmer, and the shortage did not abate. "Freedmen are generally doing well," Thompson was able to report in February 1867. "All of them who are industrious . . . can find good homes, plenty of labor, and generally good wages." He recorded monthly rates of twelve to thirteen dollars for males and five dollars for females.[5]

In Lyon County, agent William C. Noel made no mention of labor shortages, but he reported writing only fifty-one contracts employing sixty-five freedmen during April 1866. They reached agreements with former owners or other farmers to work for half of the crop or for pay, some for $8 to $16 a month, others for $75 to $200 a year. Because individual farmers made multiple contracts to obtain the workforce they needed, the number of different farmers represented in the fifty-one contracts cannot be determined.[6]

Thus, in 1866, jobs were available, but only a minority of Lyon's farmers were cooperating with the bureau, as Noel explained in May that "[s]o far as this County is concerned they are doing tolerably well," but "[t]here are several *leading rebels* . . . that won't regard the *law*. They have *verbal contracts* with freedmen, but won't bring them forward." The number of Lyon's farmers refusing to enter into contracts increased in the spring. Such failures worried Noel, leaving him "satisfied there are a number of men in this County and Trigg also that have freedmen in their employ that will never pay them what they have promised."[7]

Noel encountered even greater problems in Trigg, where the slave population had been more than three times larger than Lyon's in 1860, and he found "the Citizens (Rebels) . . . very stubborn and rebellious towards the operations of the Bureau." On an inspection tour through Trigg in May 1866, Noel arrived at Cadiz, the county seat, and was visited by "two of the most reliable *union men* in the *State of Kentucky*" to learn he "would be waited upon and requested to leave the County . . . and it would not be very healthy for me to remain." Noel returned to Trigg later in the month, again to hostile greetings, and perhaps to discover part of the reason its citizens wanted to keep the bureau at bay: "I am satisfied that they are holding some freedmen in Slavery, and treating them worse than they did before the Government set them free."[8]

Without troops, Noel could not enforce labor contracts or liberate freedmen still held in slavery or carry out the work of the bureau. He repeatedly requested military assistance, but to no avail, and became increasingly despondent in his communications. In his last report, dated June 14, 1866, he complained of what had grown to be "a good many persons" in Lyon County who would not make or respect labor contracts with freedmen. Conditions in Trigg County only deteriorated for its freedmen who

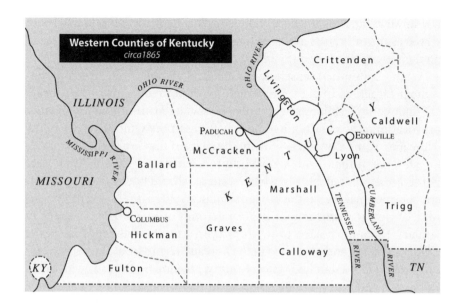

were, a bureau agent reported in 1868, "completely under the control of the whites. They dread them so much that they have never dared to erect anywhere in that county either school houses or churches."[9]

It became impossible for Noel to carry out his work in Trigg County, but the menacing conditions there appear to have been exceptional among the three Kentucky counties with land lying between the Tennessee and Cumberland Rivers, as well as in Marshall County, across the Tennessee River from Lyon and Trigg. In no county was the bureau welcomed, but while agent Thompson wrote of a "[s]trong prejudice" against the bureau in Livingston in April 1866, he also mentioned "there has been no conflict or disturbance," and no mention of personal threats appears in his reports. In May 1866, agent Noel logged without comment one outrage (an attack against blacks) involving a freedman in Lyon; otherwise, he made no mention of threats or violence against freedmen or himself in the county.[10] In both Livingston and Lyon Counties, resistance to the bureau seems to have been passive and effective, limited to farmers' refusals to cooperate with its contracting efforts, relying on the inability of the bureau to prevail in state courts or enforce its will on anyone.

In April 1866, a month before Smith returned home, bureau agent John Donovan observed, "There are some good well[-]disposed and humane men who under any circumstances would accord to the Freedmen their just rights, but they are few in comparison to the many who would not accord to the Negro any rights that a white man is bound to respect."[11] Those few, however, and other whites willing to allow Kentucky's blacks to coexist, served as the only allies available to freedmen who otherwise had to stand on their own in a violent world.

Whites committed senseless, random acts of violence against any convenient target, as in a case recorded by the bureau office in Paducah: "[T]hree colored children were shot at by a white man without the slightest provocation. The children had been bathing in the Ohio River when the white man came along in a Skiff and discharged his Gun at them, wounding all three of them with squirrel shot."[12] Fortunately, the children were not seriously injured, but elsewhere, scattered throughout Kentucky's western counties making up the bureau's Paducah subdistrict, violent felonies were committed with impunity.[13] An account of one terrible incident in January 1866, purported to be from Lyon County, was reported in the *Chicago Tribune* and preserved in the bureau's records, but the perpetrator resided and farmed in Livingston County. Freedmen's Bureau agent H. W. Cobb reported to the *Tribune* the case of Reuben Harris of Lyon County, who had informed Union officials as to the whereabouts of his master, hiding in nearby wilderness with other Confederate cavalrymen. Harris's master, Isaac Rucker, escaped, but two of his sons were captured. They returned home at war's end to learn Reuben had informed on them, and the following macabre scene unfolded:

> Isaac Rucker then took Reuben, his former slave, stripped him and tied him up by his wrists to a pole between two trees, just so that his toes could touch the ground. He then, with his own hands whipped him, and continued to whip for hours, frequently saying he would cut him in two. His wife and family were present, moaning in agony at the spectacle. The wretch turned and struck the wife ten blows, and told her to go off and mind her own business. One of the black man's sons he made bring him (the rebel) whiskey several times while he was applying the cruel lash to his father. . . . [H]e did whip on till the whole body was cut up most horribly. From 11 A. M. till sunset the martyrdom went on. . . . I should add several white men stood around, witnessing the flogging and encouraging it on.[14]

By 1868, open violence had gradually decreased as attackers began to operate in secret. In June, the bureau agent at Columbia received a report of "outrages" in Hickman County west of Between the Rivers. There Ku Klux Klan members "had killed one black man and taken guns from others." The attackers claimed to be searching for weapons, but their primary objective was to drive blacks from the state. Northeast of Between the

Rivers, during August, the Klan was active in Henderson County, having "completely overawed the Freedmen, broken up religious meetings, destroyed the school houses and driven off the teacher." A month later, Klan members returned to attack a black man, Forest Bowler, at his house, shooting him in the shoulder, "this because he had not left the County when told to do so." Soon thereafter, in adjacent Union County, another black man, "Abraham Russell . . . was shot through the neck, the ball lodging in his Breast . . . by K. K. (unknown) five in number. Russell was a peaceful farmer working on Shares and doing well. He is reported dead."[15]

Klan activity continued unabated in western Kentucky in October. "High handed outrages on Freedmen by lawless men disguised and calling themselves Ku Kluxes continue to be practiced without the slightest pretense of interference by the State authorities," the Paducah bureau agent reported. "Twenty cases of Shooting, burglary, and robbery in various parts of the district have been formally reported during the present month, but it is evident from Statements received that the cases not reported by far exceed this number."[16]

One account of Klan activity in Eddyville, reportedly carried out by Klansmen from another county, is preserved among bureau records, written to agent W. James Kay by schoolteacher Henry Bond, whose courage more than offset his command of English: "There are A Band of White Men in Town with There Pistols and Was Hear Last on The 27th [April]. And Threw Rocks on The School House and Have Sworn to Kill Me if I Continue to Teach Those Childeren. Nobody wont Tell me Ther Names [.] They say they live in Crittendon Co. . . . They Say I Had Better Stop Teachen for A While and I will not Do So without My Mind Changes Very Much[.]"[17]

SEEKING RELIEF from violence and in search of a better life, increasing numbers of Kentucky's freedmen continued the exodus begun before the war. Other thousands fled to urban areas of refuge within the state—the preferred escape plan of those living in western Kentucky. Thus, rural population declines in western counties were not evenly distributed across the region. Instead, they were concentrated in the counties of Ballard, Caldwell, Calloway, Crittenden, Fulton, and Graves as cities in other counties absorbed their escaping populations. Two cities in particular, Paducah and Columbia, served as magnets to increase the population of their counties, McCracken and Hickman, which grew by 116 percent (1,769) and 29 percent (366), respectively, from 1860 to 1870.[18]

Population increases also occurred in the three counties with land between the Kentucky and Tennessee Rivers and in adjacent Marshall County,
but not necessarily for similar reasons. Slave owners in Trigg County, with
the region's largest slave population (3,448) in 1860, maintained tight control over freedmen after the war (as in August 1866, when former slave
owners arranged for the abduction of two children from Tennessee), and
its population increased naturally by more than 9 percent (319) over the
decade.[19]

Unlike Trigg, which reported only two fugitive slaves in 1860, Livingston, Marshall, and Lyon Counties each lost a substantial number of
fugitives that year. Livingston recorded 210 fugitives in 1860, establishing
a black population total of 1,042 that grew by only ten residents in 1870.
Marshall lost 80 fugitive slaves in 1860, leaving its black population at 306.
That population grew 26 percent (79) over the decade, nearly recouping
the loss of 1860 but not experiencing additional growth.[20] A natural growth
rate in Marshall approximating that of Trigg would account for about one-
third of Marshall's increase.

Lyon County surpassed its adjacent counties. In 1860, 195 of Lyon's
1,094 slaves were listed as fugitives, of whom half were children under sixteen. Thus, the county's 1860 black population was more accurately set at
945, the combination of 899 resident slaves and 46 free blacks. By 1870,
Lyon's black population had more than doubled the loss of 1860 to reach
1,419. With an additional 474 individuals, Lyon attained the largest percentage increase (more than 50 percent) over the decade of any county except McCracken.[21] (See Appendix, page 207.)

Lyon was the only county in western Kentucky whose black population
increase cannot be explained by either the attraction of an urban center or
by the natural growth of a sizable prewar population. Furthermore, while
all counties certainly lost additional slaves during the war, Lyon's wartime
losses were both agricultural and industrial, as they included those from
among the approximately 83 male slaves belonging to the Hillman Brothers' Tennessee Rolling Mill.[22] While there is no definitive explanation of
why Lyon's black population increased after the war while other rural counties declined or grew more slowly, evaluation of the small amount of surviving evidence offers some clues.

The pattern of slaveholding in Lyon County, as in Kentucky as a whole,
differed considerably from the pattern found in the Deep South. The terrain favored farms of small and moderate size, as opposed to large plantations, and slave owners sought requisite smaller labor forces. In 1860, 53
percent (94) of Lyon's 178 slave owners had 3 or fewer slaves (of these, 50

owners had 1 slave), 30 percent (53) had between 4 and 9 slaves, and 17 percent (30) of the slave owners, including Andy Smith's owner, Elias Smith, had between 10 and 40 slaves. The largest slave owner in the county, with 121 slaves, was industrial, the Hillman Brothers' Tennessee Rolling Mill.[23] (These figures represent ownership only and are not adjusted to account for fugitive or manumitted slaves.)

Slaveholding in Lyon County (and in Kentucky at large) differed from that in the Lower South in yet another way, as explained by historian Christopher Waldrep. Kentucky law allowed for a slave-owning society, not a slave-breeding society, and slave trading was illegal in the state. Slaves might be brought into the state for personal use, but their sale within five years incurred a $600 fine. The law was not scrupulously obeyed, but when Lyon County was created in 1854, its officials followed the law's record-keeping requirement and produced a list of imported slaves, the only such document of its kind known to exist.[24]

Analysis of the list allowed Waldrep to draw a few tentative conclusions. "First, a look at the imported slaves suggests the existence—at least in tiny Lyon County—of a viable slave-based economy in need of more hands." Female slaves, resident in the area when Lyon County was created in 1854, outnumbered male slaves 58 percent to 42 percent, so it was reasonable for importers of slaves to prefer "male field hands because the existing supply of slaves was inadequate to the demand." Slave families were also imported, increasing the number already present in 1854. Roughly half of the owners possessing four or more slaves may have owned families by 1860, and "the record shows that slaves imported as families were more likely to remain in Kentucky even after emancipation than slaves imported singly."[25]

Slightly more than half of Lyon's slaves in 1860 were under age twenty (including Smith), of whom almost 40 percent were under age fifteen, suggesting, in the absence of a slave-trading society, a strong family presence. Lyon was not unique; similar higher percentages of children, and likely also families, were present among slave populations in other counties.[26] The presence of families, the difficulties of escape or leaving the state with children, or the specter of leaving loved ones behind may explain why many freedmen chose to remain not only in Lyon County but also elsewhere in Kentucky where they faced difficult economic conditions and ever-present threats to their safety. It took courage to leave, and it took courage to stay.

Thus, the presence of families, as in Smith's case, may well have been an important factor inhibiting, though not preventing, slaves and later freedmen from leaving the county during the war. But the presence of families does not account for the significant increase in Lyon's black population, which could only have been accomplished by migration or by the re-turn of once-fugitive slaves to the county.

The small amount of available evidence suggests many of Lyon County's slaves may have remained or returned as freedmen because life there was at least tolerable. Evidence of mass evictions of slaves from farms and of mob or Klan activity among county residents is not present in Freedmen's Bureau records, nor are efforts of whites to perpetuate slavery evident. Also, bureau agents did not report threatening conditions in Lyon, as they did in Trigg County. Still, Isaac Rucker's torture-murder of Reuben Harris (whether in Lyon or Livingston County) revealed the region bounded by the Cumberland and Tennessee Rivers was not immune to inhumanity.

The availability of land and opportunities for jobs—not only in field-work but also affiliated with steel and charcoal production, mining, carting, and in the timber industry and along the rivers—inevitably attracted fugi-tives and others to Lyon County after the war. Whatever remuneration the county's freedmen might have gained for fieldwork, given the resourceful-ness that had helped them survive slavery, they may have felt able to pro-vide for themselves residing where they were.

Thus, Lyon County offered Smith relative safety and the opportunity to earn a living, but there were also other enticements. He was well known within the local community, in part because of his years of operating the Eddyville ferry, and he was also widely recognized as a relation of the large white Smith family. He was close friends with several of his white cousins, upon whom he could depend for support. Smith also knew the Between the Rivers area, having spent much of his life there before his escape. Insu-lated by the rivers, it was an out-of-the-way region heavily forested and in-terspersed with small farms where he might be left unbothered to make a living and build his life.

Throughout Kentucky, between 1860 and 1870, at least fourteen thou-sand slaves and later freedmen, including veterans and their families, dealt with threats to their safety by fleeing the state to make new lives across the Ohio River, especially in Illinois, Indiana, and Ohio. Several thousand more sought safer urban areas within the state. During ensuing decades and well into the middle of the twentieth century, as part of the Great Migration, additional thousands would leave Kentucky, as well as other southern states, in search of better and safer lives. Thus, when Andy Smith left a se-cure home in Illinois to return to Lyon County in spring 1866, he followed a course that went against the tide of a century of black migration.

CHAPTER 9

BOTTOM RAIL ON TOP NOW

1866–1900

S EVEN MONTHS AFTER HIS ARRIVAL in Clinton, Illinois, Andy Smith decided to return home: "I stayed there until May 1866 when I went back to Kentucky to visit my mother and three sisters. Col. Warner and his daughter came to the train and told me to come back to Clinton whenever I was ready, as I had a lifetime home there. I went down to Cairo, Ill. and took a boat to Moses Ferry, a mile below Birmingham, about 8 or 10 miles from where I was born."

Smith returned to Between the Rivers three years and four months after his escape from slavery. From the boat landing on the Tennessee, he walked east and north for more than eight miles to his mother's home at Harrison Smith's farm on the south bank of the Cumberland River. He soon met with his sisters, learned Alf Bissell had returned home safely, and "[l]ater I went to Eddyville and saw all my former playmates, who were ex-Confederate soldiers. I then saw my former owner [William Smith], who came to me and gave me good advice. He told me that he was poor as I."[1]

Smith and the vast majority of other black veterans and former slaves from the agrarian South desired to own land. Its possession was their key to independence, self-sufficiency, and the potential for a decent life, but for many, the obstacles to obtaining land were overwhelming. Try as hard as they might, by 1870, only 4.8 percent of the approximately nine hundred thousand black families or heads of households in the South managed to acquire either rural or urban real estate.[2]

These obstacles to owning land were greatest in areas of the Lower South, where white landowners, dependent on large-scale labor to produce their crops, conspired to maintain a permanent force of dependent agricultural workers. They agreed not to hire one another's black workers nor sell or rent land to them. Violation of such agreements invited retaliation, and the relatively few blacks who managed to acquire land typically had to settle for less-fertile soil. On average, throughout these states, only one rural black family in thirty-one (16,161 black families out of a total of 503,595) owned land in 1870. Among the relatively few blacks living in cities and small towns beyond the reach of the planter class, one in nine families owned land (4,313 families of 38,846) in the Lower South.[3]

The situation was different for Smith and other freedmen who settled west of the mountains in the states of the Upper South, notably Tennessee, Missouri, and Kentucky. The region's smaller agricultural holdings did not depend on large-scale labor forces as did the production of cotton and other Lower South crops. As a result, opposition to blacks owning land in these states was not as strong among local whites, although attacks by white racists remained a threat. In Kentucky, by 1870, the ratio of rural black landowners was one in fifteen families (2,513 out of 37,713), and the ratio for the state as a whole increased to nearly one in nine families when the landholdings of rural and urban black families were combined.[4]

Compared to whites, the landholdings of a people emerging from slavery remained minuscule five years after emancipation. "[O]ne-ninth as many southern blacks owned one-fiftieth as much real property as the average white American," historian Loren Schweninger ascertained.[5] But the accomplishment of these approximately 43,268 families and heads of households was a beginning, and Kentucky was among those areas where, because blacks could purchase real estate, a market existed with demand for affordable land.

Smith's intentions on returning to Kentucky appear to have entailed more than a simple "visit" to his mother and sisters—his subsequent actions suggest he returned home with a plan. Opportunity awaited a person who had financial resources, was willing to work incredibly hard, and was well acquainted with the portion of Lyon County that lay Between the Rivers. Bounded on three sides by the Cumberland and Tennessee Rivers, the land was covered in forest interspersed with farms, an out-of-the-way rural region outsiders easily passed by.

Smith also had other internal resources to draw on. His military service had not only provided him with financial resources, but, as with many of his fellow veterans, it also imbued him with the discipline of military training, appreciation for teamwork, and the pride of having fought successfully for his freedom and the freedom of his family and race. He was also among those soldiers who experienced being in a position of leadership. He rose through the noncommissioned ranks, gaining recognition from white officers who entrusted him with responsible positions requiring judgment, independent action, and ultimately courage. Military service helped to hone his innate qualities and better prepared him for his postwar life in business and as a community leader.[6]

Like many black veterans, Smith had received his army pay in a few installments late in the war and had little to spend it on while in the service; but unlike his comrades with family living in the North, he had no way of sending money to his mother and sisters. Given his accumulated pay and his enlistment bonus, it is reasonable to assume he arrived in Kentucky with several hundred dollars in savings.

He appears to have been careful in the years following his return, not yet buying land but conserving his funds and working to add earnings to them. Prudence dictated any source of revenue be exploited, and Smith collected every dollar he could. In one instance, the Lyon County clerk recorded, "I, J. McLain do certify that on this day Andy Smith produced to me in my office the head of a grey fox . . . for which said head he is entitled to be given one dollar."[7]

Within four months of returning home, on September 5, 1866, Smith married Amanda Young. Andy and Amanda likely had known one another for years before the war. More than twenty-five slaves with the surname Young lived Between the Rivers in 1860, although Amanda's family might have resided at Birmingham, the ferry landing across the Tennessee River from Lyon County. A closer connection may have been through Amanda's cousins among the Benberry family who were well known to Smith. Beyond these suppositions and the date of her birth, May 8, 1844, no information has thus far been established about her background, including whether she had been born into slavery or freedom.[8]

The Smiths would have no children of their own, but that did not mean their home would be childless. The 1870 census records Sarah Scott, 17, living with the Smiths, her relationship to them unknown. No trade or occupation was entered, only that she could read and write. The 1880 census revealed a young girl, Dora McCracken, also seemingly unrelated to the Smiths, was living with them. The census taker, who was supposed to describe each person's "Relationship to the head of this family—whether wife, son, daughter, servant, boarder or other," selected servant from the list, instead of other, to enter on the form. Clearly, Dora was no servant; she was only ten. The census taker did not describe any work she did, entering only "at home" on the form under profession or occupation, and then recorded she was in school, attending the fifth grade. Dora certainly had chores to do, but her primary "occupation" was being a student.[9]

Within a few years, in 1883, Amanda Smith's nephew, Will Benberry, the six-year-old son of Kitty Benberry and Andy Smith's close friend Owen Benberry, joined the Smith family and became the son the Smiths never had. In 1892, when Will was sixteen, they provided for his future financial support by transferring to him title to over 62 1/2 acres of farmland on the Cumberland River, inserting into the deed, "For $1.00 and the love and affection that they have for [Will], they having taken him and raised him as one of their own family, and thus wish to provide him a home." In 1887, four children ages six to twenty were recorded living with the Smiths.[10]

The Smiths initially made a small investment in farming without buying land. Instead, they either farmed family land, possibly belonging to Amanda Smith's relatives, or rented. They slowly increased the number and variety of their livestock and initially practiced subsistence agriculture to grow food to feed themselves and their animals. In 1867, they were the owners of one cow.[11]

Tax records from 1868 reveal the Smiths had added a horse to their holdings, along with four more head of cattle, and produced 150 bushels of corn. Their taxable wealth was forty dollars (the value of the horse; five or fewer cattle and the crops were tax exempt). In 1869, they produced three hundred bushels of corn, and, to earn money, they had no choice but to turn to the production of black tobacco, from which they yielded three hundred pounds. That year their taxable wealth rose to sixty dollars (the value of their horse).[12]

Tobacco farming was a long, involved, and terribly labor-intensive process, beginning in winter when the bed was seeded to establish young plants. The plants needed constant care while germinating, and at the same time, the field had to be prepared to receive them. The ground was plowed twice at right angles, creating a pattern of squares called checks. Each check was fertilized and shaped into a hill. Once the young plantings were ready for transplant, farmers had to wait for sufficient rain to loosen the soil so each tender plant could be "drawn" and quickly taken to the field.

Family members and field hands walked down the rows to "drop" a planting on each check. Then the grueling process of "setting" would begin.

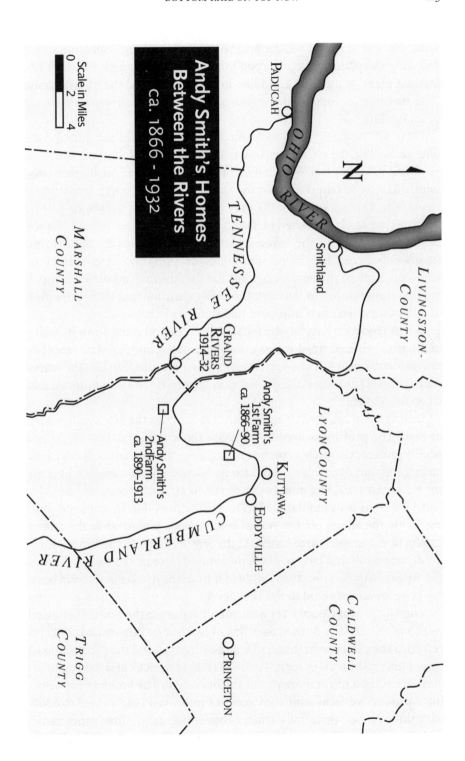

Andy Smith's Homes
Between the Rivers
ca. 1866 - 1932

Scale in Miles
0 2 4

PADUCAH

OHIO RIVER

N

Smithland

LIVINGSTON-
COUNTY

MARSHALL
COUNTY

TENNESSEE RIVER

GRAND
RIVERS
1914–32

Andy Smith's
1st Farm
ca. 1866–90

LYON COUNTY

Andy Smith's
2nd Farm
ca. 1890–1913

KUTTAWA

EDDYVILLE

CUMBERLAND RIVER

CALDWELL
COUNTY

PRINCETON

TRIGG
COUNTY

Setters would crawl on the ground with a tobacco peg, following those dropping the plants. Using the peg to punch a hole in each hill, they inserted a plant in the hole and filled in the dirt around the plant's roots. After working for long hours or even all day, setters could have a difficult time standing.

Once set, tobacco plants took unceasing care. Weeding required continuous hoeing, the soil supporting the stems had to be worked, and each plant had to be "topped"—cut off about waist high—and small leaves constantly had to be removed from the stalks to produce fewer, large, heavy leaves. The farmers were not the only ones who prized the young plants, which were eagerly devoured by tobacco worms. Families and field hands continuously walked the rows, picking off the worms by hand to be smashed between fingers or sometimes dropped into a container of kerosene. And so the summers went for the Smiths and other farmers, moving from one job to the next, nurturing their tobacco while attending to other crops, livestock, and farm maintenance in between.

When ready for harvest, the tobacco was cut and hung from its stalks in a barn and fired until it was cured to a not-quite-dry state, another process that could last the better part of two months. Finally, the leaves were stripped from the stalk, graded as to quality, bound into bundles, and taken to market.[13]

In a region of subsistence agriculture, tobacco was the only viable source of cash. The profit was used to purchase those items farmers could not readily produce themselves, such as metal, store goods, tools, and land. Following the war, dark tobacco sold for its highest average price of 13 cents per pound in 1867, but soon began to fall, to 10 cents per pound in 1872, and 5 1/2 cents per pound by 1878. During the period from war's end until the 1890s, the selling price averaged seven cents a pound while the cost of production averaged three cents.[14] If the Smiths had sold their three-hundred-pound tobacco crop in 1869, they might have netted twenty-four to twenty-seven dollars, but they withheld it from the market in the vain hope the price would rebound to the 1867 level.

The 1870 Lyon County tax assessment reported the Smiths' assessed wealth at seventy-five dollars, the value of two horses they owned, and also recorded the presence of three cows and eight hogs and the production of three hundred bushels of corn. The 1870 Federal Agricultural Census, however, described a much more promising operation. The Smiths were working a productive farm with sixty acres of improved land valued at $300, with three horses, three milk cows, two working oxen, three other cattle, and sixteen hogs. They produced 300 bushels of corn, 6 bushels of pota-

Part of a two-sided chimney and an oak tree in what was the front yard are all that remain of Smith's first house Between the Rivers. Photograph by Ray Parish. (*Shara Parish*)

toes, 150 pounds of butter, and 22 gallons of molasses, but no tobacco crop.[15]

In 1871, the Smiths reduced their livestock holdings to two horses, three hogs, and eight cattle, grew four hundred bushels of corn, and returned to growing tobacco. Their yield was six hundred pounds, and with the average price still above ten cents per pound, their profit may have been as much as forty-eight dollars had they sold the crop, but the lower price induced the Smiths to again withhold their tobacco from the market in hope the price would rise. In 1871, their taxable wealth rose to $150 (the value of their horses and cattle).[16]

Andy and Amanda Smith made their first home on a beautiful site near the river bottoms on the bank of the Cumberland. Their house rested on a wooded rise of land. A large oak tree stood in the front yard, providing abundant shade in summer and allowing afternoon sunlight to pass through its limbs and help warm the interior in winter. The house was constructed in a style common to the area. Rectangular in shape, the front room served as the living quarters. A second room was built on a brick foundation over the root cellar and served as the food-preparation and dining area. A large, double-sided brick fireplace and chimney stood at the center of the house, separating the two rooms. The kitchen was outside, convenient to the dining room door; the well was safely removed from the kitchen. The porch likely encompassed the side of the house facing the Cumberland River.

Down the hill, on the far side of the oak tree, Smith constructed out-buildings and beyond these pens for livestock. He dammed a small water cut in the nearby hillside to form a pond for the animals. Pastures stretched from the hill toward the river, several hundred yards distant. The Dover Road ran across the property, connecting the small settlement of Nickell (later to become the town of Grand Rivers, Kentucky) to the nearby Eddyville Ferry and Dover, Tennessee, about forty miles to the south.[17]

Typical for the area, the Smiths planted a garden close to the house to grow a wide variety of vegetables with a space designated therein to grow herbs. Large plots farther from the house were dedicated to varieties of potatoes and squash, corn, and other vegetables. Together with the fruit orchard, these crops were intended to feed the family. Field crops to feed livestock or tobacco to be sold for cash consumed the largest areas of land.[18]

For those looking to supplement the food produced on their farms, the countryside offered bountiful resources. County historian Odell Walker recalled his childhood, like that of numerous generations preceding him, living in a land of plenty. As spring warmed into summer, a succession of wild fruits became available. In June, residents joined flocks of birds in competing for the first of a succession of tasty berries. The wide variety of fruits gave way to nuts in the fall, augmented by sweet saps from which to make chewing gum or drinks. Wild game was also plentiful, with deer, turkey, and hogs being favorite targets. Smoked venison hams were a delicacy offered to family and friends at holidays.[19]

The Smiths increased their livestock holdings in 1872, with three horses, nine cattle plus eight studs, jacks, or bulls. They may have attempted to start a stud-service business or purchased the bulls as an investment. The 1873 records show them in possession of three horses, seven cattle, and eight hogs, but the bulls were gone. They produced three hundred bushels of corn in 1872 and five hundred in 1873, but no tobacco, as its price slowly fell in each of those years. The Smiths' taxable wealth in 1872 and 1873 was placed at $250 (the value of their livestock).[20]

After several years without selling tobacco and without the money those crops would have engendered, the Smiths faced a shortage of cash. This was a common problem farmers typically resolved by purchasing goods on credit from local merchants, providing a lien on their next tobacco crop or other property as collateral, and paying the debt once they had sold the crop. In 1873, merchant H. M. Hanson agreed to extend credit to the

The David McKenzie Log Cabin, a US National Register of Historic Places site, was built in Staffordsville, Kentucky, between 1860 and 1865. This cabin may resemble the first house in which Andy and Amanda Smith lived Between the Rivers. It is not known if their house was of log or plank construction, which was also common in the area. (*Mountain Homeplace, Staffordsville, KY*)

Smiths, but he required as collateral two thousand pounds of tobacco in Smith's possession. (Smith's own tobacco production had totaled nine hundred pounds; how he obtained the remaining eleven hundred pounds is not known.)

By July 1874, Smith had found a buyer for his tobacco, but Hanson wanted Smith to pay his debt of $85.67 with his tobacco crop, not with cash. Hanson stood to recover considerably more, perhaps double the amount of the debt, if he seized and sold the tobacco himself. Using near-hysterical language, Hanson turned to the circuit court: "Said Smith has sold his property with the fraudulent intent to cheat linder or delay his eviction; and is about to sell and or otherwise dispose of his property with Such intent. Wherefore he prays judgment for his debt and for an attachment against Defendant's estate and for all just and proper relief." While only sufficient property to pay the debt and court costs was supposed to have been taken, the deputy sheriff seized all the tobacco, "Levied the within attachment upon a lot of Tobacco in bulk supposed to [be] 2000# the property of Andy Smith." No records survive to reveal if Smith recovered the portion of his property improperly seized.[21]

Meanwhile, still in need of cash, Smith planted tobacco in spring 1874 and produced one thousand pounds, but the price was falling, and his rate of return for this his largest crop would have been less than that of earlier years, yielding perhaps fifty dollars. In 1874, he retained two horses, one less than in 1873, but he added one mule while keeping seven head of cattle and seven of eight hogs from his 1873 total. The 1874 tax records reported Smith's total taxable wealth (based on livestock) at $190, a decline of $60 from 1873. In addition to tobacco, he also produced three hundred bushels of corn.[22]

In 1875, Smith's total taxable wealth declined further, to $155. He began the year with two horses, one mule, four head of cattle, and four hogs. He produced just one hundred bushels of corn and twenty-five bushels of wheat, but no tobacco,[23] and he had his second encounter in the Lyon County Circuit Court. Smith brought a mare to N. C. Gray, owner of a stud service, but the procedure went awry, leading to the death of the mare. Smith sued Gray, who was one of Lyon County's wealthiest citizens, and his assistant James Shuff for $200 to recover the cost of the mare and lost income from his farming operations. Smith testified to being "engaged until about the first of June 1875 in cultivating a crop of corn and tobacco" having only the mare and one other horse. With the loss of the mare, "his crop has suffered for cultivation and has been greatly damaged,"[24] which explains why he produced no tobacco that year and his production of corn fell to one hundred bushels.

The jury found for the defendant, but Smith's attorney requested the verdict to be set aside and a new trial be granted on the grounds, "1st The Court erred in instructing the Jury as to the Law of the Case[;] 2nd The Court erred in refusing to give or grant the written instructions asked for by [Plaintiff's] counsel[;] 3rd The Verdict of the Jury rendered in the Case is not supported by the evidence in the Cause, and is contrary to both Law and evidence." The court refused to allow a new trial, but it did acquiesce in a request to submit the case to the court of appeals. Other than a $4.40 charge to Smith in January 1876, to cover the cost of preparing a transcript for the court of appeals, no other record of appellate action has been found.[25] Whether Smith finally decided not to appeal or the case files did not survive is not known.

Smith was also required to pay Gray's and Shuff's court costs amounting to $12.15. This charge, combined with Smith's own costs of $26.10 plus his attorney's fee, would likely have exceeded $40, a not-inconsiderable expense for Smith in addition to the loss of his mare and crops.[26] It took the Smiths nearly seven years to rebuild their taxable wealth to its level in 1873, prior to his economic setbacks and the two court cases.

No tax rolls survive for 1876–1878, but it is unlikely Smith profited from tobacco in 1878, as unusually wet conditions reduced the size and quality of the crop, and the price fell to 5 1/2 cents a pound. Smith's taxable wealth improved slightly to $180 in 1879. He had two horses, two mules, five head of cattle, and five hogs. He produced two hundred bushels of corn, sixty bushels of wheat, and four hundred pounds of tobacco, but the average price remained at 5 1/2 cents per pound, yielding a small profit of perhaps ten dollars.[27] (See Appendix, page 208.)

In 1880, Smith's taxable wealth rose to $255. He had three horses, two mules, twenty head of cattle and five hogs. He may have raised cattle for cash in 1880, as records show him with only eight head of cattle remaining in 1881. He also produced four hundred bushels of corn, twenty bushels of wheat, and five hundred pounds of tobacco, for which he may have received fifteen dollars.[28] But this would be his last tobacco crop. The pattern of his life was about to change, a transformation brought about by a combination of medical necessity and new opportunities.

ANDY SMITH RECEIVED no combat wounds while in the army, but he did endure disease and injury, most especially from his work on Morris Island. Regimental surgeons treated him for recurring fever and chills, an injury to his right hip, and injuries resulting from heavy lifting. All of these caused him occasional absences from duty while in the service and continued to trouble him throughout his life. The fever and chills were symptoms of malaria; the right hip injury, described as a dislocation, occurred in an altercation in 1864, likely in the performance of provost guard duty; and damage to muscles and other soft tissue resulted from the fatigue work on Morris Island during the siege of Battery Wagner.[29]

Physicians in Lyon County began treating Smith as early as 1868 for wartime-related problems. Treatment for rheumatism began about 1876, likely a consequence of the damage done to connective tissue and joints from the heavy lifting on Morris Island. His first treatment for a dislocated right hip is not documented, but Smith testified the hip had bothered him continuously since the original injury. He also reported a loss of hearing in his left ear.[30]

Smith's pension records reveal he was justified in applying for a disability pension well before 1880, but he delayed doing so until 1887, at age forty-five, when he was awarded a partial disability pension of four dollars per month, followed by an increase to six dollars in 1892. Payments were based on rank, with the maximum amount awarded to sergeants set at eight dollars per month. It is clear from the statements of his physicians and other testimony that lifting, general farm work, and even walking and riding were periodically very painful for him.[31]

After 1880, Smith altered his farming operations to practice less labor-intensive agriculture and began to focus on livestock production. He maintained a few horses and mules as needed to cultivate his remaining fields, a small herd of cows provided milk and meat, and in 1881, he increased the number of hogs to eleven, more than doubling the previous year's total. Hogs appear to have served the dual purpose of providing meat and serving as cash livestock, their number increasing to twenty in 1890 and again in 1892, then peaking at forty in 1895. Beginning in 1884, he also began keeping three or four sheep annually on the farm.[32]

Field crops were no longer produced for cash but for the support of livestock. Corn became the primary crop, peaking at one thousand bushels in 1890 and 1892, and hay production commenced in 1888, ranging from one to three tons annually. The planting of field crops was otherwise limited and sporadic: one hundred bushels of wheat in 1887, two hundred bushels of oats in 1889, and fifty bushels of oats in 1891.[33] New opportunities had enabled Smith to abandon the physically exhausting cultivation of tobacco.

In 1880, Lyon County officials discovered that early settlers living Between the Rivers had not adequately surveyed their landholdings. New surveys revealing available land unleashed competitors rushing to be the first to file their claims for five cents an acre at the Eddyville Court House, and Smith, who had participated in the surveying, was ready. Wanting to acquire property on or close to the south bank of the Cumberland River, he managed to be among the first to know the date when a one-hundred-acre tract was to be offered for sale in May.

Leaving home immediately, Smith used his knowledge of every back road, every shortcut, and the best water crossings. He arrived in Eddyville during the night and was the first person waiting at the entrance to the courthouse when it opened the following morning. In August, an adjoining twenty acres became available, and he repeated the process. Decades later, one of Smith's cousins recalled that on this second occasion, a friendly competitor, white landowner Matthew Nickells, came running up to the courthouse at the break of dawn only to see Smith sitting on the steps at the front door and exclaimed in exasperation, "Andy, you beat me again!"[34]

Smith surely paid the six dollars and associated costs (including those of a survey) for the combined 120 acres from savings, but soon another, far more expensive opportunity arose. The Lyon County lands of Barren

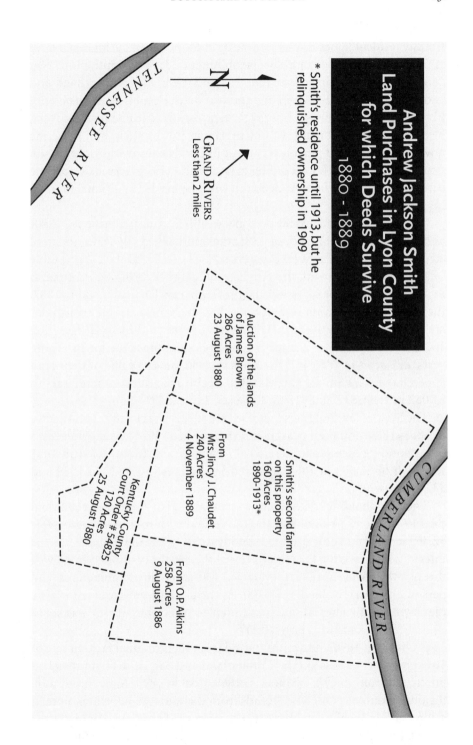

**Andrew Jackson Smith
Land Purchases in Lyon County
for which Deeds Survive
1880 - 1889**

* Smith's residence until 1913, but he
relinquished ownership in 1909

N

TENNESSEE RIVER

GRAND RIVERS
Less than 2 miles

Auction of the lands
of James Brown
286 Acres
23 August 1880

Smith's second farm
on this property
160 Acres
1890-1913*

From
Mrs. Jincy J. Chaudet
240 Acres
4 November 1889

Kentucky County
Court Order # 54825
120 Acres
25 August 1880

From O.P. Aikins
258 Acres
9 August 1886

CUMBERLAND RIVER

County resident James Brown were advertised for sale to the highest bidder at the courthouse door in Eddyville on August 23, 1880. Smith purchased 286 acres for three dollars an acre. He paid with $429 cash in hand and two notes each of $214 due in one and two years. Possibly Smith paid with his and Amanda's savings, but given their own recent financial recovery, he surely depended on at least one private investor to help him make the down payment. That person was most likely his cousin and close friend, Benjamin F. Smith, who, according to family knowledge, served as a private banker to extend credit to Andy Smith when he needed additional funding for land transactions.[35]

Smith's acreage and taxable personal wealth fluctuated during the 1880s as he bought and sold land. In 1881, the Smiths held 406 acres, the total acreage of the two recent land purchases, assessed at $760. Their taxable wealth grew by $365 with the purchase of livestock, bringing the total to $1,125, an increase of $870 over the previous year. They sold land in 1882, their holdings declining to 306 acres, but their total taxable wealth decreased only slightly, to $1,005. They sold more land in 1884, retaining 261.5 acres. Their total acreage did not change appreciably for two more years, 277 acres in 1885 and 267 acres in 1886, but the value of their land appreciated. The Smiths total taxable wealth rose during these years to $1,083 in 1884, $1,580 in 1885, and $1,577 in 1886.[36]

The Smiths' landholdings increased from 322 acres in 1887 to 545 acres in 1888–1889, and then peaked at 561 acres in 1890. They experienced a corresponding increase in their total taxable wealth from $1,791 in 1887 to a high of $2,652 in 1888, followed by declines to $2,422 in 1889 and $2,023 in 1890.[37]

Their landholdings declined by more than half to 250 acres in 1891 and then to 230 acres in 1892, but their taxable wealth rose to a comfortable $2,363 in 1892 and only dropped slightly to $2,313 in 1892. Thereafter, the intermittent surviving tax records reveal the Smiths continued to do well through the 1890s. In 1895, they owned 150 acres with combined real and personal property valued at $1,100. At the close of the century in 1900, they owned 229 acres of land, and their total taxable wealth was set at $1,329.[38] (See Appendix, page 209.)

Probably in 1890, the Smiths moved from their original farm to one of 164 acres that was also on the Cumberland and part of the land they had purchased from Jincy J. Chaudet in 1889. Also in 1890, Andy Smith took the opportunity to visit with friends from the war. A handwritten note in a copy of Fox's regimental history, *Record of the Service*, belonging to the Association of Officers of the 55th Massachusetts Volunteer Infantry, revealed Color Sergeant Andy Smith had returned to Boston to attend a Grand Army of the Republic reunion with his comrades from the 55th Massachusetts.[39]

Smith's initial purchases of land in 1880 had placed him and Amanda among the highest 10 percent of Lyon County landowners, black or white. Though their acreage fluctuated during the 1880s, they held more land than 85 percent of white landowners in 1884, 96 percent of white landowners from 1888 to 1890, and at least 85 percent of white landowners in 1891–92. In 1884, the Smiths' total taxable wealth of $1,083 exceeded that of 84 percent of the white population. Their five years of highest taxable wealth, in excess of $2,000 from 1888 to 1892, exceeded that of nearly 90 percent of Lyon County's white residents.

Yet the Smiths' 1890 assessment of $2,023 approximated that of only a very few of the 11 percent (96) of Lyon County's wealthier landowners who were either industrial, commercial, or, such as the William Stone family, among the county's established agricultural elites. Of these, 5 percent (45) had evaluations of up to $2,999; the evaluations of another 5 percent (39) extended from $3,000 to $6,999; assessments of the wealthiest 1 percent (12) ranged between $7,000 and $38,165.

Otherwise, the Smiths' wealth compared favorably with the remaining white landowners, for whom the mode fell between $300 and $349, with the median falling in the lower range of those with assessments between $550 and $599. The Smiths were by far the wealthiest black landowners in 1890, with an assessment nearly $1,500 greater than that of the second-highest landowner. Among black landowners, the mode fell among those with assessments between $50 and $99, and the median between those with assessments between $100 and $150. (See Appendix, page 210.)

The gross figures detailing the Smiths' landholdings and total taxable wealth do not tell the whole story, much of which is shrouded in the region's extensive loss of private and public records in the great flood of 1937 and thereafter by the further loss of records caused by the Tennessee Valley Authority's forced removals of people living Between the Rivers.

Between annual tax assessments, Smith engaged in considerable buying and selling of land, and many deeds that might have been made did not survive the devastations of the twentieth century.[40] His first land sale, the 100 acres from his 1880 purchases of 406 acres, was made before the midsummer tax assessment of 1882, but it is not known to whom the land was sold or for what price. It is likely Smith used his profits to help pay the balance of his two notes on the land he purchased from Barren County resident James Brown. By 1884, he had sold an additional 44 1/2 acres, but the assessed value of his remaining land had risen to $709, an increase of $139 over his 1882 assessment. In 1885, he increased his holdings by only 15 1/2 acres, yet the assessed valuation of his 277 acres increased to $1,094.

These and other unrecorded transactions made up the greater part of Smith's business dealings wherein he sold land for profit and invested in land of greater value. He thereby acquired the income freeing him from dependence on tobacco farming while increasing his landed wealth. Yet without the documentation contained in deeds, Smith's actual profits and losses cannot be known. Furthermore, his total wealth cannot be known because Kentucky taxed only real and personal property, not income. His total taxable wealth, which was a lesser amount than his total wealth, is the only measure available to follow annual fluctuations in his accumulated wealth.[41]

Smith helped other blacks acquire land, such as his close friend Owen Benberry, who first appears on the tax assessment list as a landowner in 1887 with 120 acres assessed at $580, land previously belonging to Smith but for which there was no recorded deed. In another example, Smith sold seven acres to Lucy Elmore for fifty dollars in an 1891 transaction for which there is a deed. In 1892, her seven acres were assessed at $275.[42] The few surviving records do not provide sufficient data to determine the degree to which Smith contributed to an increase in black land ownership. Instead, the tax assessment books simply record the holdings of five black landowners living Between the Rivers in 1880, expanding to seventeen in 1890, reaching a high of thirty-five in 1904, and declining to thirty in 1911.[43]

SMITH BECAME A successful businessman. In addition to farming his own homestead, county records reveal he bought and sold over one thousand acres of land, made contracts to lease mineral rights, and leased land for railroad-tie production. He served as a broker for people seeking to sell land in Lyon County, made loans to individuals secured by promissory notes, and borrowed money. Cash flow could be problematic at times, as much for those buying and selling land as it was for farmers waiting for the returns from their tobacco crops. Thus promissory notes were widely used in lieu of cash payment, a practice inevitably inviting legal disputes.

Smith and his business partners, both black and white, were plaintiffs and defendants in suits brought for the payment of promissory notes and other actions. Court records contain the plaintiff's charges but might not include the defendant's rebuttals, and sometimes it is not evident who prevailed. But in one case, brought against Smith by businessmen John Kimmel and Felix Rudolph for payment of a bill, Smith's rebuttal is among the court documents. The complete record reveals how complex these cases could be and is a warning not to draw conclusions about the motives of either plaintiffs or defendants absent full documentation.

On August 13, 1885, Smith signed a promissory note for ninety-six dollars with Kimmel and Rudolph to be paid in ninety days. Kimmel and Rudolph did not file with the court for payment of the note until November 10, 1888. Smith responded he had paid the bill: Kimmel and Rudolph had accepted from Smith as payment another promissory note in which businessmen A. R. Loud & Brothers were to pay monies due to Smith. The plaintiffs, however, claimed they had been unable to collect the payment. Smith responded that A. R. Loud & Brothers were then solvent, and the plaintiffs only had to exercise ordinary diligence to collect. Then, within a few years, the business failed, and the Loud brothers departed the area. Now, more than three years later, the brothers could not be located.[44]

Wanting evidence the plaintiffs had, in fact, not collected payment, Smith requested return of the promissory note, but the plaintiffs refused to produce it. The case continued until, in December 1891, it was dismissed on payment of the bill by Smith. Whether the promissory note was returned to him or he was otherwise satisfied Kimmel and Rudolph had not received payment from A. R. Loud & Brothers is not known.[45]

Two law cases expose complications arising in Smith's work, revealing the effort expended did not necessarily yield recompense in the end. The Sligo Iron Stove Company was one of three creditors awarded property of the Church Cart Manufacturing Company. The creditors contracted with Smith and his business partner T. J. Nickell to serve as their agents for sale of the property, but Sligo later attempted to hold Smith and Nickell accountable for the remainder of its settlement when the property was sold with Sligo receiving only $48.05, leaving $274.75 outstanding.

Smith and Nickell refuted several charges made by Sligo and revealed they had never been able to sell the property because the sheriff, responding to court orders, had retained possession and conducted the sale. They were awarded costs with the dismissal of the suit upon the application of Sligo's attorneys two days before the trial was to begin. Fortunately, Smith and Nickell recovered their expenses, yet the suit had been time consuming and distracting, being filed in October 1895, and not resolved until May 1897.[46] Smith's most exasperating legal case, however, was concurrently underway, entailing a suit he brought on August 7, 1895, against Robert L. Dulaney, a white Illinois banker and real estate agent.

In June 1892, on the front porch of N. J. Braswell's hotel in Eddyville, Smith spoke with Dulaney to request additional time to repay the balance of a judgment, possibly $194, against Smith and his business partners. According to Smith, Dulaney replied he would give Smith much more than the amount of the judgment if Smith would sell a tract of land owned by Dulaney that lay between the Tennessee and Cumberland Rivers in Lyon County. The two men reached an agreement. Smith "finally [found] a purchaser in the person of one E. L. Moore and took him over said tract of land and showed it to him [and] brought about an agreement between them, and the price so agreed . . . [was] $6,500." The sale occurred in September 1893, but after nearly two years, Smith's commission of $650 had still not been paid.

Dulaney strongly denied he had ever engaged Smith to sell the land. In his testimony, taken in a deposition in Illinois (he never appeared in court) signed on April 27, 1896, Dulaney denied that Smith "brought about any agreement between myself and Mr. Moore as to the sale of & the price to be paid for the land."[47]

While Moore and Justin Harlen, Dulaney's local land agent, each received a summons to appear at the trial, they did not do so, and no record of testimony by either is included in the court records. Surely they could have clarified whether Smith showed Moore the property, negotiated the selling price, and put Moore in contact with Harlen to close the deal. Moore's arrangement to purchase the land did, however, indebt him to Dulaney's bank, which may account for Moore's reluctance to testify.

The jury awarded Smith $300 plus 6 percent interest and court costs of $28.30, but Dulaney challenged every effort Smith made to collect. As late as 1904, Smith was still trying to collect his judgment from Dulaney's heirs.[48]

In 1901, Andy and Amanda Smith learned that Alfred Doom, a white man, had publicly accused Andy Smith of stealing Doom's corn. When asked by Amanda Smith on May 1 if he had made such a statement, Doom replied, "Yes, and he did steal my corn." Later that day he elaborated on those words when speaking directly to Smith in public: "I did say so and it is true, you did steal my corn and you are a low down stinking thief, and ought not to have a place to lay your head at night." In June, Doom repeated the accusations in public, thereby attacking Smith's character and accusing him of the crime of larceny. Smith filed suit for $1,000, the maximum amount allowed by law.

In court, Doom admitted to accusing Smith of stealing corn, his defense being it was a true statement. The judge instructed the jury that as the defendant admitted saying "the words charged in the petition . . . said words are slanderous and if the jury believe from the evidence that the same [words] were false and maliciously spoken they will find for the plaintiff." The judge further emphasized if the words "were false, then the law would assume that they were malicious." But "if the jury believes from the evidence that the words were true, or substantially, true, the law is for the defendant."

The jury struggled as a majority agreed in favor of Smith, and even among these jurors, the awarding of damages caused much consternation. Three jurors refused to acquiesce in a verdict and award of damages for Smith, but under Kentucky law, nine jurors could return a verdict if all nine signed the document. These nine reached a resolution on damages. "We the jurors find for plaintiff one cent and cost."[49]

In spite of the minuscule sum, Smith had won his case. He lost two more law cases than he won in Lyon County, but that he could at times prevail in court was a notable accomplishment in the age of Jim Crow, both for Andy Smith and for Lyon County.

CHAPTER 10

HARD TIMES

1900–1917

T HE FIRST DECADE OF THE TWENTIETH CENTURY was one of gradual fiscal contraction for Andy Smith. The 229 acres of land he owned in 1900, assessed at $1,261, declined to 156 acres assessed at $1,000 by 1904, after which his acreage fluctuated slightly but increased in value to $1,200 by 1909. By 1911, however, he owned only five acres in Lyon County. His taxable personal property also declined, from $1,329 in 1900 to $370 in 1911, and the value of his household furnishings decreased by half over the decade to $50. His livestock holdings were small in 1900—two horses, three mules, four head of cattle, and two hogs—but he had managed to retain some of each in 1911: one horse, two mules, one head of cattle, and two hogs. On the plus side, he had acquired a dog.[1]

There is no evident correlation between Smith's declining finances and the turbulence of the Tobacco Wars, engendered by the intrusion of tobacco trusts into the economy of western Kentucky and Tennessee. In 1905, tobacco farmers organized both the Planters' Protective Association (PPA) to challenge the tobacco monopolies and its vigilante wing, the hooded night riders. The vigilantes terrorized tobacco company employees and tobacco farmers selling to the trusts but did not target black farmers. Since Smith did not farm tobacco, it is highly unlikely he was entangled in the struggle between the PPA and the trusts.[2]

By 1907, however, the night rider movement had morphed into disparate groups that were unaffiliated with the PPA but copied the methods of its vigilantes: attacking using the cover of night, wearing hoods, destroying property, and whipping, beating, and even killing individuals found to be undesirable. Anyone deviating from community morals might be targeted by the new night riders, including purveyors of alcohol, gamblers, and men who failed to support their families or abused their wives. White employees of southern Lyon County's iron furnaces belonged to a night rider group focused on driving blacks from the area. In February 1908, they rode into Eddyville at night, beat and whipped ten individuals, including six who were black, and told them to leave town.[3]

For several years, until state authorities suppressed the night riders, Smith's community was vulnerable to attack, but the destruction of records obscures what can be known: no written reports appear to survive documenting threats in Smith's vicinity or in nearby Grand Rivers in Livingston County. The only remaining recourse is to consult oral history, and there the evidence is thin.

Smith's cousin by marriage, Newt Benberry, provided an oral account, but he was not an eyewitness or contemporary, speaking of events occurring a decade before his birth. According to Newt, when Andy Smith learned of night rider activity in the area, he obtained two cases of guns (whether rifles or shotguns is not evident) by mail order from Sears & Roebuck and gave them to his friends. At least one person used the weapon to repel individuals attacking his home. Another story circulating in the community, attributed to Newt's cousin, Ewing Benberry, was of a group of black residents who, learning only hours in advance of a night rider attack, took their shotguns and deployed to waylay their assailants at a bridge, but the night riders never appeared.[4]

Perhaps there is factual information in Newt Benberry's account, but if not, it may yet reveal something of interest about Smith's community, that in their collective memory, this was the type of action later generations expected Smith to have taken if his friends were threatened. The second account reveals later generations preserving a memory that their ancestors came together to defend their community. Still, given the present state of knowledge, it is not possible to know how accurate, if at all, these accounts might be.

In essence, the turmoil of the early years of the twentieth century may or may not have made some contribution to Smith's financial problems and declining landholdings. What is known is he invested his savings in land, not in bank accounts, and he relied on land sales to generate cash.

He also continued to purchase land to rebuild his holdings when possible, though not at the levels of his younger years. Then, in 1907, something went terribly wrong.

In January, he entered into an indenture to repay a note for $500 to D. S. Nowlin using the 164 acres encompassing his homestead (his second farm located a few miles south of Grand Rivers) as surety. Why he needed $500 and chose to acquire the money in this manner is not known, but he was unable to repay the debt in the allotted time. The land, identified as the Andy Smith Tract, appraised at $2,000 and was sold at a December 1909 auction in Eddyville for $634.70, the amount of the debt plus interest and associated costs. Smith made no effort in court to halt the sale and simply acquiesced in the process.[5]

The loss of his home and farm and Smith's listing in the 1911 tax assessment present a desolate picture, but his situation was not nearly as desperate as it appears. Andy Smith's second (white) cousin, J. M. (James M.) Smith, the Lyon County Clerk, conducted the court-ordered auction and sold the land to his uncle and Andy Smith's first cousin, W. D. Smith, who sold the land to J. M. Smith, who sold the land to a mutual friend, local businessman George W. Dixon.[6]

Dixon thus received a valuable tract of land for about 36 percent of its value, but Andy Smith and his family continued residing in their home with enough land to produce crops for family consumption and maintain livestock. Smith's 1911 tax assessment reveals him to be living on the farm, but in a circumscribed setting compared to his 1909 assessment. He was no longer growing field crops, such as the ton of hay and three hundred bushels of corn he had produced in 1909, and his livestock holdings were down slightly, but he still had his dog.[7]

Meanwhile, Smith was planning a move to the new community of Grand Rivers, about three miles distant, in Livingston County, where he would remake his life. He had participated in the town's early development, and on April 28, 1910, he purchased a lot in Grand Rivers' northwest district. But he remained on his farm in Lyon County for several more years. Correspondence affirms his residence there as late as June 1913, while Livingston County deeds reveal his presence in Grand Rivers by winter 1914. George W. Dixon sold the Andy Smith Tract on December 30, 1915, for $1,400.[8]

Smith's remaining five acres in Lyon County consisted of wooded land in the northwest corner of Between the Rivers, about a mile east of the Tennessee and two miles southeast of Grand Rivers. Two of those acres comprised the ground Smith dedicated to his community for Oakland

Cemetery in the 1880s. He sold the adjacent three acres in 1915 to the Lyon County Board of Education as the site of the Oakland School for black children.[9] (See Appendix, page 212.)

THE FIRST DECADE OF THE TWENTIETH CENTURY also encompassed the most difficult years of Smith's personal life. Amanda Smith, whose health had been in decline, died April 21, 1901. Andy Smith was not alone, however, as Will Benberry remained nearby. More than a year and a half later, Smith married Gertrude Catlett, a beautiful young woman who was only eighteen at the time of the wedding on November 30, 1903 (the thirty-ninth anniversary of the Battle of Honey Hill). Her surviving letters to Smith reveal her to have been much in love.[10]

Perhaps it was the difference in their ages that caused them to travel to Cairo, Illinois, to be married. They were sufficiently far enough from home so she could give her age as twenty-four, thereby adding six years, on the marriage license, and he could subtract thirteen years to report his age as forty-eight. They soon had three daughters: Laculian, born on February 12, 1905, lived only eighteen months; Susan Geneva, born on September 26, 1906; and Caruth, born on November 25, 1907. Less than four weeks after Caruth's birth, the skirt of Gertrude's dress caught on fire from the kitchen hearth, and she died of her burns on Christmas Eve.[11]

It was decided that Susan, referred to as Geneva, would continue to live with her father. Smith employed the services of a housekeeper to assist with Geneva's care, and in 1910, Will Benberry, also recently widowed, returned home to help. When Caruth was an infant, it was thought best for her to go live with Gertrude's parents, John and Jennie Catlett, who were relatively young, in their forties, and had three other children living at home. The Catletts resided in Paducah, an hour's travel by train, allowing Smith and Geneva to visit without much difficulty, but the arrangement lasted perhaps a year.

John Catlett had been enduring racial harassment and decided to move his family out of state. Over the next few years, the Catletts became a small part of the Great Migration, moving first to Evansville, Indiana. In 1910, they were living in Princeton, Indiana, after which they moved to Vincennes, and finally to Terre Haute, as John followed the Wabash River north to find employment and opportunity. Caruth grew up knowing her father only from his visits. Meanwhile, Geneva continued to live with Smith until September 1913, when she joined Caruth and the Catletts in Vincennes to begin school.[12]

SMITH'S INABILITY TO PROVIDE the best environment for Caruth at home was linked to his age, aggravated by his continuing health problems. His pension files record his afflictions, and increased payments would have helped with the cost of medical treatments, but he was unable to obtain the correct amount he was due.[13]

Smith appealed under the 1890 Dependent and Disability Pension Act, which provided pensions for injured veterans who were unable to perform manual labor, and injuries need not have been war related. His war injuries had limited his mobility and his ability to lift heavy objects, but this request too was denied, and his disability pension remained at six dollars a month.[14]

Smith's difficulties with the Bureau of Pensions appeared to be mitigated when, in 1907, Congress provided for monthly pensions based on age alone: twelve dollars at age sixty-two, fifteen dollars at age seventy, and twenty dollars at age seventy-five.[15] He made his claim under the new law and received the twelve dollar pension for his age bracket, but being illiterate, he did not realize the bureau's notary public had recorded his birth year as 1843 instead of 1842.[16]

Pensions increased again under the Pension Act of May 11, 1912, and on May 29, Smith's monthly payment rose to seventeen dollars, the amount allotted for a veteran age sixty-six to sixty-nine with two years of service. On September 6, 1912, three days after Smith's seventieth birthday, he applied for the increase to twenty-three dollars due to him under the new act. Instead of the increase, a letter arrived four months later seeking documentation to verify the date of his birth. Replying promptly by affidavit, Smith affirmed he possessed no written record of his birth date and the only document he had to establish that date was his army discharge, which recorded he enlisted on May 16, 1863, "age 20 years."[17]

Smith explained that because he could not read or write, he had always relied on someone else to determine dates, using his discharge papers to fill in the blank spaces on forms. He reasoned the error placing his birth in 1843 was made when the pension bureau clerk figured back twenty years from the 1863 enlistment date on his discharge papers without taking the month of his birth into consideration.[18]

Bureau of Pensions officials refused to accept Smith's army discharge papers as documentary proof of his age and denied his claim for a monthly pension based on having reached age seventy. Smith's pension did not increase until September 1913, when he turned seventy according to the bureau's accounting, but an official did send him a form letter providing an avenue whereby he might establish the date of his birth.[19]

The letter requested Smith to furnish the bureau with the place of his residence in 1850 and 1860, as well as the names of his parents or those with whom he resided during those years. Smith replied, saying he lived with his mother, Susan Smith, near Eddyville, Kentucky. The information was used to determine if his name was in the census records. It was not, of course, since Smith was a slave; the search was destined to fail from the beginning. Bureau officials were either unaware of or said nothing about his race when they requested census data from returns for the white population.[20]

Dr. Burt G. Wilder, c. 1910, while he taught at Cornell University. (*Cornell University Library*)

The struggle to establish his birth date in 1842 was one Smith was destined to lose. His pension increased to forty dollars in 1918, the year following his seventy-fifth birthday. Thereafter, increases were determined not by advancing age but by legislative action: to sixty-five dollars in 1926, and later, in October that year, to seventy-two dollars for disability. Yet the problem originating in a clerk's clerical error proved everlasting. It carried over into Andy Smith's medical records, onto his death certificate, and as the date of birth inscribed on his tombstone.[21]

IN EARLY 1913, former 55th Massachusetts surgeon Burt Wilder reestablished contact with Andy Smith. In the decades since the Civil War, Wilder had emerged as an outspoken advocate of racial equality. He was one of the few scientists of his day willing to take a public stance in defense of black Americans, and his profession made him exceptionally well qualified to do so. As a professor of neurology and vertebrate zoology at Cornell University, he became one of the nation's leading scientific researchers specializing in the morphology of the brain: the scientific inquiry into its form and structure (more generally, the external appearance and arrangement of its parts). One aspect of such research was to determine if the size and shape of a person's brain correlated to his or her known attributes, such as race, intelligence, or criminality.[22]

At the turn of the twentieth century, Wilder began to confront white supremacists, including scientists, who attempted to appropriate the study of brain morphology to postulate a scientific rationale for white racial superiority.[23] In his own writings and public speeches, Wilder demolished pseudoscientific ramblings equating brain size with intelligence, amassing copious data to establish, "As yet there has been found no constant feature by which the Negro brain may be certainly distinguished from that of a Caucasian," and underscored his conclusions with the observation, "[D]uring both my army and university experiences there have been occasions when I was tempted to exclaim, 'Yes, a white man is as worthy as a colored man—provided he behaves himself as well.'"[24]

Wilder carried on his crusade beyond the realm of science, arguing "[t]he American Negro is on trial, not for his life but for the recognition of his status, his rights and his opportunities."[25] For Wilder, there was no better way to enlighten his white audiences and instill self-confidence and pride in his black audiences than to write about the 55th Massachusetts. In 1905, he drew on the 55th's charge at Rivers' Causeway to illustrate "Two Examples of the Negro's Courage, Physical and Moral,"[26] and as he approached retirement in 1910, he intended to do more. Wilder wanted to write a history of the 55th to extol and preserve for posterity the collective accomplishments of a black regiment and record the names and deeds of its individual soldiers.[27] Thus, within a few years, he contacted Andy Smith, one of those about whom he would write.

The initial communications between Wilder and Smith do not survive, but Wilder did ask Smith what he recalled of Rivers' Causeway and Honey Hill. The earliest of the extant letters in the correspondence dates to February 12, 1913, in which Smith dictated his reply:

> Dear Doctor Wilder, I write you this letter to let you Know that I am trying to straighten myself Out as to the two Engagements you wrote me about. Viz. Rivers Causeway and Honey Hill. You ask me about myself and family. I am farming getting along nicely. [H]ave been married but my wife is dead, have two children, names Geneva and Ruth. Your letter brought back to my mind many things that a good soldier has to Endure. [A]nd I was delighted when I read it. Your Humble Sargeant Andrew Smith.[28]

Wilder wrote three days later, February 15, before receiving Smith's letter, but referencing receipt of an earlier card:

> Since receiving your card I have been very much occupied. I am preparing to publish my "Records and Recollections of the Civil War;" I wrote a letter nearly every day and you are often named, always with commendation. I wish to include in my book as many of your experiences

as I can, and I shall be very much obliged if you will write them out for me. Particularly do I wish your account of Rivers Causeway, on James Island, when we crossed from Long Island before day and captured two Confederate guns; Honey Hill where you saved the colors; and Charleston where you captured the deserted, Pelett[e].[29]

Wilder proceeded to inquire about Smith's family, not realizing Smith (who had enlisted in the 55th as a free man from Clinton, Illinois) had been born a slave. "Please begin by telling me about your parents and early life; have you any Indian blood? . . . How far back can you ascertain as to your family? How came you to enlist, and what were your first impressions?" Wilder also did not realize Smith could neither read nor write: "Did you write letters home, and if so were any of them kept? They would be of the greatest importance." It is apparent Wilder wrote this letter before he received Smith's letter of February 12, because he said: "If you are married tell about your wife and children. . . . What have you done since the war and where have you lived?" Wilder also wanted to know if Smith had a copy of Colonel Fox's regimental history and if other veterans of the 55th lived near him. In a postscript, he inquired, "Are any of you musical?" Wilder, a composer, returned to this subject in a subsequent letter, noting, "you do not say whether your daughters are musical."[30]

Wilder was interested not only in Smith's memories of the war but also in Smith as a person. Yet he did not realize how much he was asking of Smith, who, illiterate with no letters or other written records to evoke past events, had only his memory to draw on to recall happenings a half-century past. Smith did, however, comply with Wilder's request and dictated "a sketch" of his life, dated March 22, 1913.[31]

Wilder now learned of Smith's early life in slavery, his escape, experiences at Shiloh, and move with John Warner to Clinton, Illinois. The account also included Smith's early memory of his service in the 55th, focusing on his Long Island picket duty up to the night Colonel Hartwell allowed him to join the expedition to Rivers' Causeway and James Island. Wilder subsequently received a third-person account titled "Andrew J. Smith, Sketch of his life," dated June 1913,[32] and a "Certificate of Character from neighbors of Andrew J. Smith":

Eddyville, Ky. June 3, 1913. We, the undersigned, citizens of Lyon Co., Ky., state that we have known Andy Smith for many years; that, shortly after the Civil War, he returned to this county and still resides here; that he has the respect and confidence of all who are acquainted with him;

that he is honest, discreet, industrious, sober and law-abiding. He has generally engaged in farming or logging; he was employed for some time in the building of the town of Grand Rivers and the furnaces of the Hillman Land and Iron Company. We further say that he has lived the life of a good citizen. (Signed by)

J. M. Smith, ex Co. Clerk and vice-pres. First National Bank
B. F. Smith, [Farmer]
W. L. Crumbagh, 5 terms ex-judge
T. T. Handberry, P. M.
Geo. W. Dixon, Merchant. G. Evans, merchant, Both of Grand Rivers.[33]

Why Smith sent Wilder the certificate of character was not apparent, and Wilder commented, "I do not understand why you got others to vouch for you; I would trust you as much as any other man." Still, Wilder may have been impressed by the statement, perhaps explaining why he became overly inquisitive about Smith's affairs. "Please tell me how much land you own; whether you employ other men; whether you have money in the bank; do you vote, and for how many years?" Wilder continued to press Smith for more facts about his service with the 55th and commented, "My book will have a fuller account of you than of any other man; there will be considerable about [Private] David Lee [of Company C, 55th Massachusetts] also."[34]

No letters from Wilder to Smith are preserved in Smith's records for the remainder of 1913 and all of 1914, but Smith did respond to Wilder on November 9, 1914, returning papers Wilder had sent him to review. "I am sending you your papers. I cannot recall much more about location of our men and our moves etc. I have been trying to study them and recall something's possibly I had forgotten or I would have returned them long ago."[35]

Meanwhile, Wilder had begun to write about the 55th. On May 28, 1914, he spoke highly of Andy Smith and David Lee in a lengthy address, "The 55th Massachusetts Volunteer Infantry, Colored," presented to the Brookline Historical Society.[36] On December 10, 1914, the *National Tribune* (precursor of the veterans' newspaper *Stars and Stripes*) published a letter from Wilder correcting errors and the slighting of black troops in a recent contribution on the Battle of Honey Hill. Defending his regiment, Wilder singled out Smith as "a perfect type of soldier in all respects" and wrote of his bravery in saving the colors. The *National Tribune* even printed a recent photograph of Smith supplied by Wilder.[37]

In April 1916, Wilder read a *National Tribune* report of new legislation instructing the Bureau of Pensions to issue monthly pensions of ten dollars to certain honorably discharged Medal of Honor recipients who had reached age sixty-five. Eligibility for the pension required the recipient to have been awarded the medal "for having in action involving actual conflict with an enemy[,] distinguished himself conspicuously by gallantry or intrepidity, at the risk of his life, above and beyond the call of duty."[38] The law, which established the Medal of Honor list, was the product of Legion of Honor efforts to elevate the status of the Medal of Honor to that of the European medals and restrict awards to military acts of valor.

Later in the year, Wilder wrote Smith, offering to contact G. M. Saltzgaber, commissioner of pensions,[39] to recommend Smith for the Medal of Honor. Smith replied to Wilder on December 14, 1916, asking him "to call the pension commissioner's attention to the deed of gallantry . . . by me in saving the National flag at Honey Hill after one color bearer was killed and the other had his arm broken." Smith's letter expressed no interest in a pension. Instead, it was recognition for his actions at Honey Hill that Smith valued, revealing to Wilder the matter had weighed on him for some time: "I have always wanted a Medal of Honor and feel that I deserve one in this particular case."[40]

Smith might have learned of the Medal of Honor during the 1890s, or possibly in 1900 when Sergeant William Carney received the medal for saving the colors of the 54th Massachusetts at Battery Wagner. In subsequent letters to Wilder, Smith revealed he knew others had received the medal for acts such as his, and he was also aware awards to black soldiers were few.[41] He may not have known the exact number, but thus far the medal had been awarded to only seventeen black Civil War soldiers and seven sailors. The distribution of medals at the Battle of Honey Hill was illustrative: three officers received the medal in the 1890s, including Lieutenant Thomas Ellsworth for saving the life of Colonel Hartwell, but no medals were awarded to any of the battle's black troops.[42]

Wilder immediately took up Smith's cause with enthusiasm, but he was also clearly cognizant that while an officer of the regiment, he was not an eyewitness to Smith's actions at Honey Hill, and the officers who had been witnesses were now dead (the law did not require Wilder to be a witness). Wilder's letter, dated December 21, 1916, served not only to recommend Smith for the Medal of Honor for saving the colors at Honey Hill but also cited other incidents of Smith's meritorious conduct and testified to Smith's service as that of an exemplary soldier: "I am told that, for acts of conspicuous gallantry during the Civil War, there are awarded medals or other tokens of government recognition. If so I have the honor to recommend a member of Co. B. 55th Reg't Mass. Vol. Infantry, colored." Wilder

then referenced Fox's regimental history to document Smith's act: "Color
Sergt. Robert King, a brave, handsome lad of eighteen, was blown to pieces
by the explosion of a shell; but the colors were snatched from his hand and
sustained by Corporal Andy Smith." Wilder next quoted his own *National
Tribune* article of December 10, 1914, to present Smith as the exemplary
soldier:

> Andrew Jackson Smith enlisted at the age of 20 from Clinton, Ill., private
> in Co. B. 55th Mass.; promoted to corporal, sergeant, and color sergeant;
> a perfect type of soldier in all respects. While private at "Yellow Bluff"
> (now New Berlin) Florida, he was for a time detailed as my orderly, but
> at the alarm of an attack by the enemy, he begged to be permitted to go
> to his company. At the bloody battle of Honey Hill he took the colors
> from the slain Color-sergeant and saved them. Sent alone to arrest a de-
> serter he warned the latter of the result of attempting to escape and
> when he disobeyed shot him, but (unfortunately) not fatally. He never
> took liquor, even when prescribed by me.[43]

War Department clerks in the Adjutant General's Office began processing Smith's recommendation on January 2, 1917, a procedure lasting all of
three and a half hours wherein the clerks made notations on the form ver-
ifying the search, which they passed among themselves. Without a search
of the archives, each clerk signed the form declaring no record of Smith's
actions at Honey Hill existed among the documents in the government's
possession, thereby sending the recommendation on a journey to oblivion.
On January 3, 1917, Adjutant General Henry P. McCain responded to
Wilder to explain the Medal of Honor could not be awarded under law because "the evidence . . . must be derived 'from official records in the War
Department,'" and "[a]n exhaustive examination of the official records has
resulted in failure to discover any evidence of the incident referred to
within, or of gallant conduct on the part of Mr. Smith."[44]
      Wilder delayed writing Smith to begin his own pursuit for documen-
tation, searching through the vast collection of records in his possession.
He found the after-action report for Honey Hill, written by Colonel
Hartwell, but it was disappointing. Unfortunately for Smith, Hartwell had
written the report less than a week after the battle while in the hospital at
Hilton Head. He had singled out for special praise only the officers about
him whose acts he had witnessed. Separated from the regiment at Boyd's
Landing, Hartwell had not even learned the name of the officer, Lieutenant
Ellsworth, who had carried him off the battlefield. Thus, it was doubtful

he yet knew who had saved the colors or even that Color Sergeant King had been killed.[45]

After more than a week, Wilder wrote to Smith enclosing the adjutant general's response and reporting on his futile search for documentation. Smith replied, enclosing a clipping on awards of the Medal of Honor from the *National Tribune* and commenting, "I know there have been medals granted to others for [deeds] that were no more Gallant by reading the list in the *National Tribune*." Wilder and Smith soon agreed the only remaining chance was to seek the few surviving eyewitnesses, in the hope War Department officials might relax their regulations and accept such testimony.[46]

Wilder poured through his extensive collection of letters in search of evidence from deceased officers, but again, fate did not favor Smith. Captain Soule was with his company in the woods on the Union right at Honey Hill and did not witness the 55th's charge. In vain, Wilder read a letter Lieutenant Ellsworth had written his wife—"My Color Corporal saved the colors; the sergeant and two corporals were killed"—but he did not mention Smith's name. "Of course," Wilder wrote in frustration to Smith, "you were the color corporal."[47]

Captain James Thurber responded to Wilder, revealing his memory was failing. "All I know is that he [Smith] was a splendid soldier and if he says he saved the Colors at Honey Hill, I should believe him." Lieutenant William DuPree wrote to Wilder revealing he was not at Honey Hill, but Sergeant Major Trotter had told him, "Corp. Smith showed conspicuous bravery in sustaining the colors when the Color Serg't was killed in that action." Sergeant Major Trotter was, however, deceased. David Lee of Company C wrote to Smith, "I was in the Honey Hill fight but did not see anyone pick the colors up; but know that you carried them throughout the fight."[48]

John Warner was deceased, but his son Vespasian was also a person of considerable standing, a Civil War veteran who had been elected to the US House of Representatives for five terms and had served as commissioner of pensions between 1905 and 1909. Vespasian remembered Smith and wrote to Burt Wilder, supplying a character reference and an account of Smith's actions at Shiloh in support of Smith's recommendation, but character references would have been of little use to the adjutant general.[49]

In April, after several attempts, Wilder finally received a reply from Charles E. Grant, whose potential importance as captain of company was negated because he was not present at Honey Hill. Yet Grant did what he could: "Have ransacked what few old time papers remain from several removals, but cannot find, nor do I remember special incidents regarding Andy Smith. Of course I do remember him as an extra good soldier and especially faithful. Am sorry I cannot be of more help. Andy was an honest man, and personally, I should believe anything he said."[50]

Grant's letter effectively ended the quest for Smith's medal, and Wilder wrote as much in a letter to Smith in late April or May 1917, concluding: "It is too bad. But I really see no use in making further efforts. Under some conditions there might be secured some special action of Congress, but surely not now. I am returning all the papers I have and advise you to keep them together in a box or stout envelope, so that they may be preserved for your descendants and the public."[51] Wilder could not have known his act to preserve and transfer these papers to Andy Smith would ultimately lead to Smith's receiving the Medal of Honor.

Having abandoned all hope, Wilder finally received the affidavit of an eyewitness, Jordan M. Bobson, who had been the sergeant of Company C, the color company. No better witness could have been found, for Sergeant Bobson had charged up Honey Hill with the color guard: "My Company was in front, I was to the left of Sergt. King when he was killed. [H]e was the Color Sergt. & obliqued a little to the left of the color guard, and I was a few feet from Sergt. King when he was killed, and Corpl. Andrew J. Smith of Co. B, 55th Mass, Picked the flag up, this was our last charge in that Battle. This is as near as I now remember, at this late day, and I here Sign my name and affix my official Seal this 14th day of May, A.D. 1917."[52]

Sergeant Bobson was the only eyewitness whom either Smith or Wilder had been able to locate (he may have been the only living eyewitness to Smith's saving of the colors). His testimony was impressive, but in the absence of official records, it could not be enough. On June 20, 1917, Smith replied to Burt Wilder: "Dear Doctor. Since there has not been any record made of the Heroic or Gallant Conduct of Colored Soldiers, I feel that it is not necessary to try any longer for a Medal of Honor. I thank you from the depths of my heart for your helping me. I don't feel that I can Ever repay you for your kindness. Anytime I can in my Humble way do anything for you, I am at your service. If I come to the reunion at Boston would I get to meet you there[?]. With best wishes, I am Humble comrade, Andrew J Smith."[53]

Wilder and Smith exchanged a few more letters as Wilder sought answers to specific questions for his book. The final letter to Wilder in Smith's papers was written on March 4, 1918, in which Smith related his memory of Rivers' Causeway. Wilder died in early 1925, after several years of failing health, without publishing a fully developed history of the 55th Massachusetts.[54]

Wilder did annotate and revise his 1914 address to the Brookline Historical Society, "The 55th Massachusetts Volunteer Infantry, Colored," for publication as a pamphlet in 1917 and with additional revisions in 1919. Therein Wilder expanded his remarks on Smith to include, "had it been *officially reported at the time*, Smith probably would now hold a 'Medal of Honor for Distinguished Gallantry in Action' under the Act of Congress of April 27, 1916."[55] More significantly, Wilder amassed an impressive body of documents without which significant portions of the history of the 55th Massachusetts and the legacy of Andy Smith would have been lost.

CHAPTER 11

THE SECOND TIME AROUND: GRAND RIVERS

1914–1932

EVEN WHILE HE WAS LOSING HIS FARM, Andy Smith had begun to build a future for himself and his family in Grand Rivers. The agreement J. M. Smith had arranged with George W. Dixon provided Smith with a respite of several years to rebuild his savings, probably from his livestock operations, but he may also have had other assets, perhaps returns on investments or continuation of his business activities. Whatever the cause, Smith appeared to be in an upbeat mood as he wrote Burt Wilder in February 1913, "I am farming getting along nicely." When he arrived in Grand Rivers in winter 1914, he was by no means destitute.[1]

The founders of Grand Rivers, incorporated in 1890, strove to create a regional industrial and commercial center. Assuming the new community would attract a massive influx of new residents, the town's surveyors designated four substantial residential districts to surround the business and commercial center. They divided each district into a grid with rows of rectangular blocks and, in turn, subdivided the blocks into lots for houses. The frontages and depths of the smaller lots, as in the northwest district where Smith would own land, were approximately 25 feet by 125 feet (slightly more than 7 percent of an acre), while larger lots were about twice as wide with approximately the same depth. Yet, within a few years, the Grand Rivers development scheme failed, leaving the community without the industry, business, and jobs necessary to prosper, and with much vacant land for sale.[2]

Smith had known years before the loss of his farm that unimproved land in Grand Rivers sold for only a few dollars. As early as 1905, Will Benberry purchased six adjacent lots for $100, the price set at $16.66 2/3 per lot, and one other lot with a house for $75. He may have lived in this house with his first wife until her early death or derived income from rent on the dwelling. Otherwise, he suffered a loss on the investment when he sold all seven lots in 1909 for $160.[3]

Benberry's experience was not unusual. Thus, when Smith purchased his first lot in Grand Rivers, in April 1910, for $11.75, he was investing in his future in a community where land was affordable but unlikely to appreciate in value to yield profits such as he had realized in his Lyon County land sales. His goals and pattern of buying and selling land would, therefore, be different.

In February 1914, on the cusp of his arrival in Grand Rivers, Smith purchased two adjoining properties, one with a house, for $100, Lots 3 and 4 next to his own Lot 5 on Block 21. In May, he bought Lot 17 on Block 21 for $5 and a half-acre of unsubdivided land for $10. His next purchase, four parcels on Block 20, Lots 28, 29, 30, and 31, cost only $10 and was not made until December 1916. He assigned joint ownership of each of these properties to Geneva and Caruth, assuring his daughters an inheritance.[4]

It was not only the opportunity of obtaining a house that had attracted Smith to Grand Rivers but also the prospect of buying affordable farmland with which he could support himself and generate income. The land surveyed for the community by the defunct Grand Rivers Land Company remained mostly rural, and the black community living in the northwest corner of town was small, perhaps twenty-five families.[5]

Thus, Smith could buy adjoining vacant lots of land for farming without intruding on the homes of his neighbors. The half-acre of unsubdivided land Smith purchased for Geneva and Caruth in May 1914 likely served as the initial site of his farming operations. He owned a fruit orchard in Grand Rivers, from which he harvested apples, peaches, and perhaps other fruits for sale. The location of the orchard is not known, but the plat of Grand Rivers reveals eight of his lots on Blocks 20 and 21 were mostly wooded and two others partially so.

Smith purchased land on only two more occasions for which there are recorded deeds, each made in his name only (to be inherited by Geneva and Caruth). The first, in August 1920, included five parcels, Lot 32 on Block 20, and Lots 26, 27, 30, and 31 for $23. His largest and possibly last land purchase in Grand Rivers came in June 1923 when he acquired 21 lots on Block 4. The deed does not specify the price Smith paid to E. E. Redd for these lots, stating only "in consideration of one dollar and other valuable considerations which is paid excepting One hundred dollars ($100.00) payable by note."[6]

Assuming Redd exacted a profit, Smith would have paid more than Redd's 1918 purchase price of $235 ($11.19 per lot). Smith enclosed his land on Block 4, indicating he had purchased the property to use for grazing livestock. The enclosure included not only Smith's land but also several unimproved lots subsequently claimed by others. After his death, disputes arose over several of these parcels, but all were resolved in favor of Geneva and Caruth, affirming Smith possessed all or nearly all of Block 4.[7]

In total, Smith purchased eight lots and an unsubdivided half acre in the names of Geneva and Caruth and twenty-seven other lots in his own name. Of all of the properties Smith acquired in Grand Rivers, Lots 3, 4, and 5 on Block 20 were the only ones he sold. In December 1928, he oversaw their sale from Geneva and Caruth to Arthur Benberry for $251, of which Smith received $1. Geneva received an immediate payment of $110, and Caruth received $140 a year later.[8] Smith, therefore, was no longer attempting to profit from the sale of land but to support himself from its possession through a viable farming operation centered on livestock and the processing of meat supplemented by the sale of fruit from his orchards. He used other unimproved lots to grow crops to feed his livestock.

Smith also allotted sufficient land to grow vegetables, fruits, and seasonings for his household. In this, Smith and his neighbors, like virtually anyone with access to land in a rural community, grew much of their own food. Except for the house on Lot 4 and a two-story house on the half-acre lot, the town's plats do not otherwise record the construction of any houses or commercial buildings on Smith's property. He soon made his home in the large two-story house, locally known as The Ark, which he opened to serve as a home for several other families.[9]

Given his age, his infirmities, and the size of his operations, Smith, of necessity, provided welcomed jobs for people in his community. Geneva, returning home for visits in the 1920s, recalled seeing black and white people working for Smith, including white women working at the house. Her young daughter, Dolores, born in 1926, recalled similar memories from visits to her grandfather in the early 1930s when he

> would take me out and watch some of the workers who worked for him when they were harvesting some of the crops, and during harvest time

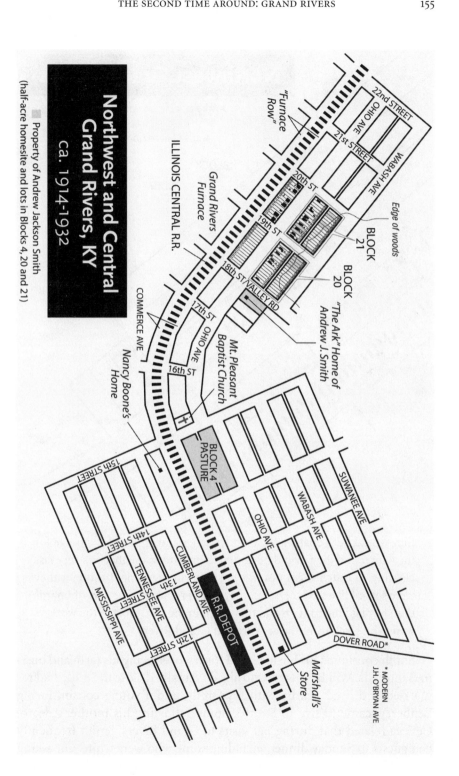

Northwest and Central
Grand Rivers, KY
ca. 1914-1932

Property of Andrew Jackson Smith
(half-acre homesite and lots in Blocks 4, 20 and 21)

22nd STREET
OHIO AVE
WABASH AVE
21st STREET
"Furnace Row"
Edge of woods
20th ST
BLOCK 21
19th ST
Grand Rivers Furnace
BLOCK 20
ILLINOIS CENTRAL R.R.
18th ST/VALLEY RD
"The Ark" Home of Andrew J. Smith
17th ST
OHIO AVE
16th ST
COMMERCE AVE
Mt. Pleasant Baptist Church
Nancy Boone's Home
BLOCK 4 PASTURE
15th STREET
SUWANEE AVE
WABASH AVE
14th STREET
OHIO AVE
TENNESSEE AVE
13th ST
CUMBERLAND AVE
R.R. DEPOT
DOVER ROAD*
MISSISSIPPI AVE
12th STREET
Marshall's Store
* MODERN
J.H. O'BRYAN AVE

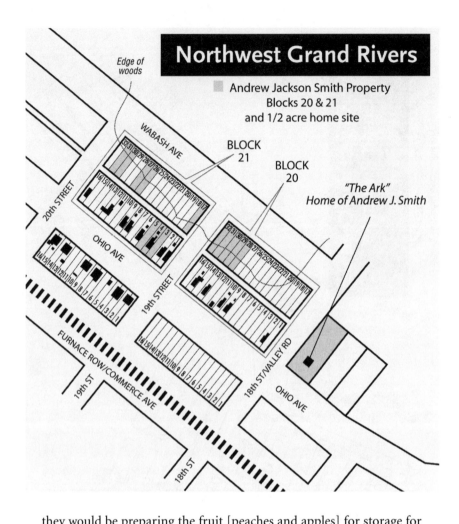

Northwest Grand Rivers

Edge of woods

Andrew Jackson Smith Property
Blocks 20 & 21
and 1/2 acre home site

WABASH AVE

BLOCK 21

BLOCK 20

"The Ark"
Home of Andrew J. Smith

20th STREET

OHIO AVE

19th STREET

FURNACE ROW/COMMERCE AVE

19th ST

18th ST

18th ST/VALLEY RD

OHIO AVE

they would be preparing the fruit [peaches and apples] for storage for the winter and they would be drying them, and to me that was very fascinating to watch them put out the fruit on these big, I thought they were sort of like stretchers, but they were probably some sort of boards that they laid the fruit on and they dried in the sun. Most of the workers were white folk from the area around Grand Rivers.[10]

Smith continued his life in Grand Rivers, overseeing his farm and business interests. Will Benberry, who always remained close to Smith, had remarried and lived nearby with his family, and a young cousin, Ewing Benberry, came to live in Smith's home following his mother's death. Geneva related that during her visits to Grand Rivers, Smith frequently had guests to Sunday dinner, including some who were white. On asking her father, "Who are those white people," he replied, "Relatives."[11] Smith continued to enjoy good relations with his white cousins, the children of his father's brother Edward, especially Benjamin F. Smith and J. M. Smith, who were also business partners, and their sister Nancy Smith Timmons Boone, who had been a lifelong friend.

The Grand Rivers home of Nancy Boone and her husband, Albert L. Boone, was high on a ridge immediately south of a ravine wherein the tracks of the Illinois Central Railroad followed a course inland from its crossing of the Tennessee River. Smith's neighborhood was atop the ridge on the ravine's north side. On summer evenings, Smith crossed the ravine, stepping over the railroad tracks, to visit with Nancy Boone and her granddaughter Golda on the cool, wide front porch of their home. Decades later, in 2003, Golda Beaman recalled those summer visits, filled with friendly banter and stories about growing up in Lyon County:

> I was seven, ten, eleven, and twelve hearing Andy and Grandmother tell their tales out on the front porch. They were just like that. They argued a lot about dates and everything. Just so human. But all I remember about him—everybody had lots of respect for him. He really was a gentleman. Even as young as I was at that time, I knew he was unique. And I looked up to him. That's unusual in those days. But I was always so pleased when I was there, and I would see Andy coming up the hill to have a conversation with my grandmother. And they just had the best time. . . .
>
> I could see the house where he lived. We could see his house from Grandmother's porch. He lived just a little distance from there. Like I said, I was so pleased when I'd see him coming. I would have said, and even now, he was so aristocratic that I would have said that he was a school teacher or something like that, you know, a man, someone with education.
>
> Andy was a Baptist, and Grandmother was a Methodist, and they were strong people, and they would never agree. . . . They would talk about their churches and they didn't agree at all, but it was all levity. They never got mad or anything like that. I can see my grandmother now, pulling up her chair like this, it was a straight chair, "Now Andy," when she was talking about pouring water over the head, you know, she got out of her chair and she raised . . . up like that, and she said, "Now Andy, you know I'm a Methodist." He'd say, "Yes, I know you are Nancy, and I'm a Baptist, and I believe in immersion."

Andy required "full immersion," Golda related, the simple sprinkle of water on the head "wasn't good enough for him. He was a typical Baptist." Golda added:

> [E]verybody had so much appreciation for him and for his character, and for his integrity . . . . and you'll have to realize that I was very young at the time. . . . But I had enough sense to sit down and listen to those two, I thought old people, old enough to die, you know, especially my grandmother. Now Andy didn't look [old], he was a good looking man. . . . I think [because] he had so much dignity, and I was so impressed with the way he handled himself.

A last recollection by Golda Beaman is probably the portrait many residents of Grand Rivers retained of Andy Smith: "I remember him [at] Marshall's store, and he was always laughing and telling stories to all ages, adults as well as children, but he did seem to like children. . . . [He] always had candy or money for children. He gave [them] a nickel, and they could buy their own candy."[12]

Smith's fondness for children was affirmed by Mary White, who remembered sharing in "Uncle Andy's" generosity while growing up in Grand Rivers. "Well Every Saturday or every other Saturday he would have a gathering right down there in front of his house on the side of the street, and they would have . . . something like a little picnic." Smith could then "bring out all these pennies that he had as well as change, [but] mostly pennies, and he would have all the kids come together." Smith then took the pennies and tossed them out among the children to "see how many pennies they could gather up, and they could keep [them]." Mary White also remembered that Uncle Andy carried candies for the children, "little things to make them happy."[13]

In a time when income and profit often amounted to a few dollars, candy was a special treat for children, reserved for only a few times a year. Smith took great joy in providing small treats for children, but he also took pleasure in providing for all those living in his community. Hattie Benberry, who was a young girl in Grand Rivers during the 1920s, told of times Smith slaughtered cattle to feed people when they did not have a source of meat, and the community came together for a good meal.[14] One of the "fondest memories" of Smith's young granddaughter, Dolores,, "was [in] the spring of the year . . . [when] my grandfather would have a lamb roast, and he would invite all of the people in the area to come in and share a roast with the family."[15] In his later years, Uncle Andy remained at the cen-

ter of his community, surrounded by relatives and friends, always willing
to help make the lives of others a little better.

DOLORES SHELTON BROWN was Geneva's eldest child and the only one of
Smith's grandchildren to have retained memories of him. Decades later,
She offered a few glimpses into his final years:

> Well, I have many memories of my grandfather. Of course, he died when
> I was six years old. But as a youngster, I used to go down there with my
> mother and visit all the time, and he was always very fond of me because
> I was his first grandchild, and he always called, always referred to me as
> his "Little Chap." I don't know whether he wanted a boy child or a little
> girl child as his grandchild, but he loved to help me learn about life and
> about things that happened on the farm. . . .
>
> And I remember one morning when my mother went into the town
> to do some shopping, and when she came back, there was a whole
> bunch of encyclopedias left at the house. She asked my grandfather,
> "Where did these encyclopedias come from?" He said, "Well, Little Chap
> needs some encyclopedias." And she said, "Well, she doesn't know how
> to read as yet." And he said, "Someday she will."
>
> And he always wanted me to be able to learn and appreciate education
> and appreciate life. And also when I was little he loved to take me in the
> kitchen and let me learn to cook, and Mother used to come in some-
> times and see the flour and the ingredients all over the kitchen, and
> she'd say, "What happen to the kitchen?" And he said, "Well, Little Chap
> needs to learn how to cook, and she wants to learn how to cook. So I
> just let her." And so we would have that kind of interchange between
> each other at all times. And then he was just a warm and loving grand-
> father, and I always loved being with him. Sometimes he would take me
> out to the pond, and we'd go fishing together, and those were the days
> that I really enjoyed being with him. And, I don't know, I really regretted
> when he passed away, and I [no longer had] . . . that kind of interaction
> with my grandfather. I always thought that he was like, almost like a
> second father to me when I was a little girl.[16]

Dolores may have idealized the remembrances of her grandfather. By
the time she was old enough to form memories, Smith had been in failing
health for several years, his injuries from the war and arthritis aggravated
by advancing age. In 1926, his physician diagnosed him as suffering from

"general arteriosclerosis" as evidenced by frequent attacks of vertigo. He was also "very short winded" and "very weak," in need of the care of an attendant.[17]

In December 1928, Smith wrote to the commissioner of pensions, evidently in the belief he was eligible for an increase in his pension from seventy-two to ninety dollars a month as "now I am totally helpless, so that I must even have an attendant at night." The letter appears to have been occasioned by Smith's injury in an accident in November about which there are no details, but Smith wrote, "the doctors say it will be a hard fight for me to recover, as I am 85 years old."[18]

Smith apparently did recover to some degree, but he needed assistance in those years, especially at night, and Will Benberry was always there to help, as was Will's wife, Cora. As early as 1926, they had been helping Smith dress and undress, activities made difficult by his rheumatism, and helped him move up and down the stairs to his home, and stayed with him at night. During the day, however, Smith may have concealed his medical problems from friends, neighbors, and the community at large. Neither Ewing Benberry nor his cousin Newt Benberry, who also grew up in Grand Rivers in the 1920s, thought of Smith as being in poor health or infirm in his final years.[19] It would have taken an incredible effort for Smith to have been the presence in Dolores's life that she remembered, but he evidently managed to do so sufficiently to meet the needs of a small child.

Andy Smith died on March 4, 1932, of arteriosclerosis. On Sunday, March 6, a cold late winter day with a high temperature of 32 degrees, his family and friends gathered at Oakland Cemetery, Lyon County, on the land he had donated to his community, about two miles south of Grand Rivers. They laid him to rest singing, "Gonna lay down my sword and shield, Down by the riverside. . . . I ain't gonna study war no more."[20]

PART 3

HONOR

CHAPTER 12

RECLAIMING THE LEGACY

1932–1986

I N LATER LIFE, CARUTH WROTE SHE "seldom saw her father during her growing up years." Over time, the arrangements made for her care following Gertrude Smith's death became increasingly less advantageous for the relationship between father and daughter. Andy Smith had sent his children away from home to give them a better quality of life than he could provide, but he was forced to do so at a time when advancing age made the rigors of traveling increasingly difficult, and visits came less often. John and Jennie Catlett encouraged him to move to Terre Haute, but, as Caruth complained, "He would not leave Kentucky."[1]

Certainly, her father seemed tied in a special way to the land Between the Rivers, but he also needed to manage his businesses to support himself and his daughters. When he did arrive in Indiana for visits, it was a grand occasion. "He came with gifts," Andy Smith's grandson, Andy Bowman, related, "things that would make a young girl, a young person, really proud." There were gifts for others as well; one time he brought silverware for Jennie Catlett and "very special gifts" for Caruth. "I don't think he visited very often," Bowman surmised, "but when he did, she was delighted to see him, to recognize that he was her father."[2]

As Smith and the Catletts desired, life in Terre Haute provided Caruth, Geneva, and the Catlett's surviving children, Nellie, Ruby, and Charles, with the opportunity for a better future. Indiana afforded them six additional years of public schooling beyond that available to black children in Kentucky. Caruth was a talented child with a beautiful singing voice, and she learned to play the piano. Geneva joined her sister and grandparents in Terre Haute to begin elementary school and benefited immensely from the experience.

Geneva completed high school and, nearly six months later, in November 1923, married college student Henry Shelton. Caruth, however, did not take full advantage of the formal education her father wanted her to have in Indiana. In July 1923, at age sixteen and after two years of high school, she married Richard Robinson. In 1927, they had their only child, Richard, but were separated and probably divorced by 1929. At the time of Andy Smith's death in 1932, she was living with her son in Buffalo.[3]

When Caruth returned to Grand Rivers to attend her father's funeral, she was taken aside after the service and given his papers, a "'keepsake' to remember her father by."[4] As she turned the pages, she found information that helped fill the void in her knowledge about Andy Smith's life. Here were official documents, a pamphlet history of the 55th Massachusetts, letters from Civil War comrades, a body of correspondence from Burt G. Wilder, his letter recommending her father for the Medal of Honor, and another from the adjutant general denying the award, events about which Caruth had no prior knowledge. The moment would not allow the thorough examination she wanted, so she returned the pages to their case and carefully conveyed them back to Buffalo. There she had the privacy to examine the contents and reflect on her discovery.

Caruth could not have known it at the time, but the information she found was priceless. Without these papers, it is inconceivable she and her family would have ever learned about her father's recommendation for the Medal of Honor. Except for a file buried deep in the archives of the Adjutant General's Office, she now possessed the only other extant records documenting Andy Smith's recommendation and the rationale for its denial. She did not question the medal's denial or entertain any effort to reverse the decision. She needed time—more than five decades—to comprehend the potential those pages held.

Overjoyed with possessing new knowledge about her father, she was also overwhelmed by the responsibility of preserving his legacy. Caruth "decided that she would keep [the papers] with the future plan to have them published or codified in some manner for library or museum donation in the interests of Afr[ican] American History," but this endeavor would have to wait. "At the time it was during the Great Depression and hard economic times," Caruth wrote, and she "had a young son to support and educate alone, so the project was deferred for many years—but never forgotten." She would not risk the loss of Andy Smith's papers, and she placed them in the care of a friend, Wardner H. Jones, an undertaker who stored them in a protected place for far longer than either he or Caruth ever anticipated.[5]

Caruth then married Henry Lawson, a porter, and the family moved to New Rochelle, New York, in the 1930s. Within a few years, while waiting at a bus stop, Henry was accidentally struck by a car and killed. In addition to the emotional toll, Caruth once again faced the necessity of raising her son as a single parent. She persevered and continued to reside in New Rochelle through the 1940s, filling her life with service to St. Catherine's A. M. E. Zion Church and to her community. She applied her artistic talents in support of dramatic clubs; contributed to community service through the Empire State Federation of Women's Clubs, in which she served as president of the Westchester, New York, region; and was an avid supporter of the NAACP and the Urban League.

By the time Caruth moved to New York City in the 1950s, she had expanded her involvement in communal groups to include active participation in the Daughters of Union Veterans of the Civil War, the Daughters of the Grand Army of the Republic, and the National Society of Daughters of the Union 1861–1865. These organizations served to perpetuate the memory of the Civil War and provide assistance to Union veterans and their descendants.[6] Interaction with other descendants of Union veterans not only enabled Caruth to learn more about the war but also provided a means to honor and keep her father's memory alive.

While Caruth was building her life in New York, Geneva and Henry Shelton had moved to Detroit with their two daughters, Dolores and Henrietta, and son James. In 1935, Andrew was born, and another son, Walter, followed. Norman Hodges, a childhood friend of the family's, related his memories of Geneva Shelton at this stage of her life: "Mrs. Shelton was a very intelligent, personable, and maternal individual, who was a voracious reader of fiction, non-fiction, and historical literature."[7]

Hodges spoke affectionately of Geneva Shelton as an important figure in his formative years:

> Above all, she was a font of wisdom and learning and orientation for adulthood for the peers and friends of the Shelton children. She contributed a great deal to my personal maturation with respect to . . . love for books . . . a deepening appreciation for culture and the impact of

culture (reading, art, the legitimate theater, museums, and an intellectual curiosity about the world and domestic and international issues). She never ceased to encourage us to read and to think critically about what we read. She also told us many stories about her generation and about life in general.[8]

Geneva Shelton was as yet unaware of the Medal of Honor recommendation, but she generally knew more about Andy Smith's life and accomplishments than did her younger sister. Geneva, unlike Caruth, also possessed a handwritten account, which she called "the journal," that resembled the text of the March 21, 1929, *National Tribune* article, "Adventures of a Colored Boy in War."[9]

Hodges recalled that Geneva Shelton used the "journal—a rather nondescript and worn notebook," to help keep the memory of her father alive. "What I remember most about the times when Mrs. Shelton would take out this old journal and begin to talk of Andrew Jackson Smith and his life and exploits was the enthusiasm with which she told her father's story (reading from the journal) and the very obvious pride she felt over his repudiation of slavery and his determination to make his personal contribution to its demise. Sometimes, Mrs. Shelton would have tears in her eyes when she told these stories from the journal of Andrew Jackson Smith."[10]

The story of Andy Smith was, therefore, an important influence on his daughters, his grandchildren, and their friends. Young Andy, however, would not know about his grandfather. Henry and Geneva Shelton, struggling financially to raise their children during the Depression, accepted an offer from Bob and Babe Bowman, close friends who resided nearby and were childless, to have Andy live with them. This was not an unheard-of practice, and much as Andy and Amanda Smith had taken Will Benberry into their family, the Bowmans took in young Andy as if he were their own child.

Everyone assumed Andy would eventually be made aware of the arrangement, but he thought of himself as Bob's and Babe's son and as a "cousin" of the Sheltons: "I grew up knowing [Geneva] as my aunt, someone [in whom] I could confide my hopes and dreams. I understood that she and Babe Bowman made a pact that they would live within walking distance."[11] Andy visited Geneva Shelton's house often, without ever realizing she was his mother and that family stories told about a Civil War soldier were actually about his grandfather. He retained no memory of the name Andy Smith.[12]

Shortly before Andy Bowman's sixth birthday in 1941, the Bowman family moved about two miles away from the Sheltons' neighborhood, considered to be within walking distance, and Andy made return visits to their home. The Bowmans enrolled Andy in first grade at a school in their new neighborhood, which Babe managed to accomplish without supplying a birth certificate. Andy Shelton became Andy Bowman, and the need to address his parentage receded.

Young Andy spent the rest of his childhood growing up in a wonderful environment with loving parents who sacrificed to make a better life for him. They must have found it too difficult to reveal the truth to Andy, and the Sheltons allowed the deception to continue. Meanwhile, Caruth Smith and Geneva Shelton drifted apart and would have little contact for the next forty years.

In 1953, near the end of his senior year in high school, Andy began searching for career opportunities. He decided to join the US Air Force, but the recruiters required him to present a birth certificate before he could sign his enlistment papers. When he returned home to ask the Bowmans for the birth certificate, they first told him they could not find it. Then, a few days later, they told him they needed to talk to him. It was then he received the shock: "Andy," Babe Bowman told him, "you're not our son."

Andy listened numbly as he learned his real mother was his "Aunt" Geneva Shelton, the woman whose home he had so often visited. Decades later, he described the news as "devastating." Coming in the crucial years when a young man begins to forge his own independent identity, the timing of the revelation could not have been worse. Strong family identity and knowledge of his heritage would have helped ease the sting of rejection, but Bowman had neither. Compounding the loss he felt, the lack of a birth certificate prevented his enlistment in the air force, leaving him without the career he was planning to enter and the requisite pay accompanying it. He was drifting, rudderless, and without the family ties he thought were his.

Andy soon found an outlet for his feelings of anger and abandonment in pool halls and made friends with those in the local gambling scene, spending an increasing amount of time with them. He began drinking and hustling people at blackjack and poker, developing skills as a cardsharp. Andy was on a track leading only to trouble, but this portion of his life abruptly came to an end when he found himself about to cheat a good friend out of a considerable amount of money. He realized "this path was not the one" and walked away. Remaining close to Bob and Babe Bowman, he searched for a new direction forward. He eventually gained the assistance of an attorney and legally changed his surname to Bowman. With documentation in hand, he was finally able to enlist in the air force in 1955 and became a specialist in electronic countermeasures.

Bowman received his honorable discharge from the air force in 1959 and returned to civilian life to begin a career with the Federal Aviation Administration in Indianapolis. Two years later, he met Esther A. Long. They married and soon began to raise a family: Catherine, Andrew, and David. They lived in a nice house in an Indianapolis suburb and had all the responsibilities that came with a home and family. Meanwhile, Bowman's career in the FAA progressed nicely, and he eventually became the first black supervisor at the Indianapolis air traffic control center, in charge of all electronics during his shift.

Living in Indianapolis placed Bowman within driving distance of Detroit, allowing him to make periodic visits home to see Bob and Babe Bowman and to strengthen relations with his biological family, especially his mother. But he remained troubled by the deceptions of his younger days. Sensing he was still not at ease, Geneva occasionally tried to talk to Bowman about Andy Smith in the hope he would find meaning in the life of his grandfather, a successful person and community leader who had also been a soldier. To Bowman these stories meant little.

Bowman had not studied the Civil War and was suspicious of his mother's stories about his grandfather having been a soldier and landowner. The latter ran contrary to the standard tales of black Americans' lives as sharecroppers in southern states. He decided his mother was either mistaken or attempting to glorify her father. In any case, the people he knew to have owned land in his family had only owned houses in Detroit. "I thought it was all a fairy tale." He also could not understand why some people were so interested in the Civil War, and it appeared to Bowman those people were always white. "I thought anyone who talked about the Civil War was a bigot—it seemed they were longing for a return to slavery."

Bowman remained a man seeking his identity as he built his own successful life in Indianapolis, but in the early 1970s, his world began to change. Geneva Shelton decided to move back home to Kentucky to live near her birthplace. She and Henry settled in Kuttawa, across the Cumberland River from where Andy Smith had, many years before, established his first farm. They resided in the midst of families who had once lived Between the Rivers before the Tennessee Valley Authority appropriated their property in conjunction with construction of two new dams near Grand Rivers.

Thus, when Andy Bowman visited, often with Esther and their children, he entered into the company of people who either had known Andy Smith or knew of him. Bowman became friends with some of these individuals, in particular cousins Ewing and Newt Benberry, who had grown up in

Grand Rivers and knew Smith for much of the final two decades of his life. Ewing had even lived in Smith's home as a youngster. Both told Bowman stories about Andy Smith and life in Grand Rivers, and Newt drove him along the route he thought Andy Smith might have followed to escape from slavery in 1862.

Geneva Shelton now began to talk extensively about her father, and Bowman began to listen. The stories were true, Bowman realized. Andy Smith had created a successful life, but more than being a prosperous landowner, he had provided jobs, he made land available so people might have small farms, he was a benefactor to his community, he had opened his home to children in need of a family, he had been respected by members of both races, and he had even entered into business arrangements with whites. More than successful, his grandfather had been a decent person whose memory was respected and even cherished within his community. Andy Bowman wanted to learn more about Andy Smith, but his grandfather's service in the Civil War remained of little concern to him. That, too, would change in another decade.

ANDY BOWMAN'S JOURNEY of discovery began in 1982 with an eighth-grade school assignment for Andrew S. Bowman Jr. The students in young Andrew's class were to write a paper about an ancestor. Upon learning of his son's project, Andy Bowman told Andrew, "You know, your great-grandfather was a soldier in the Civil War." The two decided to investigate. They drove to Kentucky to visit his mother and search for evidence.

At the Lyon County Clerk's office, they found some of Andy Smith's land deeds. They took handwritten notes, which, together with Geneva Shelton's recollections about his Civil War service, provided the basis for a tidy paper, though without mention of the Medal of Honor denial. They still did not know about Andy Smith's Medal of Honor recommendation and denial, information only Caruth possessed. Indeed, each daughter had knowledge about their father's Civil War service that the other lacked, but the sisters, who had not been close as children, had grown even further apart as adults, separated for decades by different interests and long distances.

Caruth, meanwhile, had continued to live an active life in New York City. She had married Dr. Edward L. Washington, a prominent educator in the New York City public schools, and, in the early 1980s, they decided to retire to Los Angeles. On their journey to California, they drove first to Buffalo, providing Caruth the opportunity, after more than five decades, to retrieve her father's papers.

Over time, she began to work with the documents, inserting each page into a Mylar sleeve to protect and preserve the paper and then organizing the pages into an album: Letters and Memorabilia of Color Sergeant Andrew J. Smith ("Andy") Civil War Soldier, 55th Volunteer Regiment, Company B., of the Massachusetts Volunteers, Union Army (1984). She compiled an annotated table of contents for the documents and wrote a biography of Andy Smith, attempting to re-create his life as best she could. Lacking many facts, including those possessed by Geneva, Caruth relied on faint memories and conjecture to fill gaps in her knowledge, and the resultant biography reveals how little accurate information she possessed about much of her father's life. It also reveals how desperate she was to fill that void.

Upon completion of the project, Caruth changed her intended disposition for her father's papers. She realized the simple placement of the album and biography with a public archive did not ensure it would ever be discovered, and she wanted to honor her father's participation in the Civil War, not risk it being lost to history. Therefore, she retained possession of the album and began an effort to interest historians in its documents and in writing about her father's life.

Two years later, in 1986, Caruth's and Geneva's aunt, Nellie Catlett Ransome, died in San Francisco, and both sisters attended the funeral. Caruth called Geneva soon thereafter, and the two began corresponding. This led to Caruth making plans to visit Geneva, who began to contact family members and arrange a small reunion in Chicago. Andy Bowman agreed to attend, anxious to meet his mother's sister.

The day finally arrived, and the family gathered at a relative's house in Chicago. Bowman arrived first, then Caruth. To attest to the success of her life thus far, Caruth wore her finest. Two luxurious stoles covered her shoulders, diamond rings glittered from her fingers, and an expensive watch adorned her wrist. Introductions were made all around, and then Andy's own moment arrived to greet Caruth. After exchanging names, Andy took note of Caruth's watch. "That's a nice watch," he said to her. "It's a lot like mine." He held out his wrist where his watch was secured, the face of Mickey Mouse smiling at Caruth. She had a good chuckle and took an instant liking to Andy.

Bowman was unaware Caruth possessed her father's papers or had any particular interest in his Civil War service. Then someone raised the subject of Andy Smith, and Bowman mentioned the school paper his son Andrew had written, spurring a positive reaction from Caruth that Bowman had not anticipated. She was ecstatic that Bowman had suggested that his son write about Andy Smith and then drove him to Kentucky to do research. Caruth believed that in Bowman she had found a kindred spirit, and she would not lose the opportunity to develop their relationship.

Meanwhile, Geneva Shelton overheard the conversation, and, as Bowman later recalled, "This led to a debate between Geneva and Caruth about how Andy Smith had traveled to Massachusetts to enlist in the 55th." To everyone's amusement, "the two got to friendly arguing, which eventually petered out." But that day, within the humor and camaraderie of a family gathering, the alliance that led to the reversal of the denial of Andy Smith's Medal of Honor was forged.

CHAPTER 13

PASSING THE TORCH

1987–1997

A CLOSE FRIENDSHIP, sustained by long-distance telephone calls, developed between Caruth Smith Washington and Andy Bowman in the years following their family's reunion in Chicago. Typically, their conversations took place at night when Bowman called Caruth around midnight from Indianapolis, 9:00 PM for her in California. They usually talked for an hour or two, learning about each other's lives and thoughts, but conversations always turned to family and Andy Smith. Caruth supported Bowman's nascent interest in his grandfather's life and encouraged him to study the Civil War. She even offered to buy him a uniform so he could become a reenactor. At the time, Bowman had no interest in reenacting, but he took her words to heart: he had much to learn.

Another matter of conversation was Caruth's inability to find anyone who would write a book to honor her father's Civil War service. She had talked or written to educators, including university professors and at least one prominent African American historian, as well as to authors and journalists, but she was never able to interest anyone in writing about the Civil War career of Andy Smith. Caruth's album, even with precious, vital information, was in itself insufficient to support a fully developed biography. Assuming additional documents could be found, far more data, entailing extensive research, needed to be amassed. The busy, successful professionals whom she contacted were already committed to other projects, and no one seemed drawn to the story of a soldier denied the Medal of Honor.

In 1989, as Caruth entered her eighty-second year, she felt increasingly unable to continue the search for an author. She mailed the album containing Andy Smith's papers to Bowman and, in an accompanying letter, wrote simply, "I'm going to choose you to carry the flame for me."[1] Thus, the woman who had preserved and defended her father's memory chose the man in search of his own identity to carry on her work. Bowman believed that if he were to become an effective advocate for his grandfather, he would have to learn much more about the service of black troops and the 55th Massachusetts.

He began his search in libraries, only to discover that much of the information he needed was not available in books. The war in the Union's Department of the South had been largely ignored by historians, as had the service of the 55th Massachusetts and other black regiments. Indeed, until the 1989 release of the motion picture *Glory*, few Americans had known that black troops had fought for the Union. Bowman decided, therefore, to educate himself. He took journeys of self-instruction during much of the next decade, traveling to other states in search of archives and historic sites, and, most importantly, to visit people who could help him learn and understand what he could not yet find in books.

Bowman's early breakthroughs, however, were made close to home in Indianapolis, where a 1991 conversation with fellow FAA employee Jerry Nelson laid the foundation for future discoveries. Nelson knew from his military service that Bowman could make a telephone call to the National Archives and obtain his grandfather's military records. A copy of Andy Smith's Compiled Military Service Record soon arrived, containing data abstracted from the regimental books of the 55th Massachusetts with his enlistment, discharge, physical description, special duty assignments, and promotions.

Nelson took Andy Smith's service record to a meeting of the Indianapolis Civil War Round Table, where members concluded Smith had been an exemplary soldier. The bimonthly muster roll abstracts revealed that he was never absent or subject to disciplinary action, was detailed to special duty on several occasions (a demonstration of trust in Smith by regimental officers), and from enlisting as a private was promoted to corporal and then to color sergeant.

Nelson conveyed these impressions to Bowman, together with the insight that the color sergeant was typically the most highly respected enlisted man in a regiment. Bowman's interest in his grandfather swelled. He became driven by the desire to find out everything possible about the life of Andy Smith, and he also began to wonder if the missing records from the War Department might be found.

Bowman's next opportunity came a few months later when, in August, the Sons of Union Veterans of the Civil War held their 110th Annual Encampment in Indianapolis. He arrived with Caruth's album to share the contents of Andy Smith's papers with two leading members of the Civil War community: Jerry Orton, a member of the Sons of Union Veterans, and his wife, Lorraine Orton, a member of the Daughters of Union Veterans of the Civil War. The Ortons suggested army historians might like to see the documents in Caruth's album and directed Bowman to the US Army Military History Institute (now called the US Army Heritage and Education Center) at Carlisle Barracks, Pennsylvania.

In early 1992, archivists at Carlisle Barracks cordially welcomed Andy and Esther Bowman. John Shonaker asked to copy his grandfather's records for their collection, and Bowman began his initial research into the institute's vast holdings. On a subsequent visit with Esther at his side, Bowman was searching through microfilm of the 1914 *National Tribune*, slowly turning the reel by a hand crank. An article by Burt Wilder began to come into view, followed by the top of a photograph of a man's head. "The further I rolled the film," Bowman related, "the more of the picture we saw." He had just found the first image he had ever seen of his grandfather. It was a photograph of an older Andy Smith, his wizened gaze staring out from the page as if to greet Andy Bowman with dignified approval. "It was," Bowman said, "a life-changing moment."[2]

Unknown to the Bowmans, someone else was interested in the life of Andy Smith. Historian Katherine Dhalle had undertaken extensive travels conducting archival research on soldiers of the 55th Massachusetts. Having received confirmation that Cornell University housed a collection of photographs of black soldiers, Dhalle took the first of what would be many drives from her home in Rome, New York, to visit Cornell's Rare and Manuscript Collections, wherein resided the Burt Green Wilder Papers.[3]

"The first time I saw Dr. Wilder's collection," Dhalle recalled, "I couldn't believe my eyes. What a goldmine of information it contained. I don't think anyone had been through it in ages. . . . As I progressed through the collection, I found many interesting tidbits and people [whom] I tried to research further. One of those was . . . Andy Smith. I remember writing to a couple of historical societies in Kentucky to see if they had any information on Andy Smith, but I never received any replies back. From Andy Smith's correspondence to Dr. Wilder, I learned that Dr. Wilder had tried to get

the Medal of Honor for Andy Smith, but . . .
nothing could be done."

Dhalle's travels included a trip to Carlisle
Barracks to examine the holdings of the US
Army Military History Institute, but she had
arrived before the Bowmans' initial visit and
did not find records pertinent to her interests. Then, during a second visit on April 22,
1992, she searched the card file again to determine if any new acquisitions had been
cataloged and found a listing for the letters
of Andrew Jackson Smith. Dhalle was ec-

Andrew Jackson Smith, age 72,
in the *National Tribune*, the first
picture Andy Bowman saw of
his grandfather. (*Cornell University Library*)

static. "When the papers were brought to me
to view, I discovered that the letters Carlisle
held were the letters that Andy Smith had received from Dr. Wilder. Cornell had Andy
Smith's letters, and now Carlisle had completed the circle by being in possession of Dr.
Wilder's letters. How often does that happen?"

Dhalle promptly conferred with the curator, Dr. Richard Sommers, and
"told him about my previous attempts at tracking down Smith's descendants, and asked him if there was a way I could get in touch with the person
who had donated the papers to Carlisle. He told me while he couldn't give
me their name and address, he could, in fact, send a letter for me. So I sat
down, penned a letter explaining everything, put it in an envelope provided
by the library, put a stamp on it, and gave it to the curator."

Andy Bowman replied to Dhalle's letter by express mail, and she responded by telephone the day his letter arrived. They agreed to meet in
Washington, DC, within two weeks. Dhalle would be there to research
records in the National Archives, while Andy and Esther Bowman already
had a trip scheduled to visit their son David at Howard University.

They met outside the National Archives gift shop, introduced themselves, and moved to the cafeteria to talk and review copies of documents
from the Wilder collection that Dhalle had made for the Bowmans. During
their initial telephone conversation, Dhalle had told Bowman "about the
photo of the little girl that I'd found with the letters, and he told me that
it was his mother. He couldn't believe it as he'd never seen a picture of her
as a child. I made sure I had a copy made and brought it with me to that
first meeting. That was the beginning of our friendship and the sharing of
information on his grandfather and the 55th."

Bowman knew he must eventually search at the National Archives, and he took this opportunity to make his first attempt. His telephone call in 1990 to order records had been easy, and now, as he entered the archives nearly two years later, he hoped for a similar experience: he could walk in, order what he wanted, and it would be brought out. But no one's first visit to the National Archives is ever that simple.[4] The Bowmans logged in, were photographed and issued identification cards. They had to deposit in a locker their coats, briefcase, purse, and anything else that might conceal papers. With notepaper and pencils in hand, they proceeded to rooms where bibliographic guides and archivists were available to help direct their research. Some documents were accessible on microfilm, which they might retrieve and read by themselves, but they had to submit request forms to see the original documents housed in the stacks. Then, waits of one or two hours or more—even to the following morning—ensued, depending on the scheduled time for the next retrieval of records. Finally, carrying only a slip of paper with research notes, they passed through the controlled entry into the Central Reading Room to view the documents they had requested.

Bowman emerged three days later, a little frustrated and still struggling with identifying the correct words to define his search, but he and Esther had at least found Andy Smith's pension file. The process, at first daunting, became more comprehensible on return visits as the Bowmans learned to manage procedures designed to protect and make accessible the nation's historical records. During these visits, they also brought Caruth's album with them, and using those documents with the help of archivists, they began to find useful evidence: documents from the Adjutant General's Office pertaining to the denial of Andy Smith's Medal of Honor. Yet they found no account of his actions at Honey Hill.[5]

While visiting African American historical sites in Washington on the day following their first visit to the National Archives, the Bowmans encountered amateur historian Wilbert H. Luck. The meeting was a charming happenstance for all. In retirement, Luck had become interested in the 55th Massachusetts and, appalled at the dearth of information published about it, wrote and self-published a short history of the regiment. He was delighted to meet the grandson of Andy Smith and presented Bowman with an inscribed copy of his book, *Journey to Honey Hill*. Bowman, in turn, was excited to meet someone knowledgeable about the regiment and, finally, to possess a book he could study. Later, eagerly examining its contents, he found a quotation describing Andy Smith's saving the colors at Honey Hill. Here was yet another claim in support of his grandfather's actions, Bowman thought, and evidence must exist somewhere.[6]

wounded, as they were bearing him off. Lieut. Hill, Col. Hartwell's aide, was blown from his horse by the concussion of a shell
and taken to the rear; but he soon returned to the field. Color-
Sergt. Robert King, a brave, handsome lad of eighteen, was blown
to pieces by the explosion of a shell; but the colors were snatched
from his hand, and sustained by Corp. Andy Smith. The loss in
these charges was heavy, as in each one the enemy fired grape and
canister at short range. In the mean time Companies K, E, and I

Andy Smith's heroism at Honey Hill as his regiment suffered severe casualties is described
on page 43 of the official *Record of Service of the 55th Massachusetts Volunteer Infantry. (Library of Congress)*

Bowman's search bore fruit sooner than he expected and in unexpected
circumstances. A few months later, on Sunday, August 30, he saw an inter-
state sign for Manassas National Battlefield Park while he was driving a
friend to Dulles International Airport. He knew the battles at Manassas,
fought in 1861 and 1862, were unrelated to the history of the 55th Massachusetts, but on the return trip, he decided to see the battlefield simply to
learn more about the war. Late in the afternoon, he drove into the park
against the tide of an overflow crowd of departing visitors who had been
participating in events commemorating the 130th anniversary of the Battle
of Second Manassas. As the Bowmans entered the Henry Hill Visitor Center, a senior park ranger kindly interrupted his paperwork to greet and engage them in conversation.

Upon learning about Bowman's ties to the 55th Massachusetts, the
ranger went into a back room and reemerged to present Bowman with a
photocopy of *Record of the Service of the 55th Regiment of Massachusetts
Volunteer Infantry.* The regimental history had been originally published
in 1868, and, although reprinted in 1971, it was possessed by few libraries
and remained difficult to find. With his own copy of the text in hand, Bowman discovered more evidence, in the words of Lieutenant Colonel Fox,
that "Color-Sergt. Robert King, a brave, handsome lad of eighteen, was
blown to pieces by the explosion of a shell; but the colors were snatched
from his hand, and sustained by Corp. Andy Smith." Furthermore, Fox's
statements were not his alone, as the text of the regimental history had
been reviewed by a committee representing the Association of Officers of
the 55th Massachusetts.[7]

The Bowmans and Dhalle began to consider enlisting the assistance of
the US Army in their search for evidence. Perhaps Lieutenant Colonel Fox's
statement in the regimental history might serve to instigate a new search

for the missing military documents. They did not know how to request an investigation into the denial of a Medal of Honor, or if such an investigation was possible, or whom to ask about these matters.

Dhalle decided to write for direction to the person at the very head of the US military command: "In September or October of 1992, I wrote to General Colin Powell, who was then Chairman of the Joint Chiefs of Staff, regarding the pursuit of the Medal of Honor for Andy Smith. On October 26th, 1992, I received a personal reply from General Powell. He advised me that there was a special branch that handled those requests and was kind enough to forward a copy of my letter to the Military Awards [and Decorations] Branch for their consideration."[8]

On March 1, 1993, Dhalle received a letter from an officer in the Military Awards and Decorations Branch, Alexandria, Virginia, stating "there are no provisions under existing law whereby this request may be honored." The officer explained that the Act of Congress of July 9, 1918, ended the period in which recommendations for the Medal of Honor based on Civil War actions could be considered and set new guidelines and timelines for any future requests.[9] However, Dhalle's letter was a preliminary request for procedural information—not for an application supported by documentation for a new recommendation, but the procedure for a reconsideration. Although Congress had established time limitations in 1918 prohibiting any new Civil War recommendations, the Department of Defense's Manual of Military Decorations and Awards has long provided for reconsideration of denials of the Medal of Honor in cases involving possible "error or impropriety."[10] Dhalle and the Bowmans were unaware of this provision and did not challenge the officer's response, but neither did they accept it. They continued their efforts and planned to meet next at Cornell University so Andy Bowman could examine the Burt Wilder papers.

A few months later, the Bowmans had their first, stunning view of Cornell's vast campus, the college buildings looming high in the distance over Ithaca, New York, from atop East Hill as they approached the small city. Rendezvousing with Dhalle in the town, they drove up University Avenue to the Cornell campus and made their way to Olin Library. There, elevators descended three stories below ground to the Carl A. Kroch Library's Division of Rare and Manuscript Collections. As the elevator doors opened, they stepped out into daylight emanating from skylights high above a central atrium, brightening the surrounding research rooms and creating a pleasant atmosphere for the study of archival records.

The Bowmans began working their way through Burt Wilder's extensive collection, rich in information on Andy Smith and the 55th Massachusetts.

Here were descriptions of everyday life in the regiment, internal stresses, personalities of officers and men, Wilder's scientific investigations, medical work, diet and general health of the men, his views on service in a black regiment, and drawings of camp life.

Wilder's interest in the regiment's history produced a substantial post-war correspondence with officers and enlisted men, as well as with Confederates they had once opposed. His visit to Charleston decades after the war enabled Wilder to produce accurate maps of troop movements in the engagement at Rivers' Causeway. Also present was his collection of photographs that had originally attracted Dhalle's attention.

Bowman increasingly wanted to know more about his grandfather and his grandfather's war, and he next went to Boston in search of additional information. The Bowmans visited the State Library of Massachusetts, which houses the Alfred S. Hartwell Collection, and the Massachusetts Historical Society, to which Charles B. Fox donated his war letters to his wife and his manuscript history of the 55th Massachusetts. Both archives served as sources for Massachusetts's black troops in the war, not only for their military actions but also for their thoughts and motivations.

Bowman interspersed his travels to Washington, New York, and New England with continued visits to Kentucky to spend time with Geneva and to learn more about Andy Smith's life there. Research in the Lyon County Clerk's Office yielded Andy Smith's marriage certificate to Amanda Young and records of transactions wherein he had bought and sold land. Subsequent research at the Livingston County Clerk's Office revealed land transactions made later in his life when he had settled in Grand Rivers, and his death certificate. But Bowman did not fully appreciate the extent of Andy Smith's land holdings until he met Ray and Shara Parish.

Ray Parish, having grown up Between the Rivers in the 1950s and 1960s, shared memories of the final years of the community Andy Smith had helped build before it was demolished by the Tennessee Valley Authority, preparatory to flooding much of the region by newly constructed dams. He was also president of Between the Rivers Inc., a citizens' group caring for the cemeteries, virtually the only remaining vestiges of the community that was once there. Parish took the Bowmans on a pilgrimage to Andy Smith's grave in Oakland Cemetery. There they found his grave next to those of Gertrude and Laculian; a walk of a few yards brought them to Amanda's grave, and farther on was the grave of Susan, Andy Smith's mother.

Ray and Shara Parish became wonderful friends and strong supporters of the Bowmans in their quest to learn more about the life of Andy Smith.

Parish's knowledge of Between the Rivers was unsurpassed, and he conveyed the Bowmans to the scenes of Andy Smith's life, including the remote remains of his first farm.

ANDY BOWMAN'S LIFE had changed in the years since he had taken young Andrew to Kentucky to research his paper assignment. The knowledge that his grandfather, one among thousands of black troops, had participated in the Civil War and made a contribution to the freeing of his race transformed the quality of Bowman's life. He threw off the stereotype imposed on generations of black Americans—that they had done nothing to achieve their freedom—to embrace a sense of self-respect and determination:

> Just knowing our ancestors fought for their freedom, that it wasn't just handed to them, gave new meaning to my life. I took greater pride each day in my job, in everything that I did. . . . [Before] I knew of my grandfather, . . . I had no concept of who I was. This made me somebody. I felt very proud that my family had made their contribution. I liked myself now. I had also never considered myself as a black American before, but I became more relaxed, and I felt more connected. I paid more attention to my actions, and I became more concerned about the product of my life.

That knowledge instilled more than pride; it enabled him to realize his own sense of competence. He represented himself more assuredly to his colleagues at the FAA and even to his family. "My children picked up on this and developed more confidence in themselves and became even better students. They didn't need to go searching for heroes because they already had Andy Smith in their family."

Bowman wanted to share the knowledge of his ancestor and the impact it had made on his life and his children. He was particularly concerned about communicating with children who, not knowing that their ancestors had fought for their freedom, were without pride in their heritage from which they might draw strength and self-confidence.

In February 1992, while attending FAA training in Florida, Bowman discovered that a Civil War reenactment of the Battle of Olustee was being staged nearby. He made his way to the site, where he had his first encounter with reenactors who, fortuitously, included those representing the 54th Massachusetts. Bowman talked at length with the participants and departed with an appreciation of the educational potential of living history.

Bowman's friend, Khabir Shareef, shared his feelings: "I never knew there were black soldiers in the Civil War. I thought all black folks were slaves, and Abraham Lincoln had freed them. We want people to know the black man fought for his own freedom—it wasn't given to him." This knowledge gave Shareef "a different perspective; it gave me a sense of pride and dignity, and I wanted to share that with others." To that end, they formed a small reenacting troupe, with Shareef assuming the persona of Major Martin Delany, a physician who recruited thousands of black troops for the Union cause and was the only black officer to hold the rank of major in the Civil War, and Bowman the persona of Color Sergeant Andrew Jackson Smith.

In uniform, they staged performances for school children to tell them about the United States Colored Troops. Eventually titled "The Major and the Color Sergeant," their performance became a greater success than they had ever anticipated, and they went on to perform before thousands of children at schools and civic events for more than twenty years.

Decades later, having become a parent and established a successful life, David Bowman reflected on his mother and father, grandparents, and great-grandfather's legacy:

> I am standing on the shoulders of my segregation era parents, who are standing on the shoulders of my Jim Crow era grandparents, who were standing on the shoulders of my enslaved great-grandparents in order for me to be able to reach this level. I thought about what it took for them to overcome what they had to overcome. . . . Knowing that Andy Smith took so many courageous actions before, during and after the Battle of Honey Hill, it encourages me to also be courageous in my own actions as well. For me, it's not just that some vague historical characters contributed to American history, but my own flesh and blood that makes me proud. I hope not only to be the manifestation of my great-grandfather's dreams, but to ensure that my own descendants make me and the country proud as well.[11]

Meanwhile, another of Andy Bowman's travels yielded important results. While in Washington, DC, in 1995, he visited the Anacostia Museum and came upon a display about Woodrow Wilson. Bowman soon discovered that there was more to the president whom his high school books had lionized as a champion of democracy, world peace, and the League of Nations. These books had ignored a dark side of Wilson's presidency: he was also a racist whose administration drove African Americans from federal service and imposed segregation in federal workplaces and public facilities.

The information was stunning. Bowman returned home, read each of the documents relating to the denial of Andy Smith's Medal of Honor, and arrived at a conclusion that he did not want to reach: Andy Smith had been denied the Medal of Honor because Burt Wilder, in all innocence, had recommended him for the medal during the presidency of Woodrow Wilson, and, given the racism inherent in the Wilson administration, officials in the War Department perhaps knew not to recommend to the president that a black soldier be awarded the Medal of Honor.

Only two Medals of Honor were awarded to black Civil War soldiers after 1874: in 1900 to Sergeant William H. Carney, 54th Massachusetts, for saving the colors at Battery ("Fort") Wagner, and in 1914 to Private Bruce Anderson, serving with the white 142nd New York Volunteer Infantry. Anderson's award was one of three made to a small group of soldiers cooperating in one action, and there is no indication War Department personnel were aware of Anderson's race. He was simply one of three soldiers from a white unit.[12]

Contrasting the account in the regimental history of the 55th Massachusetts, wherein Colonel Fox clearly stated that Corporal Smith had saved the colors at Honey Hill, with Adjutant General McCain's assertion that "[a]n exhaustive examination" had failed to uncover any evidence, Andy Bowman concluded—in an understatement—that, "Someone had not told the truth."

Determining why Andy Smith had been denied the Medal of Honor led to the breakthrough in the search for the missing evidence. Bowman reasoned that McCain and the clerks in his office simply denied the existence of evidence already in their possession. So the place to search was where, in 1917, the evidence was said not to be: in the Civil War military records of the US government, specifically in the regimental books of the 55th Massachusetts (the bound records of day-to-day operations, including written orders, letters, company descriptive books, and morning reports) housed in the National Archives. Kathy Dhalle reached these conclusions at virtually the same time as did Bowman and sent him a message: "Look in the Descriptive Book and Order Books of the 55th Massachusetts."[13]

A few months later, in March 1996, the Bowmans made their next visit to the National Archives. They scheduled three days to search the records, but what should have been a rewarding process turned into an exasperating experience. By now seasoned researchers, the Bowmans requested the Descriptive Book, Order Book for Company B, and the regimental Order

Book of the 55th Massachusetts, but when they arrived in the Central Reading Room, they were told that the books could not be found. They repeated their requests the following day without success.

On the morning of their final day in Washington, with only a few hours remaining, they were told once again that the documents were unavailable, but this time their conversation was overheard by archivist Cynthia Middleton. She knew that the regimental books had been temporarily removed for binding but was able to make them accessible to the Bowmans. They worked quickly but methodically. He began searching for Andy Smith's entry in the Descriptive Book, which was easily found: "Promoted for bravery in action at Honey Hill, Nov. 30, 1864."[14] Meanwhile, she began working through the pages in the regimental Order Book.

Searching regimental books is not necessarily a quick or easy task. Typically, they contain hundreds of pages of documents with multiple entries per page, handwritten in faded ink, often difficult to discern. Middleton eased their way by turning the Order Book to the starting date for the search, November 30, 1864. Taking care not to damage bound pages whose age exceeded more than 130 years, the Bowmans began reading each entry, searching for any mention of Andy Smith. Fortunately, the items were few in December and January because the regiment had been in the field, but nothing appeared in the records for December; nor did it seem anything would appear for January until they reached the final day of the month. Esther was the first to find Lieutenant Colonel Fox's order promoting Corporal Andrew Smith to Color Sergeant for saving and sustaining the colors after the death of Sergeant King.[15]

Esther Bowman then saw another bound book, less than half the size of the large regimental books. "I wonder what's in here," she said to her husband and began turning the pages. She had found an appendix to the regimental Order Book, and under the date of February 8, 1865, she located Special Order No. 17 in which Sergeant Andrew Smith was among the soldiers Colonel Hartwell recognized "for especial gallantry under the enemy's fire."[16]

The Bowmans departed the National Archives that day with photocopies of three documents, any one of which should have sustained Burt Wilder's recommendation of Andy Smith for the Medal of Honor. Finally, they had the evidence to obtain reconsideration of the medal's denial, but they had yet to overcome the inertia of official indifference.

THE PROPER PROCEDURE to request reconsideration of the denial of a Medal of Honor is to initiate an inquiry with the appropriate military service through a member of Congress, but the staffs of Bowman's and Caruth's senators and representatives would not place Andy Smith's case before the US Army Military Awards and Decorations Branch. "It's too late," staff members repeatedly told Bowman—an answer given either in ignorance or disinterest.

These senators, representatives, and their staffs could not have been unaware of the current national debate about the role of racism in failures to award the Medal of Honor. Cases relating to Asian American and African American soldiers in World War II were of particular concern, and Congress had responded, including legislation in the National Defense Authorization Act for Fiscal Year 1996 to facilitate review of potential irregularities in past incidents. The law specifically provided for senators and representatives to submit individual cases to the military award branch of the respective services.[17] In failing to comply with this legislation, Bowman's and Caruth's political representatives and their staffs seemed unable to grasp that a soldier from an earlier war was as much entitled under law for reconsideration as one who had served in World War II, Korea, or Vietnam.

Without the support of his political representatives, both white and black, it was difficult for Bowman to know how to proceed, but he kept searching. Certainly, these people had demanding schedules and pressing matters to resolve, yet Bowman only needed someone to write a short cover letter and enclose his documents. Eventually, he was referred by a deputy legislative assistant to the chairman of the Joint Chiefs of Staff. After several attempts to talk with the officer, Bowman was met with a stinging rebuff. "This is never going to happen," the officer said, "the Medal of Honor was impossible to get," the case was "not worthy," and it was "too late to try."[18]

The response was terribly demoralizing, almost shattering. During the course of seven months, Bowman's mood had gone from exhilaration to despondency. He and Esther had located the evidence in the government records that Adjutant General McCain claimed could not be found, but now no one, not his representatives, not an army congressional liaison officer, would help him place Andy Smith's documents before the US Army's Military Awards and Decorations Branch. Bowman later wrote in his logbook, "I nearly gave up."[19]

Bowman needed time to think, to prepare a course forward. At the urging of friends, in what would be a prophetic act, Bowman joined the Indianapolis Civil War Round Table in October, soon after the army officer's rebuke. He was heartily welcomed, and members invited Caruth to the December meeting as their honored guest. Bowman hoped that membership would foster his course of self-education to learn more about the war and bring him into contact with others in the Civil War community who might help him find a way to gain a hearing for Andy Smith.

In early 1997, at Dhalle's urging, he decided to travel with Esther to the scenes of Andy Smith's Civil War service. After visiting Charleston, the Bowmans paid a special visit to Dhalle's friend James Island historian Willis "Skipper" Keith. An authority on the history of Charleston's Sea Islands, Keith has long been active in local historical research and preservation. As a lifelong resident, he is familiar with the Civil War sites and movements of armies through the islands, even recalling from his youth the physical remains of military operations now obliterated by wind, tide, and human activity.

Keith guided the Bowmans to sites on Folly Island; the places of infantry movements on Peas Island (Tiger Island), Sol Legare Island, and James Island, including the location of the Confederate defense line that incorporated earthworks at Rivers' Causeway and Grimball's Causeway; the sites of Forts Lamar, Pemberton, and Johnson; McLeod's Plantation; and Battery Means. Keith's patient guidance and depth of knowledge enabled the Bowmans to envision Andy Smith's movements, to be present at places where his grandfather and the 55th Massachusetts had served, and to empathize with the experience of serving in the siege and occupation of Charleston.

The Bowmans next traveled to Parris Island to meet another of Dhalle's friends, Stephen Wise, curator of the Parris Island Museum. Wise arranged permission for the couple to visit Honey Hill (the land being on private property with restricted access), and then led them on a guided tour of the battlefield. Andy Bowman was able to walk the ground where the 55th Massachusetts charged and stand where his grandfather had saved the regiment's colors. Following his pilgrimage to Honey Hill, Bowman returned home to Indianapolis determined to persevere.

During these months, Bowman decided to revive Caruth's effort to find someone to write about Andy Smith's life. Perhaps a book would build interest and help convince political representatives or someone else to place his case before the army's Military Awards and Decorations Branch. He began to seek a historian who would write about his grandfather's accomplishments.

CHAPTER 14

THE QUEST FOR RECONSIDERATION

March 1997–May 1999

R OBERT BECKMAN FIRST MET Andrew Bowman through Sharon MacDonald. MacDonald had been a panelist for a discussion sponsored by the Indianapolis Civil War Round Table in March 1997. Among its issues, the panel deliberated whether the state of South Carolina had the right to fly the Confederate battle flag (the actual flag flown was a rectangular naval jack, not the square battle flag) over the dome of its statehouse. MacDonald maintained the South Carolina legislature had the legal right to fly any flag it chose—the question ought to be whether South Carolina should fly a flag that at least a third of its citizens found objectionable.

Bowman responded from the audience, providing the perspective of those who perceive the Confederate flag as the emblem of a government that existed and fought to perpetuate slavery. Seeing that emblem flying atop the state's capitol, the building wherein laws were made, left Bowman with a chilling feeling, as if the flag heralded a possible return to the repression of earlier times.

As the discussion progressed, Bowman later explained, he began to think perhaps MacDonald might be interested in his grandfather's story. "She was very knowledgeable, firm and positive," he later said. "She was also from Illinois, a state with ties to Andy Smith, so I decided to try to enlist her help." Later, they had a productive talk. He told her he had been seeking someone to write the history of his grandfather, an escaped slave who had fought for the Union. She replied it might be a good thesis subject for a high school teacher she knew who was completing his master's degree. As they concluded their conversation, Bowman said quietly, almost as an afterthought, "He was recommended for the Medal of Honor," and then added, his voice softly trailing off, "but he didn't get it."

Two weeks later, Beckman and MacDonald traveled to Indianapolis to meet with Andy and Esther Bowman and learn about Andy Smith. The Bowmans had done an impressive amount of research, and the historians left late in the afternoon with photocopies of documents—a stack nearly a foot high—and curiosity about the story of the Medal of Honor. During the three-hour drive home, Beckman began to leaf through the papers. Here was Burt Wilder's December 21, 1916, letter of recommendation and the January 5, 1917, official letter of denial, addressed to Wilder from Adjutant General Henry P. McCain.[1] The Medal of Honor had not been awarded to Smith because "an exhaustive examination" did not produce the required substantiating documentation in the official records of the War Department.

Here also was the internal paperwork of the War Department's Adjutant General's Office, revealing an examination that, far from exhaustive, was cursory and yielded an incomplete accounting of the War Department's holdings. The clerk assigned to search public records failed to access Lieutenant Colonel Fox's regimental history of the 55th Massachusetts from the Library of Congress. He simply noted, "Nothing found in the published records relative to the man or the incidents mentioned." Another clerk, recording fifty-five minutes to search the archives, wrote, "No record found, as claimed." The clerk assigned to examine the books of the 55th Massachusetts similarly concluded, "no record of incident found, or mention for gallantry," but he also made additional notations exposing his search for the charade it was.[2]

This last clerk began his task, appropriately, with the Compiled Military Service Records of the Adjutant General's Office, wherein data for each volunteer soldier had been abstracted from military records, entered onto cards, and placed in individual jacket envelopes. These envelopes provide ready access to information on individual soldiers and act as a guide to more-detailed accounts in regimental books. The clerk consulted Color Sergeant Robert H. King's compiled service record, which is evident from his close paraphrase of the abstract from the Company Muster Roll following King's death, "killed in action while carrying the Colors Nov. 30, 1864, at Honey Hill."[3]

The clerk had ascertained the circumstances of King's death at Honey Hill, which should have been preparatory to a thorough investigation of Andy Smith's exploits in the battle and subsequent promotion to Color Sergeant. But the clerk's only action was to consult Smith's Compiled Military Service Record, noting simply, "Claimant is reported as sgt 'D. D. [detached duty] Color' Sgt."[4] Correct procedure required the clerk to obtain the document referenced in the compiled record, which, in the case of Smith, the clerk failed to do. The clerk began and ended his search into Andy Smith's military records with a brief perusal of Smith's compiled service record.[5]

Given Adjutant General McCain's citation to the 1904 law—the evidence had to be "derived from official records in the War Department"— the findings of the clerks' search of military records, archives, and published accounts would be determinative. Thus, the brevity of the search appears intentional, as if its very purpose was to find nothing of substance.

As Beckman continued working through the stack of papers, he turned a page and saw the missing evidence: photocopies of the records the Bowmans had found in March 1996 at the National Archives in Washington, DC. Here were pages from the regimental books of the 55th Massachusetts, documents in possession of the War Department, which the clerk should have easily found in 1917 had he properly searched. Had the clerk consulted the regiment's Descriptive Book that provides the name, physical description, hometown, occupation, enlistment data, and remarks for each enlisted man by company, he would have found the entry for Andy Smith with the statement, "Corporal June 1864, Serg[eant] Feb. 1st 1865, Promoted for bravery in action at Honey Hill, Nov. 30, 1864."[6] Had the clerk simply followed the citation in Andy Smith's compiled service record to General Orders No. 3 in the 55th Massachusetts Order Book as he was supposed to, he would have located the record that, evidently, neither he nor his superiors wanted to find:

Head Qrs. 55th Mass. Vols.
Fort Burton, Ga. Jan. 31, 1865
Gen. Orders No. 3
    The following promotions of Non Commissioned officers are hereby made on the recommendation of the Comd'g Officer of Company B for distinguished gallantry in action at Honey Hill S. C. Nov. 30th 1864 . . . Corporal Andrew Smith to be Sergt. . . . Sergt. Andrew Smith having as Corporal of the Color Guard taken the Colors after the fall of Sergt. King and carried them through the rest of the action, is hereby detailed

as Color Sergt. in recognition of his conduct on that occasion.
By Command of
Chas. B. Fox
Lieut. Col. Comd'g Regt.[7]

A perusal of the regimental Order Book should also have uncovered
Special Order No. 17, issued by Colonel Hartwell a week later, on February
8:

> The Col. Commanding desires to express his pleasure to the Officers
> and men of the 55th Mass. for their good conduct in the recent opera-
> tions and especially at Honey Hill. . . . Among those who distinguished
> themselves at Honey Hill . . . the Colonel commanding cannot omit to
> mention before the Regiment the names of Lieut. Ellsworth, Sergt. An-
> drew Smith (Co. B) and Private Elijah Thomas Co. [B] for especial gal-
> lantry under the enemy's fire.[8]

Beckman looked at MacDonald and remarked, "They said they didn't
have proof of Andy Smith's actions. It's all right here. He should have got-
ten the medal."

Those who told Andy Bowman it was too late or impossible to gain a
new hearing for the denial of Andy Smith's Medal of Honor were wrong.
Department of Defense regulations specifically provided for reconsideration of denial in cases where "there is evidence of material error or impropriety in the original processing or decision on a recommendation for
award of the MOH."[9] Clearly, the failure of War Department officials in
1917 to conduct, as claimed, "[a]n exhaustive examination of the official
records" and produce government records in their possession constituted
commission of material error.

Providing even more support for Andy Smith's case, the Department
of Defense regulation included "proven gender or racial discrimination"
among examples of such transgressions.[10] Adjutant General McCain and
his clerks served in the administration of Woodrow Wilson, well known
for acts of racial discrimination and segregation of the federal civil service.
Even if the War Department had approved Andy Smith's recommendation,
it is difficult to believe President Wilson (who once held a private White
House showing of *Birth of a Nation* for friends and government officials)
would have condoned an award of the medal to Smith, whom they would
have known was African American due to his regiment and rank.[11] The
need now was to find someone who could place this body of evidence before the current US Army's Awards and Decorations Branch.

In July 1997, Beckman presented the case of Andrew Jackson Smith in a letter to Congressman Thomas W. Ewing, who represented Clinton in the Fifteenth Congressional District of Illinois.[12] Within a few weeks, an encouraging reply arrived, dated July 29, 1997: "This will acknowledge receipt of your very interesting and unusual request for a reconsideration of Color Sergeant Andrew Jackson Smith's nomination for the Medal of Honor. I have contacted the appropriate authorities on his behalf and as soon as my office has any additional information, you will be notified."[13]

The original letter had arrived on the desk of staff member Carol Fraker in Congressman Ewing's Bloomington, Illinois, office. Andy Smith's case could not have been placed in better hands:

> Mr. Beckman's letter came to me as I was doing all the Veterans' Administration work for the District at that time. I did what I normally do and made the initial contacts. I faxed the letter from Mr. Beckman to the Washington office and asked if I could pursue this and got a positive response. I spent a couple of days making the letter as appealing as I could. When I got a letter we were all comfortable with, I sent it to Congressman Ewing. He signed the letter and we sent it in with virtually no hope of anything coming from it. We got a quick response and they requested a copy of the whole package, and we had to get a letter of request from a member of the family and contacted Mr. Bowman.
>
> The whole office got caught up in it. It was such an unusual request, and I was so touched by it. I was immediately emotionally involved. It was fascinating, and my husband is a Civil War fanatic who is working on his own book on Lincoln, so I was familiar with the subject and particularly interested in the minority aspect.[14]

In September 1997, the army's legislative liaison informed Congressman Ewing of the acceptance of Andy Smith's case for reconsideration under a provision of the FY1996 National Defense Authorization Act, Section 526, which enabled Ewing to request the secretary of the army to consider the award of a military decoration, which otherwise could not be considered due to time limitations. Although time limits had not been a factor in 1917, strict limitations did exist in the modern era requiring army recommendations be made within two years of the act of valor and awards made within three years.[15]

Section 526 required the secretary of the army to make "a determination . . . as to the merits of approving the award," a process requiring Andy Smith's reconsideration being heard by the Senior Army Decorations Board. The board's decision would be subject to review within the Department of Defense. Once the final determination was made, the secretary of the army was to submit the findings to the appropriate House and Senate committees and to Congressman Ewing. If the award warranted approval, Ewing would introduce a bill containing the waiver of time limitations, thereby enabling the president to award the medal.[16]

Eighty years had passed since Andy Smith's first recommendation had been denied. His daughter Caruth was ninety years old, and her health was beginning to fail. She had endured two knee operations, and the anesthetic seemed to take a lot out of her. She became confused more often, developed fainting spells, and generally appeared weaker. At one point, her neighbors found her unconscious on the floor. Caruth eventually moved to a nursing home in New Jersey to be near her family, who worried she might not live to see her father honored.

Months passed, and Smith's family and supporters began to ask if there was a way to move the process along. They did learn the Senior Army Decorations Board had quickly approved and forwarded the review to the secretary of the army, apparently by January 1998. The process does not allow for the failing health of family members or even of recipients, and delay is supposedly built in to allow time for errors of fact or other problems to surface. So the family waited, knowing Caruth's health could take a turn for the worse at any time.

Much of an agonizing year went by as Andy Smith's recommendation advanced through the Department of Defense to arrive at the office of Secretary of Defense William S. Cohen. There it stalled. Andy Bowman sought again, without success, to contact officials in the Department of Defense and stress there was an elderly woman in poor health who had been waiting years to see her father receive his award. Beckman and MacDonald then turned to Senator Richard Durbin of Illinois, who graciously came to Andy Smith's assistance. Durbin received no reply to a letter he wrote Secretary Cohen, but, as a member of the Senate Appropriations Subcommittee, Durbin could question the secretary when he appeared before Congress. The next opportunity occurred on May 11, 1999. Once Durbin concluded his questions on military appropriations, he turned to one final matter:

> Senator DURBIN. I see my time is up, but I would like to ask just one final comment or question. I wrote to you a little over a year ago about an extraordinary situation where they had identified a sergeant, a black sergeant who served in the Civil War, who many people had researched and believed that he should have been eligible for a Medal of Honor.
>
> We are waiting, not to prompt any specific reply, but waiting for a reply. As hard as it may be to believe, the daughter of that Civil War sol-

dier is still alive today, in her nineties, and we are hoping to get some answer back from the Pentagon about our request on a timely basis because of her advancing age.

His name is Andrew Jackson Smith, and if you would be kind enough to check into that, I would appreciate it.

Secretary COHEN. Senator Durbin, let me say of all the reforms that I have tried to institute at the Pentagon, the one I have failed at magnificently is getting a timely response to inquiries coming from Members of Congress.

And I will say publicly, as I have said privately, if you really have an issue that you want me to address, call me.

Senator DURBIN. How about face-to-face? Is that good?

Secretary COHEN. This is great.

Senator DURBIN. Thank you. Thank you very much.[17]

Three days later, on May 14, the Department of Defense released "Misc. 2915, Proposed Legislation to Award the Medal of Honor to Andrew J. Smith for Action in the Civil War." Secretary Cohen informed the Committee on Armed Services of the Senate, the Committee on National Security of the House of Representatives, and Congressman Ewing that Corporal Smith's recommendation for the Medal of Honor merited approval and recommended a waiver of the legal time restrictions.

Andy Bowman could at last place a telephone call to Caruth with the news they were close to obtaining final approval for her father's medal. "She cried, and she cried," he recalled. "For a while, she just couldn't speak, she couldn't say anything." At last, she responded, saying, "I worked so hard, I worked so hard, and finally, finally, all my efforts have paid off. I knew I was right; I knew I was right." Caruth recognized the work Bowman had accomplished. "I'm so happy I gave those papers to you," she said. "I made a good choice, and I'm very happy you decided to take this up. I'm very, very appreciative." Bowman believed Caruth's life's calling had been to gain for her father the recognition he had been denied.[18]

CHAPTER 15

THE MEDAL OF HONOR

September 1999–January 2001

A WEEK AFTER CONGRESS RETURNED from its summer recess, on September 14, 1999, Congressman Thomas W. Ewing introduced to the House of Representatives H.R. 2858, a waiver of time limitations "[T]o authorize the award of the Medal of Honor to Andrew J. Smith for acts of valor during the Civil War."[1]

As Congress's only role in the approval of Medal of Honor recommendations is to waive time limitations required by law, the passage of these bills is not controversial and does not require debate. Congress often expedites this type of legislation, such as the naming of federal buildings, under what is called suspension of the rules. As recently as November 4, 1997, H.R. 105–2813, a waiver of time limitations to award the Medal of Honor to navy corpsman Robert Ingram, had been introduced into the House under suspension of the rules. In Vietnam, on March 28, 1966, Ingram had exposed himself for hours to enemy fire to treat wounded soldiers, even as he was wounded himself. The navy lost the paperwork containing his recommendation for the Medal of Honor, and the mistake was not rectified for more than thirty years. It passed the House on November 8, and the Senate on November 10, and was signed by President William J. Clinton on November 20.[2]

H.R. 2858 was initially referred to the House Committee on Armed Services, but two weeks later, on September 28, it was referred to the House

Armed Services Subcommittee on Military Personnel.[3] The bill was expected to pass from committee to votes in the House and Senate under suspension of the rules by the end of the first session of the 106th Congress on November 22, 1999, and be presented to President Clinton for his signature. The difficult part of the process appeared to be over.

Five weeks passed, and the bill was still held in the House subcommittee. The silence was puzzling. Finally, a congressional aide revealed the bill was being delayed, along with the awards of all other medals, as leverage to force approval of another medal. The aide would not identify who was conducting the delay, but he did say the purpose was to obtain approval of a Medal of Honor for President Theodore Roosevelt.

Roosevelt's Medal of Honor recommendation, like Andy Smith's, had been denied the first time it was considered, in 1898,[4] for reasons some said were politically motivated, and his family had fought for years to obtain another hearing from the army. On September 8, 1997, only weeks after Ewing submitted Andy Smith's case to the US Army Awards and Decorations Branch, New York representative Rick Lazio submitted a request for reconsideration of the denial of Roosevelt's Medal of Honor.[5] When, a year later, the Senior Army Decorations Board did not support the reconsideration, unlike Smith's application, congressional supporters of a Medal of Honor for Roosevelt moved to obtain it by other means.[6]

On September 28, 1998, the Subcommittee on Military Personnel held a hearing on H.R. 2263, introduced by Pennsylvania representative Paul McHale on July 25, 1997, with 162 cosponsors,[7] "A bill to authorize and request the President to award the congressional Medal of Honor posthumously to Theodore Roosevelt for his gallant and heroic actions in the attack on San Juan Heights, Cuba, during the Spanish-American War." [8] Under a motion to suspend the rules, H.R. 2263 passed the House by a voice vote on October 8, 1998.[9] Less than two weeks later, on October 21, again under suspension of the rules, the bill passed the Senate by voice vote without dissent, but in the accompanying discussion, Strom Thurmond of South Carolina spoke "to clarify what we are doing. This bill does not award the Medal of Honor to Theodore Roosevelt. It does authorize the President to award the Medal of Honor to then Colonel Roosevelt," but, Thurmond argued, the "task" of determining whether Roosevelt's actions merited the Medal of Honor "can only be performed by the military services." Thurmond then received unanimous consent to provide a letter expressing these views, signed by himself and four other members of Congress, including Representative McHale, to accompany H.R. 2263 to the president.[10]

On November 12, 1998, President Clinton signed H.R. 2263 into law in the Roosevelt Room of the West Wing with Theodore Roosevelt's great-grandson, Tweed Roosevelt, in attendance. In keeping with the consent of Congress as expressed in the letter, Clinton referred consideration of the denial of Theodore Roosevelt's award of the Medal of Honor to the secretary of the army.[11]

Congress had not quite usurped the military's authority to award the Medal of Honor to Theodore Roosevelt, but the pressure placed on the army by the unanimous passage of this law was tremendous. The original recommendation would be reopened and additional evidence considered, and if the army should find against Roosevelt's recommendation, its justification had to be irrefutable. Unless the army could produce compelling reasons to the contrary, Theodore Roosevelt would almost certainly receive the Medal of Honor. A deadline of May 31, 1999, was imposed for submission of evidence to the Senior Army Decorations Board.

The question remained, why was Smith's award being held in committee, hostage to the award of Roosevelt's medal? A press release issued by Representative Lazio's office in 1998 included a quotation from a member of the House Armed Services subcommittee that held a clue to the mystery: "The time has come to challenge the Army on this long overdue matter [the award of Medal of Honor for Roosevelt]."[12]

MacDonald sent a letter to the subcommittee, explaining the passage of H.R. 2858 would correct an injustice dating back to the early years of the century and enable the recipient's ailing daughter Caruth to witness the Medal of Honor bestowed upon her father.[13] No response was received. Over time, members of Congress attempted to deal with the matter quietly and away from the public view, but time was not working in Caruth's favor. Thus, after consulting with Congressman Ewing's aide, Andy Bowman agreed to speak openly to bring public pressure on the subcommittee in the hope of gaining passage of H.R. 2858 before the congressional session ended on November 22.

The *Lafayette (IN) Journal and Courier* became interested in the story, and one of its reporters, Azura Domschke, obtained an open admission from the subcommittee's press secretary:

> [T]he Army is taking its time on the legislation . . . and Congress is asking to halt Smith's bill and all proposals in the meantime. "The [House Armed Services Sub]committee is working with the Army to understand where they are on the Teddy Roosevelt bill. They're not taking any action on the other one [Smith's bill] until we understand why the Army is dragging its feet on the other one [Roosevelt's]."[14]

In response to the *Journal and Courier* on November 16, the chair of the subcommittee, Representative Steve Buyer of Indiana, maintained, "The fact is that I have vowed to ensure Smith is honored, which through the regular congressional approval process entails including it in the defense authorization bill this coming spring. . . . What was incorrectly interpreted as unjustified delay in the Andrew Smith case is very simply the normal process by which the Congress reviews such matters."[15] There is, however, no "normal" or "regular congressional approval process" for the medal, and medals most certainly do not have to be included in defense authorization bills. Neither Robert Ingram's nor Roosevelt's bills were tied to defense authorization bills. The committee could have allowed Smith the same consideration, but it did not do so. There was no way to expedite the bill's passage, forcing everyone to wait through the winter and into spring.

Caruth was sheltered from this information as she resided in her New Jersey nursing home. Andy Bowman admitted he "called her 'a couple of times. . . . [but] I couldn't tell her. I really didn't want to disappoint her. She's very emotional about this.'"[16]

At last, on April 6, 2000, Andy Smith's waiver of time limitations was introduced into the House of Representatives as part of the National Defense Authorization Act for Fiscal Year 2001, H.R. 4205. It was joined by another award of the Medal of Honor awaiting a waiver of time limitations. Captain Ed W. Freeman was one of two army pilots who repeatedly flew their helicopters into Landing Zone X–Ray under heavy enemy fire to provide ammunition, water, and supplies and to evacuate wounded during the Battle of the Ia Drang, Republic of Vietnam, on November 14, 1965. The authorization act passed the House on May 18[17] and was forwarded to the Senate, where a third award of the Medal of Honor, whose time limitations waiver had yet to be approved by the House, waited. Technician Fifth Grade James Okubo, an army medic with the 442nd Regimental Combat Team in World War II, had been awarded the Silver Star for treating and rescuing wounded soldiers under enemy fire in France in 1944. Okubo, who died in 1967, had been overlooked in the effort to identify those among America's *Nisei* soldiers whose awards merited upgrades to the Medal of Honor, under Section 524 of the National Defense Authorization Act of FY 1996, part of the broader legislation under which Andy Smith's award was reconsidered.[18]

Okubo's commanding officer had originally recommended him for the Medal of Honor. The award had been downgraded to the Silver Star (the third-highest army decoration) because Okubo was a medic, a noncombatant who did not carry a firearm and, supposedly, was not eligible for any higher decoration. His comrades, veterans of the 442nd Combat Team, gathered documentation and contacted Senator Daniel K. Akaka of Hawaii, who had been instrumental in establishing the original Section 524 legislation.

The Department of Defense approved the award of Okubo's Medal of Honor in May 2000 as Smith's and Freeman's waivers of time limitation were advancing through the House. Little time remained, however, for Senator Akaka to obtain Okubo's time waiver. On May 12, Secretary of the Army Caldera announced twenty-one of the 104 awards of the Distinguished Service Cross merited upgrades to the Medal of Honor. Akaka wanted Okubo's widow, Nobuyo, and his children and grandchildren to be in attendance and receive his medal in the company of the other families. He was as concerned for Nobuyo as the Smith family was for Caruth, and he was determined Nobuyo would be present at the awards ceremony, scheduled for June 21, 2000.[19]

Akaka did not send Okubo's waiver of time limitations to the House, and he did not ignore Ed W. Freeman and Andrew Jackson Smith. Instead, on June 13, 2000, Akaka introduced his own bill, S. 2722, into the Senate to waive time limitations for James K. Okubo and award the Medal of Honor to all three men. The bill was passed the same day by unanimous consent and sent to the House on June 14. The House held S. 2722 for a day. Then, late on June 16, the bill passed by voice vote. President Clinton signed the legislation on June 20.[20]

The next day, Nobuyo Okubo received her husband's Medal of Honor as Senator Akaka had intended, and Ed Freeman and Andy Smith received their waivers of time limitations from both houses through Public Law 106–223. It finally seemed Andy Smith would receive his medal.

Meanwhile, the House Armed Services subcommittee was still endeavoring to obtain the results of the army's review of Theodore Roosevelt's recommendation for the Medal of Honor. Secretary of Defense Cohen had forwarded a memorandum to President Clinton on February 22 recommending that Theodore Roosevelt be posthumously awarded the Medal of Honor, but Clinton had yet to act on Cohen's recommendation. Addressing the House on June 13, the chairman of the committee urged President Clinton "to announce the award now."[21] It was more than a month, however, before the army recommended Roosevelt be awarded the Medal of Honor.[22]

Surely the president would soon make time for the ceremony to present the long-awaited awards to Freeman, Roosevelt, and Smith. Then summer turned to autumn without any presentations being scheduled, and it soon became apparent the award of Andy Smith's Medal of Honor was being held hostage in yet another political quagmire.

Representative Rick Lazio, who was running against Hillary Clinton in the general election for one of New York's US Senate seats, had criticized President Clinton for not immediately awarding Roosevelt's Medal of Honor. As the Senate campaign progressed, the Roosevelt family became increasingly certain President Clinton would not allow the award to become a political issue, thus excluding the possibility that an award ceremony would be scheduled before the election. Unfortunately, this also meant the president would not soon award Ed Freeman's or Andy Smith's medals.[23]

The November elections passed. Hillary Clinton had defeated Lazio, and the award ceremonies still were not scheduled. Clinton's second term as president was drawing to a close, and soon George W. Bush would be inaugurated as president. Further delay seemed inevitable as, with a change in administrations, the need arose for the new secretary of the army, secretary of defense, and others to review the awards. It might be months, or a year or more before the medals could be presented.[24]

In the end, it was Roosevelt's family that accelerated the process. Shortly before Christmas, Tweed Roosevelt and Senator Kent Conrad of North Dakota "decided to make a final effort to secure the Medal before the close of the Clinton administration."[25] Senator Conrad hand delivered a letter from Roosevelt to President Clinton prior to a bill-signing ceremony in the Roosevelt Room of the White House. "He stopped and read the entire letter," Conrad recalled. "I've never seen a president do that. Usually they hand it to an aide. He read it, turned to me, and said, 'We'll do this.'"[26]

The award ceremony was, at last, scheduled for January 16, 2001.

THE DAY OF THE CEREMONY dawned bright and clear. The army had ensconced the Smith family at the Ritz-Carlton in Arlington, Virginia, and the media found them there early. Andy and Esther Bowman were interviewed by reporters before they had even finished dressing for the day. News of Andy Smith's and Theodore Roosevelt's impending awards was on CNN and in many of the country's major newspapers. (Ed Freeman would receive his Medal of Honor in person from President Bush on July 16, 2001.)

After a breakfast buffet courtesy of the army, Andy Smith's and Theodore Roosevelt's families traveled to the Pentagon for a meeting with

The Bowman family at the Medal of Honor ceremony on January 16, 2001, in the Pentagon's Hall of Heroes. Left to right, David, Catherine, Andrew, Esther, and Andrew Jr. (*White House*)

Secretary of the Army Caldera and then to the White House. They entered the West Wing on the ground floor, and Andy Bowman, Caruth, and Tweed Roosevelt separated from the group to meet with President Clinton before the ceremony. The remaining family members proceeded upstairs to the Roosevelt Room, the site of the award ceremony, where news media had crowded behind seats beginning to fill with dignitaries.

In the hallway outside the Roosevelt Room, Andy Bowman, Caruth, and Tweed Roosevelt waited. Then a door opened and President Clinton appeared. Bowman later recalled, "He was a very smooth, very impressive person." Elegantly attired in a black suit and a red tie, Clinton began asking Bowman about the case. "He asked me about Andy Smith, how did I get started on this, where did we get the information." He then turned to Caruth. Bowman recalled, "She was very impressed, very wide-eyed." Until this point, Bowman had been worried about Caruth. She seemed tired and not quite cognizant of the events surrounding her. When she saw the president, all that faded away.[27]

Then came the announcement, "Ladies and Gentlemen, the President of the United States." All stood, and the president entered, followed by Bowman, Caruth, and Roosevelt. General David Hicks, chaplain of the army, led a prayer, and then Clinton stepped to the podium. He made a short speech, noting Andy Smith's heroism and the dangers facing African American troops in the Civil War. Then Andy Smith's Medal of Honor citation was read by an officer:[28]

Corporal Andrew Jackson Smith, of Clinton, Illinois, a member of the 55th Massachusetts Voluntary Infantry, distinguished himself on 30 November 1864 by saving his regimental colors, after the color bearer was killed during a bloody charge called the Battle of Honey Hill, South Carolina. In the late afternoon, as the 55th Regiment pursued enemy skirmishers and conducted a running fight, they ran into a swampy area backed by a rise where the Confederate Army awaited. The surrounding woods and thick underbrush impeded infantry movement and artillery support. The 55th and 54th regiments formed columns to advance on the enemy position in a flanking movement. As the Confederates repelled other units, the 55th and 54th regiments continued to move into flanking positions. Forced into a narrow gorge crossing a swamp in the face of the enemy position, the 55th's Color-Sergeant was killed by an exploding shell, and Corporal Smith took the Regimental Colors from his hand and carried them through heavy grape and canister fire. Although half of the officers and a third of the enlisted men engaged in the fight were killed or wounded, Corporal Smith continued to expose himself to enemy fire by carrying the colors throughout the battle. Through his actions, the Regimental Colors of the 55th Infantry Regiment were not lost to the enemy. Corporal Andrew Jackson Smith's extraordinary valor in the face of deadly enemy fire is in keeping with the highest traditions of military service and reflect great credit upon him, the 55th Regiment, and the United States Army.

Upon the conclusion of the reading, President Clinton turned to Andy Bowman with the small wood-and-glass case used to display the Medal of Honor and, shaking his hand, passed the case to Bowman. The president then turned to Caruth, who was seated, and took her hand. Caruth looked up at him gratefully and said a simple and earnest, "Thank you." Andy Bowman then turned to Caruth and placed the case in her hands. At that moment, Andy Smith's Medal of Honor became the most belated award of the medal in US history.[29]

President Clinton next awarded Theodore Roosevelt's Medal of Honor, presenting it to Tweed Roosevelt, and concluded the ceremony by stating, "This is a good day for America. I'll leave you with this one thought. . . . In the case of the black soldier in the long-ago Civil War, it sometimes takes a long time to get things right. But Theodore Roosevelt reminded us that the only way we do that is by constantly focusing on the future. And that's really what we're celebrating here today, two people who changed America in more ways than one by their personal courage, from very different vantage points."[30]

President William J. Clinton presents the Medal of Honor for Andrew Jackson Smith to Andrew S. Bowman, top. Moments later, the medal is presented to Caruth Smith Washington, Smith's daughter. (*The White House*)

Following the ceremony, the press requested the family to join them on the north foyer of the West Wing. In his interview, Andy Bowman chose to point out the racial progress being made in America. "Only in America can the sons of a slave and the daughters of a slave receive the same honor at the time that a president's sons and daughters receive theirs. We stood on that same stage and received the same medal. It's just amazing."[31]

At the moment Caruth's interview was conducted, she was not an old woman in failing health, who before the ceremony had seemed so tired. She was instead alert and well spoken, again the forthright and sophisticated woman of years past. A television reporter knelt in front of her wheelchair, gently placed his microphone before her, and asked why she thought officials had denied the Medal of Honor to her father in 1917. She responded in a few words conveying the essence of the ignorance that spawns racism. "Because they didn't know us. We are not who they thought us to be."

EPILOGUE

TO MANY AMERICANS, even as we live in the world that men like Andy Smith made, the events of their times seem to have faded into the dusty past. Yet the country in which we live is not so far separated from the people and times discussed in this book, and, if one knows where and how to look, evidence of the struggles of that era remains all around us. There is much right there under our feet or passing beneath the wheels of our cars. Places and things we take for granted may have much deeper meanings and richer pasts than we know.

In May 1987, a developer began building a road for a housing development on Folly Island where the 55th Massachusetts was camped for much of the Civil War. As the bulldozers tore into the earth, the operators unknowingly revealed an unexpected discovery. After the bulldozers had been shut down for the day, relic collectors quietly stole into the construction site and began scanning the ground. Just below the surface of the disturbed soil, they found human bones.

The bones belonged to African American troops who camped on Folly Island during the Civil War, including some members of the 55th Massachusetts. Archaeologists were called in, and eventually eighteen bodies were removed from the site and taken to Beaufort National Cemetery at Beaufort, South Carolina. The soldiers were accorded a military funeral, and members of the cast of the movie *Glory*, which was just then filming in South Carolina, served as the honor guard.

Folly Island and its surrounding islets are a very different place today than when Andy Smith and the 55th spent their days working and fighting to capture Charleston. The beachfront on Folly is crowded with vacation rental houses, and tourists enjoy the beaches and sea breezes. On Sol Legare Island, a supermarket now sprawls where the 55th crossed on its way to the fight at Rivers' Causeway. Parts of the modern road to Folly Island follow the same path as the 55th's troops did on that July day in 1864 when the men had to flounder through the mud to reach Sol Legare Island. When traveling from Folly Island to James Island, modern tourists now pass in seconds what took the 55th hours to traverse.

Morris Island is deserted today, and there is little or nothing visible there to spark a memory of the heroic actions of the 54th Massachusetts or the long hours of labor the men of the 55th spent digging trenches. The site of Battery Wagner now lies beneath the sand and waves a few yards off-shore, as the sea islands shift at the whim of wind, waves, and currents. Occasionally, when a strong storm hits the Charleston area, the crashing of the waves will reveal relics of the battles that once took place there.

Morris Island was a burial ground long before the carnage of the Civil War, but by the time the war ended the island was a virtual charnel house. The men of the 54th who were buried under the parapet of Wagner, including Robert Gould Shaw, were never moved, and hundreds of Confederates were interred in shallow graves during the fighting on the island. There was an attempt to recover Confederate remains from the island after the war, but even that effort left numerous bodies beneath the sand dunes. The keepers of the Morris Island lighthouse had the sad duty of picking up remains that were disinterred by storms. After heavy storms, they reported picking up barrels full of bones, which were removed for reburial. Morris Island has never been excavated or conserved, but James Tucker, former superintendent of the Fort Sumter National Monument, believes many bones still lie beneath the surface of its sands.

On James Island, a housing development sits where Confederate troops manned the defenses the 55th charged in their fight at River's Causeway. Further inland, golfers at the Country Club of Charleston play hole number eleven unaware that beneath the manicured green lie the bones of men of the 55th Massachusetts.

Charleston is today a scenic city with a reputation for fine dining and southern charm. Battery Park and Rainbow Row draw admiring visitors, many of whom are probably unaware of the blood and sweat expended to capture the city from 1862 to 1865. Fort Sumter still sits brooding at the harbor entrance. The plantations in the regions near Charleston where men of the 55th chased the Confederate "scouts" are mostly gone, covered by the Santee-Cooper reservoirs or subsumed by the housing developments that encircle the lakes. Mexico Plantation is now a wilderness on the edge of Lake Marion.

Until recently, the site of the Battle of Honey Hill was on private property, but the land is now owned by the town of Ridgeland. The intent of Ridgeland's leaders is to preserve the battlefield and make it publicly ac-

Andrew Jackson Smith's headstones. (*W. Robert Beckman*)

cessible, but this process is just beginning and may take years to complete. A historical marker placed at the side of Route 336 informs passing drivers that a battle was fought nearby. The ruins of the battery Andy Smith charged with Robert King on that fateful November day are only a short distance into the woods, but most drivers speed by, not realizing the road cuts right through the field of conflict.

The sacrifices of Andy Smith and the men of the 55th helped put an end to slavery, but they could not extinguish the racism that was part of slavery's justification. It would take another one hundred years to begin the move toward true equality for the descendants of the freedmen.

The region around Orangeburg, where the 55th attempted to achieve a peaceful restructuring of southern society, has played a pivotal role in the evolution of race relations in the United States. A legal case begun in nearby Summerton, *Briggs v. Elliot*, helped change the country forever when it reached the US Supreme Court in 1954. It was the first of four cases challenging school segregation that were eventually combined into *Brown v. Board of Education*, in which the court struck down segregation in education facilities.

In Orangeburg itself, a racial protest in 1968 turned deadly. White highway patrol officers responding to the disturbance fired into the crowd, and three black students were killed; twenty-seven people were wounded. A student who was present described the incident as like being caught in a

Andrew Jackson Smith's great grandchildren at the dedication of the Kentucky state highway renamed in his memory. (*W. Robert Beckman*)

wave of falling soldiers. Federal charges were filed against the police officers
involved, but all nine were acquitted.

In Kentucky, much of Andy Smith's old farmland now lies under the
waters of Lake Barkley. His first home site sits on a small rise that has been
turned into a peninsula by the creation of the lake, and his pastures and
fields have been reclaimed by the forest. All that remains of his house is a
foundation and a chimney standing lonely sentinel in the woods. Much of
the land owned by Andy Smith's father and brothers—his owners—now
lies under water as well. Grand Rivers, where Andy had his last home, sits
partially submerged between two lakes instead of the two rivers that existed
when it was founded.

A national recreation area now encompasses the area Andy Smith knew
as home, and also contains his gravesite. Beyond the far southern end of
the park near Dover, Tennessee, is Fort Donelson National Battlefield. Farther south lies Shiloh National Military Park, where Andy Smith received
his head wound while helping his benefactor, Colonel Warner.

More than two miles from the north entrance to the Land Between the
Lakes National Recreation Area stands a sign marking the beginning of the
Andrew Jackson Smith Memorial Highway. A traveler following this road
south nearly four miles would come upon a historic marker on the left side
proclaiming that the grave of a Medal of Honor recipient lies just a short
distance into the woods.

APPENDIX

Population Figures for Free Blacks and Slaves in Western Kentucky, 1860–1870, Adjusted for the Absence of Fugitive Slaves in 1860

County	1860 Free Blacks	1860 Slaves	1860 Fugitives/ Manumitted*	1860 Resident Total	1870 Resident Total	1860/70 Increase/ Decrease
Ballard	31	1,718	0/0	1,749	1,477	-272 (-16%)
Caldwell	39	2,405	0/1	2,444	2,078	-366 (-15%)
Calloway	14	1,492	3/2	1,503	812	-691 (-46%)
Crittenden	19	937	0/2	956	809	-147 (-15%)
Fulton	19	1,078	140/0	957	937	-20 (-2%)
Graves	2	2,845	0/0	2,847	2,329	-518 (-18%)
Hickman (Columbia)	20	1,249	0/5	1,269	1,635	+366 (29%)
Livingston	36	1,222	216/2	1,042	1,052	+10 (1%)
Lyon	46	1,094	195/0	945	1,419	+474 (50%)
Marshall	35	351	80/2	306	385	+79 (26 %)
McCracken (Paducah)	68	1,738	286/0	1,520	3,289	+1,769 (116%)
Trigg	41	3,448	2/0	3,487	3,806	+319 (9%)
Totals	370	19,577	922/14	19,025	20,028	+1,003 (5%)

*Whether manumitted slaves remained to increase local free black populations or departed is undetermined. They totaled 14 individuals for all of western Kentucky, a number too small to be statistically significant. For these reasons, they are not included in the tabulations.

Andrew Jackson Smith's Agricultural Production & Assessed Wealth, 1867–1880

Year	Gold/Silver Clocks	Horses/Value	Mules/Value	Cattle/Value	Bulls/Studs	Hogs/Value	Corn/Bsh Not Taxed	Wheat/Bsh Not Taxed	Tobacco/Pounds Not Taxed	Personal Property	Taxable Wealth
1867				1							
1868		1/ $40		5			150			$40	$40
1869		1/ $60		4			300		300	$60	$60
1870		2/75		3		8	300			$75	$75
1871		2/ $100		8/$50		3	400		600	$150	$150
1872		3/ $200		9/$50	8		300			$250	$250
1873		3/ $200		7/$50		8	500			$250	$250
1874		2/ $120	1/$30	7/$40		7	300		1000	$190	$190
1875	$5	2/ $100	1/$25	4/$25		4	100	25		$155	$155
1876	**	**	**	**	**	**	**	**	**	**	**
1877	**	**	**	**	**	**	**	**	**	**	**
1878	**	**	**	**	**	**	**	**	**	**	**
1879	$5	2/ $100	2/$75	5		5	200	60	400	$180	$180
1880	$5	3/ $125	2/$125	20		5	400	20	500	$255	$255

** Years for which Lyon County tax assessment records do not survive.

Andrew Jackson Smith, Acreage Bought and Sold Verified by Surviving Deeds, Real and Personal Assessed Property, 1880–1899

Year	Total Acres/ Value	Acres Bought/ Price	Acres Sold/ Price	Personal Property	Taxable Wealth
1880		286 / $858* 120 / $6.00*		$255	$255
1881	406 / $760			$365	$1,125
1882	306 / $570			$435	$1,005
1883	**			**	**
1884	261.5 / $709			$398	$1,083
1885	277 / $1,094			$486	$1,580
1886	267 / $1,164	258 / $1,000	69.75 / $69.75	$413	$1,577
1887	322 / $1,584		605.5 / $3,888	$207	$1,791
1888	545 / $2,075			$277	$2,652
1889	545 / $1,775	240 / $600 1/9int. / $75	444 / $3,108 109 / $300	$347	$2,422
1890	561 / $1,604	1/9int. / $80 ? / $100 ? / $100 ? / $100		$419 $419	$2,023 $2,023
1891	250 / $1,000	? / $102	57.5 / $400 7 / $50	$563	$2,363
1892	230 / $920		10.25 / $82 62.5 / $1.00	$593	$2,313
1893	**				
1894	**			**	**
1895	150 / $750			$350***	$1,100
1896	**			**	**
1897	**			**	**
1898	**			**	**
1899	229 / $1,261			$84***	$1,346

* Land purchased after the 1880 annual tax assessment
** Years for which Lyon County tax assessment records do not survive
*** $250 personal property exemption excluded from total taxable personal property
? Acreage not specified in the deed

Assessed Wealth of Lyon County Black and White Landowners in Dollars, 1890

Assessed Wealth	Landowners B/W	Assessed Wealth	Landowners B/W	Assessed Wealth	Landowners B/W	Assessed Wealth	Landowners B/W
1-49	9/12	1300-1399	0/18	3600-3699	0/1	5900-5999	0/2
50-99	40/32	1400-1499	0/14	3700-3799	0/2	6000-6099	0/3
100-149	18/28	1500-1599	0/11	3800-3899		6100-6199	0/1
150-199	10/39	1600-1699	0/6	3900-3999		6200-6299	0/1
200-249	8/49	1700-1799	0/5	4000-4099	0/1	6300-6399	
250-299	8/41	1800-1899	0/5	4100-4199	0/2	6400-6499	
300-349	8/68	1900-1999	0/2	4200-4299	0/1	6500-6599	
350-399	7/51	2000-2099	1*/7	4300-4399	0/1	6600-6699	
400-449	4/41	2100-2199	0/5	4400-4499		6700-6799	
450-499	2/35	2200-2299	0/10	4500-4599	0/2	6800-6899	
500-549	3/34	2300-2399	0/3	4600-4699	0/1	6900-6999	
550-599	0/31	2400-2499	0/6	4700-4799		7000-7999	0/1
600-649	2/24	2500-2599	0/4	4800-4899	0/2	8000-8999	0/3
650-699	0/19	2600-2699	0/1	4900-4999	0/1	9000-9999	0/1
700-749	1/30	2700-2799	0/4	5000-5099	0/1	10,664	0/1
750-799	1/20	2800-2899	0/2	5100-5199		12,855	0/1
800-849	0/31	2900-2999	0/4	5200-5299	0/2	14,361	0/1
850-899	0/11	3000-3099	0/6	5300-5399	0/1	15,840	0/1
900-949	0/25	3100-3199	0/2	5400-5499	0/3	19,150	0/1
950-999	0/12	3200-3299		5500-5599	0/1	24,518	0/1
1000-1099	0/33	3300-3399	0/1	5600-5699		30,000	0/1
1100-1199	0/21	3400-3499	0/1	5700-5799	0/1	38,165	0/1
1200-1299	0/29	3500-3599	0/2	5800-5899	0/2		

*Andrew Jackson Smith: $2,023

Andrew Jackson Smith, Acreage and Total Assessed Wealth, 1900–1915

Year	Total Acres/ Value	Acres Bought/ Price	Acres Sold/ Price	Personal Property	Taxable Wealth
1900	229 / $1,261			$168***	$1,329
1901	**		24 / $200	**	**
1902	**			**	**
1903	**		56 / $500	**	**
1904	156 / $1000			$0***	$1,000
1905	**			**	**
1906	**			**	**
1907	150 / $1,000			$54***	$1,054
1908	**			**	**
1909	56 / $1200			$88***	$1,288
1910	**			**	**
1911	5 / $25			$345***	$370
1912	**			**	**
1913	**			**	**
1914	**			**	**
1915	**		3 / $40	**	**

**Years for which Lyon County tax assessment records do not survive

***$250 personal property exemption excluded from total taxable personal property

Andrew Jackson Smith, Acreage and Total Assessed Wealth as a Resident of Lyon
County, KY, 1867–1911

Year	Acres	Assessed Value of Real Property	Money at Interest	Total Taxable Personal Property	Total Taxable Personal Property
1867				$10	$10
1868				$40	$40
1869				$60	$60
1871				$150	$150
1872				$250	$250
1873				$250	$250
1874				$190	$190
1875				$155	$155
1879				$180	$180
1880				$255	$255
1881	406	$760		$365	$1,125
1882	306	$570		$435	$1,005
1884	261.5	$709		$374	$1,083
1885	277	$1,094		$486	$1,580
1886	267	$1,164		$413	$1,577
1887	322	$1,584		$207	$1,791
1888	545	$2,075	$300	$277	$2,652
1889	545	$1,775	$300	$347	$2,422
1890	561	$1,604	$300	$419	$2,023
1891	250	$1,000	$800	$563	$2,363
1892	230	$920	$800	$593	$2,313
1895	150	$750		$350*	$1,100
1899	229	$1,261		$84*	$1,345
1900	229	$1,261		$168*	$1,329
1904	156	$1,000		$0*	$1,000
1907	150	$1,000		$54*	$1,054
1909	156	$1,200		$88*	$1,288
1911	5	$25		$345*	$370

*$250 of personal property exempt from taxation excluded from total taxable personal property

NOTES

PREFACE

1. Caruth Smith Washington, Biographical Introduction to Letters and Memorabilia of Color Sergeant Andrew J. Smith ("Andy") Civil War Soldier, 55th Volunteer Regiment, Company B., of the Massachusetts Volunteers, Union Army (1984), Andrew Jackson Smith Papers, Abraham Lincoln Presidential Library, Springfield, IL (hereafter cited as AJS Papers).

2. Modern Civil War history contains few works focused on individual black soldiers. Only six books were published in the twentieth century, including a 1969 reprint of a nineteenth-century biography of Major Martin R. Delany, who was notable not as a frontline soldier but as a political leader and recruiter of black troops: Frank A. Rollin, *Life and Public Services of Martin R. Delany* (1868, 1883; New York: Arno Press, 1969). A. H. Newton, *Out of the Briars: An Autobiography and Sketch of the Twenty-Ninth Regiment Connecticut Volunteers* (Philadelphia: A.M.E. Book Concern, 1910) was written by a literate, free black soldier. Works on two black Reconstruction-era politicians, with only passing reference to their military service, were published in the 1970s: James Haskins, *Pinckney Benton Stewart Pinchback* (New York: Macmillan, 1973), and Peter D. Klingman, *Josiah Walls: Florida's Black Congressman of Reconstruction* (Gainesville: University Press of Florida, 1976). Two exceptional books did appear in the 1990s, based on the wartime writings of literate black soldiers of the 54th Massachusetts Volunteer Infantry, Lieutenant George E. Stephens and Corporal James Henry Gooding: Donald Yacovone, ed., *A Voice of Thunder: The Civil War Letters of George E. Stephens* (Urbana: University of Illinois Press, 1997, 1998), and Virginia Matzke Adams, ed., *On the Altar of Freedom: A Black Soldier's Civil War Letters from the Front: Corporal James Henry Gooding* (Amherst: University of Massachusetts Press, 1991, 1999). Two other biographical works have been published, but neither subject served in the US Army and both were literate: William B. Gould IV, *Diary of a Contraband: The Civil War Passage of a Black Sailor* (Stanford, CA: Stanford University Press, 2002); Robert Smalls served as a pilot, but remained a civilian, Edward A. Miller Jr., *Gullah Statesman: Robert Smalls from Slavery to Congress, 1839–1915* (Columbia: University of South Carolina Press, 1995, 2008).

3. Benjamin Quarles, *The Negro in the Civil War* (Boston: Little, Brown, 1953, 1969; New York: Da Capo Press, 1989); Dudley Taylor Cornish, *The Sable Arm: Negro Troops in the Union Army, 1861–1865* (Lawrence: University Press of Kansas, 1956, 1987); James M. McPherson, *The Negro's Civil War: How American Negroes Felt and Acted During the War*

for the Union (Urbana: University of Illinois Press, 1965, 1982); Joseph T. Glatthaar, *Forged in Battle: The Civil War Alliance of Black Soldiers and White Officers* (New York: Free Press, 1989); Edwin S. Redkey, *A Grand Army of Black Men: Letters from African-American Soldiers in the Union Army 1861-1865* (Cambridge: Cambridge University Press, 1991, 1992). Noah Andre Trudeau, *Voices of the 55th: Letters from the 55th Massachusetts Volunteers 1861–1865* (Dayton, OH: Morningside House, 1996); Noah Andre Trudeau, *Like Men of War: Black Troops in the Civil War: 1862–1865* (Boston: Little, Brown, 1998); Keith P. Wilson, *Campfires of Freedom: The Camp Life of Black Soldiers During the Civil War* (Kent, OH: Kent State University Press, 2002); John David Smith, ed., *Black Soldiers in Blue: African American Troops in the Civil War Era* (Chapel Hill: University of North Carolina Press, 2002); John David Smith, *Lincoln and the U.S. Colored Troops* (Carbondale: Southern Illinois University Press, 2013). Inexplicably, the subtitle of Trudeau's *Voices of the 55th* includes the years 1861–1865, but the unit did not come into existence until May 1863.

PROLOGUE: MARCH 6, 1932

1. Caruth Smith Washington, Biographical Introduction, AJS Papers; Caruth Smith Washington, videotape interview, July 16, 2001, AJS Papers; Andrew S. Bowman, interview, by W. Robert Beckman, September 29, 2001, AJS Papers.

CHAPTER 1: ESCAPE BETWEEN THE RIVERS

1. Andy Smith's tombstone and death certificate incorrectly give his birth year as 1843, the result of a clerical error in his military records. Entry no. 86, 55th Massachusetts Regimental Descriptive Book, Record Group 94, National Archives and Records Administration (hereafter cited as RG and NARA), and Andrew Jackson Smith Pension File, RG 15, NARA. For Elias Smith's land transactions, see the Deed Books, Caldwell County Clerk's Office, Princeton, Kentucky. Andy Smith wrote Burt Wilder that Elias Smith had about nineteen slaves when he died. Andrew J. Smith to Burt G. Wilder, March 22, 1913, Burt Green Wilder Papers, Division of Rare and Manuscript Collections, Carl A. Kroch Library, Cornell University, Ithaca, NY.

2. Andrew J. Smith to Burt G. Wilder, March 22, 1913, Wilder Papers. Andy Smith gave Lyon County as the place of his birth in his letter to Burt Wilder, but Lyon County was formed out of western Caldwell County in 1854. Discrepancies may have occasionally occurred in the recording of Andy Smith's dictated statements. Locating his birthplace southeast of Eddyville, and thus east of the Cumberland, was incorrect. He was born in the northeastern quadrant of Between the Rivers, southwest of Eddyville. In another statement, Smith said Moses Ferry, on the Tennessee River, was about eight to ten miles from where he was born, which puts his birthplace Between the Rivers, southwest of Eddyville. Andrew [Jackson] Smith, "Adventures of a Colored Boy in War," *National Tribune* (Washington, DC), March 21, 1929, reprinted in Trudeau, *Voices of the 55th,* 187–191. A handwritten account resembling the *National Tribune* article is in the AJS Papers.

3. Frederick Douglass, *Narrative of the Life of Frederick Douglass, An American Slave. Written by Himself* (Boston: Published at the Anti-Slavery Office, 1845), in *The Frederick Douglass Papers,* ser. 2: *Autobiographical Writings,* vol. 1: *Narrative,* ed. John W. Blassingame et al. (New Haven, CT: Yale University Press, 1999):13–14.

4. Will of Elias Smith, Will Book, vol. 1: 1854–1941, Lyon County Clerk's Office, Eddyville, KY.

5. Joanne Smith Evans Carnes, interview by Sharon S. MacDonald, May 20, 2003, AJS Papers.

6. Andrew J. Smith to Burt G. Wilder, March 22, 1913, Wilder Papers.

7. Ibid.; 55th Massachusetts Descriptive Book, entry no. 86, RG 94, NARA, lists Andy Smith's occupation as boatman. Smith, "Adventures."

8. Will of Elias Smith, Lyon County Will Book. Andy Smith recalled Elias died in 1859 (Andrew J. Smith to Burt G. Wilder, March 22, 1913, Wilder Papers), but Elias was alive in August 1860 according to the 1860 census. His will was processed on February 25, 1861.

9. William Johnson Stone, William Johnson Stone Papers, 1864–1953, Special Collections, University of Kentucky Library, Lexington; Odell Walker, *In Lyon County, Saturday Was Town Day: A Collection of Writings from Lyon County's Historian* (Kuttawa, KY: Lyon County Historical Press, 2002), 80–93, printed Stone's memoir; Andrew J. Smith to Burt G. Wilder, March 22, 1913, Wilder Papers; J. Milton Henry, *The Land Between the Rivers* (n.p.: Taylor, 1970s), 130, for the roster of Company G, 1st Kentucky Cavalry, September 1861. William J. Stone assisted Captain Morrison D. Wilcox and Lieutenant Ben Dyer Terry in recruiting Company G. The men came from Lyon County and Caldwell County. "Capt. Ben Dyer Terry," *Confederate Veteran* 14 (1906): 516–517. William Smith's older brother, Harrison Smith, did not serve in either army.

10. US Naval War Records Office, *Official Records of the Union and Confederate Navies in the War of the Rebellion*, ser. 1, vols. 1–27 (Washington, DC: Government Printing Office, 1894–1917), 22:357, 371, 383–384 (hereafter cited as *OR* Navy); Jay Slagle, *Ironclad Captain: Seth Ledyard Phelps & the U. S. Navy, 1841–1864* (Kent, OH: Kent State University Press, 1996), 126–127, 133–136.

11. *OR* Navy, 22:371; US War Department, *The War of the Rebellion: A Compilation of the Official Records of the Union and Confederate Armies*, 4 ser. (Washington, DC: Government Printing Office, 1880–1901), ser. 1, vol. 4:463–464 (hereafter cited as *OR*; unless otherwise stated, references are to ser. 1).

12. *OR*, 4:458–459; 536–537; John Y. Simon, ed., *The Papers of Ulysses S. Grant*, 32 vols. (Carbondale: Southern Illinois University Press, 1967–2012), 3:71–72; *OR*, 3:556.

13. *OR* Navy, 22:379; *OR*, 4:218; Slagle, *Ironclad Captain*, 136.

14. Report of Major Jesse J. Phillips, 9th Illinois Volunteers, *OR*, 4:216–217.

15. *OR* Navy, 22:379–382; *OR*, 4:215–219; Slagle, *Ironclad Captain*, 136–137; Marion Morrison, *A History of the Ninth Regiment Illinois Volunteer Infantry* (Monmouth, IL: John S. Clark, Printer, 1864), 15–16, gives incorrect dates for this action. A Union report, *OR*, 4:217, incorrectly listed Company G commander Captain M. D. Wilcox among those killed. William J. Smith's devotion to the Confederate cause is reflected in the name of his youngest son, Jefferson Davis Smith, who was born the following summer.

16. *OR* Navy, 22:379–380, 382–383; *OR*, 4:217–219.

17. *OR* Navy, 22:379–380, 382–383; *OR*, 4:217–219.

18. Smith, "Adventures."

19. *OR* Navy, 22:457–458; John Cimprich, *Slavery's End in Tennessee* (Tuscaloosa: University of Alabama Press, 1985), 14.

20. Ira Berlin, Barbara J. Fields, Thavolia Glymph, Joseph P. Reidy, and Leslie S. Rowland, eds., *Freedom: A Documentary History of Emancipation, 1861–1867: Selected from the Holdings of the Archives of the United States*, ser. 1, vol. 1, *Freedom: The Destruction of Slavery* (New York: Cambridge University Press, 1985), 521.

21. Smith, "Adventures." William Smith's sons, William and Harrison, were ages ten and thirteen.

22. Ibid.

23. J. Winston Coleman, *Slavery Times in Kentucky* (Chapel Hill: University of North Carolina Press, 1940), 96–101; Sam Steger, *Selections from Sam Steger's Historical Notebook*

(Princeton: Caldwell County Kentucky Historical Society, 2001), 56–57; William McWhorter, interview, in George P. Rawick, ed., *The American Slave: A Composite Autobiography*, 19 vols. (Westport, CT: Greenwood, 1972–1981), vol. 13, *Georgia*, part 3:98. "Patterollers" was perhaps the most widely used term, but it was only one of the variations of patrollers.

24. James Green, interview, in Rawick, *American Slave*, vol. 16, *Texas*, part 2:88.

25. Henry Waldon, interview, in Rawick, *American Slave*, vol. 2, *Arkansas*, part 7:15–16.

26. Smith, "Adventures." How accurate Smith's estimate of 2:00 AM was for their arrival at Smithland is unknown.

27. Ibid.

28. Ibid.

29. *Chicago Daily Tribune*, January 4, 1862.

30. For opinions held by those in the army's high command, see *OR*, ser. 2, vol. 1:776–777, and Ulysses S. Grant to Jesse Root Grant, November 27, 1861, Simon, *Papers of Ulysses S. Grant*, 3:227.

31. *OR*, 8:451; and *OR*, ser. 2, vol. 1:789–790, Major George E. Waring Jr. to General Alexander S. Asboth, December 19, 1861, reprinted in Berlin, *Freedom: Destruction of Slavery*, 422.

32. *OR*, 8:370; and *OR*, ser. 2, vol. 1:778, reprinted in Berlin, *Freedom: Destruction of Slavery*, 417. See also *OR*, 8:465, and *OR*, ser. 2, vol. 1:476.

33. Smith, "Adventures"; Isaac C. Pugh to his wife, April 8, 1862, 41st Illinois Volunteer Infantry Papers, Kip A. Johnson, private collection, Effingham, IL (hereafter cited as Johnson Collection).

CHAPTER 2: FORT HENRY, FORT DONELSON, AND SHILOH

1. Job Roberts, "The Experience of a Private in the Civil War," memoir, Johnson Collection; Isaac C. Pugh to his wife, February 10, 1862, Johnson Collection; Ira Blanchard, *I Marched with Sherman: Civil War Memoirs of the 20th Illinois Volunteer Infantry* (San Francisco: J. D. Huff, 1992), 41; Slagle, *Ironclad Captain*, 156.

2. Roberts, "Experience of a Private," Johnson Collection; Isaac C. Pugh to his wife, February 10, 1862, Johnson Collection; Blanchard, *I Marched with Sherman*, 41; Slagle, *Ironclad Captain*.

3. *OR*, 7:126; Daniel Leib Ambrose, *History of the Seventh Regiment Illinois Volunteer Infantry* (Springfield: Illinois Journal Company, 1868), 25.

4. Ambrose, *History of the Seventh Regiment*, 26; Captain Jesse Taylor, "The Defense of Fort Henry," in Robert Underwood Johnson and Clarence Clough Buel, eds., *Battles and Leaders of the Civil War* 1887–1888 (Secaucus, NJ: Castle, 1982), 1:371.

5. *OR*, 7:140–141; Taylor, "Defense of Fort Henry," in Johnson and Buel, *Battles and Leaders*, 1:368–370; Rear Admiral Henry Walke, "The Gun-Boats at Belmont and Fort Henry," in Johnson and Buel, *Battles and Leaders*, 1:362.

6. *OR*, 7:129–130.

7. Lew Wallace, *Lew Wallace: An Autobiography* (New York: Harper and Brothers, 1906), 369–370; *OR*, 7:122–123; Walke, "Gun-Boats," 1:362–363.

8. Wallace, *Autobiography*, 369.

9. Ibid., 370; Walke, "Gun-Boats," 1:364; Taylor, "Defense of Fort Henry," 1:372.

10. Wallace, *Autobiography*, 369, 370.

11. *OR*, 7:140–142; Taylor, "Defense of Fort Henry," 1:370–371; Walke, "Gun-Boats," 1:367.

12. Wallace, *Autobiography*, 370–371.

13. Roberts, "Experience of a Private," Johnson Collection.

14. Isaac C. Pugh to his wife, February 10, 1862, Johnson Collection.

15. Roberts, "Experience of a Private," Johnson Collection; Smith, "Adventures." The article quoted Smith saying they stayed at Fort Heiman "about three weeks." Either Smith's memory, after more than sixty years, was incorrect or the person recording his dictation made a transcribing error.

16. Roberts, "Experience of a Private," Johnson Collection.

17. Ibid.; Smith, "Adventures."

18. Roberts, "Experience of a Private," Johnson Collection; Smith, "Adventures."

19. Ibid.; Brevet-Major Henry G. Hicks, "Fort Donelson," in *Glimpses of the Nation's Struggle: Papers Read before the Minnesota Commandery of the Military Order of the Loyal Legion of the United States, 1892–1897,* ed. Edward D. Neill (St. Paul, MN: H. L. Collins, 1898), 4:447; *OR* Navy, 22:584–586; Rear Admiral Henry Walke, "The Western Flotilla at Fort Donelson, Island Number 10, Fort Pillow and Memphis," in *Battles and Leaders,* 1:433–436.

20. Roberts, "Experience of a Private," Johnson Collection.

21. *OR,* 7:295; William Johnson Stone, Papers; Kentucky Adjutant-General's Office, *Report of the Adjutant General of the State of Kentucky, Confederate Kentucky Volunteers, War 1861–65,* 2 vols. (1915; Hartford, KY: Cook & McDowell, 1979), 1:376.

22. Smith, "Adventures."

23. Andrew J. Smith to Burt G. Wilder, March 22, 1913, Wilder Papers; Smith, "Adventures"; *OR,* 7:650; Isaac C. Pugh to his son, March 8, 1862, and Isaac C. Pugh to his wife, April 8, 1862, Johnson Collection.

24. Roberts, "Experience of a Private," Johnson Collection.

25. Leander Stillwell, *The Story of a Common Soldier of Army Life in the Civil War, 1861–1865* (Kansas City, MO: Franklin Hudson, 1920), 41.

26. Roberts, "Experience of a Private," Johnson Collection; *OR,* 10–1:22–25, 28; Ambrose, *History of the Seventh Regiment,* 46.

27. Smith, "Adventures"; Isaac Pugh to his wife, April 8, 1862, Johnson Collection.

28. Captain Robert H. McFadden to the Editor, [*Mattoon (IL)*] *Gazette,* April 18, 1862, Johnson Collection.

29. *OR,* 10–1:203, 211; McFadden to the Editor, April 18, 1862, Johnson Collection.

30. *OR,* 10–1:203; Smith, "Adventures."

31. Vespasian Warner (son of John Warner) to Burt G. Wilder, March 10, 1917, Wilder Papers; Smith, "Adventures"; Andrew J. Smith to Burt Wilder, March 29, 1917, Wilder Papers.

32. Roberts, "Experience of a Private," Johnson Collection.

33. Vespasian Warner to Burt G. Wilder, March 10, 1917, Wilder Papers.

34. Smith, "Adventures."

35. Andrew J. Smith to Burt G. Wilder, March 29, 1917; Smith, "Adventures"; Andrew Bowman interview, March 26, 1997, AJS Papers; Andrew J. Smith to Burt G. Wilder, March 29, 1917.

36. *OR,* 10–1:204; Roberts, "Experience of a Private," Johnson Collection; C. H. Floyd letter to Friend Turner, July 6, 1862, C. H. Floyd Letters, Abraham Lincoln Presidential Library, Springfield, IL; Morrison, *History of the Ninth Regiment,* 29–30.

37. Roberts, "Experience of a Private," Johnson Collection.

38. McFadden to the Editor, [*Mattoon (IL)*] *Gazette,* April 18, 1862, Johnson Collection.

39. Chaplain John M. Garner, "History of the 18th Missouri Volunteer Infantry," *Unionville (MO) Republican,* August 2, 1893.

40. Ibid., July 19, 1893.

41. Ibid., July 19 and 26, 1893.

42. Ibid., August 2, 1893.
43. Ibid., July 19, 1893.
44. Ibid., August 23, 1893.

CHAPTER 3: ILLINOIS TO NORTH CAROLINA

1. According to *History of DeWitt County, Illinois* (Philadelphia: W. R. Brink, 1882), 163, Warner ate the goose while at Shiloh. Dr. Christopher Goodbrake, surgeon of the 20th Illinois Volunteer Infantry, reported Warner to be "in good health and fine spirits" on March 14, after his arrival at Pittsburg Landing. Christopher Goodbrake to Isaac N. Coltrin, editor, *Clinton (IL) Central Transcript*, March 20, 1862, Johnson Collection. Warner became seriously ill within the next two weeks and applied for medical leave on March 27, but it was not granted until after the battle. Warner was discharged for health reasons on December 12, 1862, and continued to suffer lingering effects of the illness for years after the war. John Warner Pension File, RG 15, NARA; Smith, "Adventures."

2. Peter Josyph, ed., *The Wounded River: The Civil War Letters of John Vance Lauderdale, M.D.* (East Lansing: Michigan State University Press, 1993), 46; Stillwell, *Story of a Common Soldier*, 33; Edward Dicey, *Six Months in the Federal States*, 2 vols. (London: Macmillan, 1863), 2:118.

3. Eugene H. Berwanger, *The Frontier Against Slavery: Western Anti-Negro Prejudice and the Slavery Extension Controversy* (Urbana: University of Illinois Press, 1967), 48–51. See also V. Jacque Voegeli, *Free but Not Equal: The Midwest and the Negro During the Civil War* (Chicago: University of Chicago Press, 1967), 89.

4. Mrs. D. C. Freeman to Milo Custer, October 17, 1916, McLean County Museum of History, Bloomington, IL; *Bloomington (IL) Daily Pantagraph*, March 26, 1862, reprinted in Don Munson, *It is Begun!: The Pantagraph Reports the Civil War* (Bloomington, IL: McLean County Historical Society, 2001), 61.

5. William H. Russell, *My Diary North and South*, ed. Eugene H. Berwanger (1863; Baton Rouge: Louisiana State University Press, 2001), 216–217; William Ferguson, *America by River and Rail, or Notes by the Way on the New World and Its People* (London: James Nisbet, 1856), 379–383.

6. James Wilson to the *Centralia (IL) Sentinel*, March 29, 1890; *Centralia (IL) Sentinel*, February 10, 1903; Dr. George Ross, "Centralia Was Terminal along the 'Underground Railroad,'" *Centralia (IL) Sentinel*, April 20, 1997.

7. Russell, *My Diary*, 217; Dicey, *Six Months*, 2:110.

8. Russell, *My Diary*, 217.

9. *The Biographical Record of DeWitt County, Illinois* (Chicago: S. J. Clarke, 1901), 26–29; *History of DeWitt County, Illinois*, 163; "End of a Busy Life," *Clinton (IL) Public*, December 22, 1905; Guy C. Fraker, *Lincoln's Ladder to the Presidency: The Eighth Judicial Circuit* (Carbondale: Southern Illinois University Press, 2012), 96–97.

10. *Biographical Record of DeWitt County*, 26–29; *History of DeWitt County*, 163; "End of a Busy Life," *Clinton (IL) Public*, December 22, 1905; Fraker, *Lincoln's Ladder*, 5–6; *Republicans of Illinois: A Portrait and Chronological Record of Members of the Republican Party* (Chicago: Lewis, 1905), 80.

11. *Biographical Record of DeWitt County*, 10–11, 26–29; *History of DeWitt County*, 159, 163; "End of a Busy Life," *Clinton (IL) Public*. Warner entered banking after the Civil War and acquired considerable wealth, large sums of which he returned to his community in charitable donations.

12. See *Clinton (IL) Public*, October 23, 1862; *Bloomington (IL) Weekly Pantagraph*, October 15, 1862.

13. *Clinton (IL) Public*, May 7, 1863.

14. John Warner Pension File, RG 15, NARA.

15. Isaac Pugh to his wife, October 14, 1862, Johnson Collection.

16. Rinaldo Pugh to his mother, August 18, 1862, Johnson Collection, and Isaac Pugh to his wife, September 19, 1862, and March 6, 1864, Johnson Collection.

17. Rinaldo Pugh to his mother, October 22, 1862, Johnson Collection. See also Jane Martin Johns, *Personal Recollections of Early Decatur, Abraham Lincoln, Richard Oglesby and the Civil War*, ed. Howard C. Schaub (Decatur, IL: Decatur Chapter Daughters of the American Revolution, 1912), 153–154.

18. *Clinton (IL) Public*, March 20, 1891.

19. Obituaries for Henry and Nancy Mann were published, respectively, in the *Clinton (IL) Public*, March 20, 1891, and January 25, 1895; *Clinton (IL) Weekly Register*, March 20, 1891, and January 25, 1895. Information provided to authors by Clinton local historian Joey Woolridge, October 25, 2006.

20. Militia Act, July 17, 1862, *US Statutes at Large*, 12:599; *OR*, ser. 3, vol. 2:281–282.

21. Abraham Lincoln, "The Emancipation Proclamation," January 1, 1863, in *The Collected Works of Abraham Lincoln*, 9 vols., ed. Roy P. Basler (New Brunswick, NJ: Rutgers University Press, 1953– 55), 6:28–31; Allen C. Guelzo, *Lincoln's Emancipation Proclamation: The End of Slavery in America* (New York: Simon & Schuster, 2004), 257–260.

22. See Smith, *Lincoln and the U.S. Colored Troops*, 75–76.

23. *Bloomington (IL) Daily Pantagraph*, May 21, 25, 26, 1863; *Bloomington (IL) Weekly Pantagraph*, May 27, 1863, reprinted in Munson, *It is Begun!*; Smith, "Adventures."

24. *Clinton (IL) Public*, May 7, 1863.

25. Smith, "Adventures."

26. Nancy H. Hannan, *Readville: A Mysterious Providence* (Hyde Park, MA: Albert House, 1990), 12. This work and a pamphlet, "The Black Regiments of Camp Meigs" (1995), are in the collection of the Massachusetts State Library, Boston; [Charles B. Fox], *Record of the Service of the 55th Regiment of Massachusetts Volunteer Infantry* (Cambridge, MA: Press of John Wilson and Son, 1868), 1.

27. Norwood P. Hallowell, *The Negro as a Soldier in the War of the Rebellion* (Boston: Little, Brown, 1897), 9; [Fox], *Record of the Service*, 1, 95–96.

28. Entry no. 86, 55th Massachusetts Descriptive Book, RG 94, NARA.

29. Hannan, *Readville*, 12.

30. [Fox], *Record of the Service*, 110, 112. An additional 153 recruits and 22 officers joined the regiment during the war.

31. Burt G. Wilder, Diary, May 10, 11, and 18, 1863, Wilder Papers (hereafter cited as Wilder Diary).

32. Luis F. Emilio, *A Brave Black Regiment: The History of the 54th Regiment of Massachusetts Volunteer Infantry* (1894; New York: Da Capo Press, 1995), 3. For appointment of black officers, see Cornish, *Sable Arm*, 214–217.

33. General Orders No. 1, No. 8, No. 11, 55th Massachusetts Regimental Order Book, RG 94, NARA. A trencher was a wooden plate.

34. Ibid., General Order No. 20.

35. For the color guard, see Captain August V. Kautz, *The 1865 Customs of Service for Non-Commissioned Officers and Soldiers* (2nd ed. 1865; Mechanicsburg, PA: Stackpole, 2001), 130–131.

36. See Frances H. Casstevens, *Edward A. Wild and His African Brigade in the Civil War* (Jefferson, NC: McFarland, 2003).

37. Secretary of War Edwin Stanton to William Schouler, Adjutant General of Massachusetts, Telegram, July 16, 1863, Massachusetts National Guard Military Museum and Archives, Concord, MA.

38. General Order No. 21, 55th Massachusetts Order Book, RG 94, NARA.

39. [Fox], *Record of the Service*, 7; *Christian Recorder* (Philadelphia), June 11, 1864.

40. [Fox], *Record of the Service*, 7–8.

41. Charles B. Fox, "Extracts from Letters to my Wife during my connection with the 55th Regiment Massachusetts Volunteers," Charles Barnard Fox Papers, 1861–1865, Massachusetts Historical Society (hereafter cited as MHS), Boston: vol. 1, July 23, 24, 25, 1863 (hereafter cited as Fox Letters); [Fox], *Record of the Service*, 9; Wilder Diary, July 25, 26, 1863; Captain Charles B. Bowditch, "War Letters of Charles B. Bowditch," *Massachusetts Historical Society Proceedings* 57 (1924): 422–423.

42. [Fox], *Record of the Service*, 9; Bowditch, "War Letters," 423.

43. Bowditch, "War Letters," 423; Fox Letters, 1: July 26, 1863.

44. Bowditch, "War Letters," 424.

CHAPTER 4: BATTERY WAGNER, THE SEA ISLANDS, AND FLORIDA

1. Bowditch, "War Letters," 425–426.

2. Ibid.; [Fox], *Record of the Service*, 11.

3. Quincy A. Gillmore, "The Army before Charleston in 1863," in *Battles and Leaders*, 4:52–71; *OR*, 28–1:16–29, 271–335; Stephen R. Wise, *Gate of Hell: Campaign for Charleston Harbor, 1863* (Columbia: University of South Carolina Press, 1994), 139–204; Earl J. Hess, *Field Armies and Fortifications in the Civil War: The Eastern Campaigns, 1861–1864* (Chapel Hill: University of North Carolina Press, 2005), 259–288.

4. Gillmore, "Army before Charleston," 4:60; *OR*, 28–1:21–22, 271–273, 280; Wise, *Gate of Hell*, 145–147, 236–238.

5. Bowditch, "War Letters," 426–427.

6. Wise, *Gate of Hell*, 145–147; Gillmore, "Army before Charleston, 4:60; Bowditch, "War Letters," 429.

7. Bowditch, "War Letters," 434–435; Wise, *Gate of Hell*, 148–149; "Most of the walkway was constructed through the soft organic mud of the tidal marsh. In the 1950s and 1960s, the supporting posts for this 'bridge,' broken off level with the mud, could still be seen. About 1965 they were buried under a 'spoil area' by the U. S. Army Corps of Engineers." Willis J. Keith to authors, AJS Papers.

8. Bowditch, "War Letters," 436; William S. Stryker, "The 'Swamp Angel,'" in *Battles and Leaders*, 4:73; Wise, *Gate of Hell*, 149–150, 169–173.

9. Wise, *Gate of Hell*, 156, table 18, 236– 238. Naval batteries participated in the bombardment.

10. Wheelock Pratt to his wife, September 27, 1863, Wilder Papers.

11. Andrew Jackson Smith Pension File, RG 15, Records of the Veterans Administration, NARA.

12. Corporal James Henry Gooding, October 24, 1863, in Adams, *On the Altar of Freedom*, 70; [Fox], *Record of the Service*, 15–16; Fox Letters, 1: September 23, 1863.

13. [Fox], *Record of the Service*, 13; Fox Letters, 1: August 27, 29, 1863, September 19, 20, 21, 23, 30, 1863; Bowditch, "War Letters," September 20, 23, 1863.

14. [Fox], *Record of the Service*, 12; James Henry Gooding to the *New Bedford (MA) Mercury*, September 9, 29, October 3, 1863, in Adams, *On the Altar of Freedom,* 58, 65–66.

15. Fox Letters, 2: June 23, 1864; Wilder Diary, September 5, 1864; Andrew Jackson Smith Pension File, RG 15, NARA; Burt G. Wilder to Hon. C. W. Saltxeaber, Commissioner of Pensions, December 21, 1916, Andrew Jackson Smith, Medal of Honor Application file, Adjutant General's Office, No. 251199C, RG 94, NARA; Wilder Diary, June 1, 1864.
16. 55th Massachusetts Company B Day Book, October 13, November 22, 1863, RG 94, NARA; Special Orders No. 28, October 12, 1863, and Special Orders No. 51, November 21, 1863, 55th Massachusetts Order Book, RG 54, NARA; Special Orders No. 57, November 22, 1863, African Brigade Order Book, RG 94, NARA; Andrew Jackson Smith, Compiled Military Service Record, October and November, 1863, RG 94, NARA; Wilder Diary, March 13, 1864. The Compiled Military Service Record was the document wherein the War Department abstracted and recorded data from Civil War soldiers' military records.
17. [Fox], *Record of the Service*, 39.
18. Charles B. Fox, "Records of the 55th Regiment Massachusetts Volunteer Infantry," manuscript, vol. 1: November 7, 1864, in Records of the Association of Officers of the 55th Massachusetts Volunteer Infantry, MHS, microfilm (hereafter cited as Fox, "55th Massachusetts"); Fox Letters, 3: November 8, 1864.
19. Ovid Leon Futch, "Salmon P. Chase and Civil War Politics in Florida," *Florida Historical Quarterly* 32 (January 1954): 163–188; Mark F. Boyd, "The Federal Campaign of 1864 in East Florida," *Florida Historical Quarterly* 29 (July 1950): 3–37.
20. *OR*, 35–1:480–481; [Fox], *Record of the Service*, 21; Fox Letters, 1: February 8–14, 1864; Richard W. White to the *Christian Recorder*, March 14, 1864, Trudeau, *Voices of the 55th*, 72–75.
21. [Fox], *Record of the Service*, 21, 22–24; Fox Letters, 1: February 16–17, 18–22, 1864.
22. Wilder Diary, March 13, 1864. The following accounts of the alligator hunts and Andy Smith's early experiences with Burt Wilder are from entries in the Wilder Diary, March 9, 11, 16, 17, 19, 24, 25, and April 16, 1864.
23. [Fox], *Record of the Service*, 24–25.
24. Special Order No. 18, April 20, 1864, 55th Massachusetts Order Book; [Fox], *Record of the Service*, 25; Fox, "55th Massachusetts," 1:57.
25. Militia Act, July 17, 1862, *Statutes at Large*, 12:599; *OR*, ser. 3, vol. 2:281–282, vol. 5:632–633; Herman Belz, "Law, Politics, and Race in the Struggle for Equal Pay in the Civil War," *Civil War History* 22 (September 1976): 197–213.
26. Fox Letters, 1: August 14, 1863; Alfred S. Hartwell to Edward W. Kinsley, April 7, 1864, unidentified newspaper clipping in the Edward W. Kinsley Papers, Rare Book, Manuscript, and Special Collections Library, Duke University.
27. Wilder Diary, May 30, 1864; see also Fox Letters, 2: May 30, 1864; Entry no. 86, 55th Massachusetts Descriptive Book; Special Order No. 41, June 14, 1864, 55th Massachusetts Order Book, RG 94, NARA.
28. [Fox], *Record of the Service*, 26, 28, 29; Fox Letters, 2: June 15, 1864.
29. Alfred S. Hartwell, Memoir, 12, Miscellaneous Collections, US Army Military History Institute, Carlisle Barracks, PA (hereafter cited as Hartwell Memoir); Wilder Diary, June 18, 1864; Fox Letters, 2: July 14, 1864; [Fox], *Record of the Service*, 33.
30. *OR*, ser. 3, vol. 4:448; War Department Circular, Number 60, August 1, 1864 *OR*, ser. 3, vol. 4: 565; Fox, *Record of the Service*, 34–35.
31. Fox, *Record of the Service*, 35.
32. Emilio, *Brave Black Regiment*, 220; Hallowell, *Negro As a Soldier*, 18–19; Andrew Jackson Smith, Compiled Military Service Record, August 1864, RG 94, NARA; [Fox], *Record of the Service*, 34–36.

CHAPTER 5: RIVERS' CAUSEWAY TO HONEY HILL

1. Andrew J. Smith to Burt G. Wilder, March 22, 1913, and February 19, 1918, Wilder Papers; [Fox], *Record of the Service*, 29; Wilder Diary, July 4, 1864; Hartwell Memoir, 13–14.

2. Andrew J. Smith to Burt G. Wilder, March 22, 1913, for quotations, and February 19, 1918, Wilder Papers.

3. [Fox], *Record of the Service*, 29–30.

4. *OR*, 35–2:157–158; *OR* 35–1:14–15.

5. *OR*, 35–1:87, 92; Willis J. Keith, "Fort Johnson," *Civil War Times Illustrated* 14, no. 7 (November 1975): 32–39; John Johnson, The *Defense of Charleston Harbor, Including Fort Sumter and the Adjacent Islands, 1863–1865* (Charleston, SC: Walker, Evans & Cogswell, 1890), 215.

6. James M. Trotter to Edward W. Kinsley, July 18, 1864, Edward W. Kinsley Papers; Charles C. Soule to Burt Wilder, account of the action at Rivers' Causeway, May 27, 1895, Wilder Papers; [Fox], *Record of the Service*, 30.

7. The map in Trudeau, *Voices of the 55th*, 120, places Rivers' Causeway near Fort Lamar, more than a mile to the east of its actual location. The map in Trudeau, *Like Men of War*, 259, places Rivers' Causeway correctly, but the actual forward progress of the brigade beyond Rivers' Causeway was only 333 yards, a small portion of that indicated on the map. James M. Trotter to Edward W. Kinsley, July 18, 1864, Kinsley Papers; Soule, Rivers' Causeway, 1895, Wilder Papers; [Fox], *Record of the Service*, 30; Major Joseph Morrison, 103rd New York Volunteer Infantry, report, *OR*, 35–1:78.

8. Morrison, 103rd New York Infantry, report, *OR*, 35–1:78; [Fox], *Record of the Service*, 30; Soule, Rivers' Causeway, 1895, Wilder Papers; Wilder Diary, July 4, 1864; Warren Ripley, ed., *Siege Train: The Journal of a Confederate Artilleryman in the Defense of Charleston* (Columbia: University of South Carolina Press, 1986), 157, 191.

9. Charles B. Fox, Rivers' Causeway account, Wilder Papers; Soule, Rivers' Causeway, 1895, Wilder Papers; Morrison, 103rd New York Infantry, *OR*, 35–1:78; [Fox], *Record of the Service*, 30.

10. Andrew J. Smith to Burt G. Wilder, April 25, 1917, Wilder Papers; [Fox], *Record of the Service*, 30; Soule, Rivers' Causeway, May 1895, Wilder Papers; Wilder Diary, July 4, 1864.

11. Andrew J. Smith to Burt G. Wilder, December 22, 1917, Wilder Papers.

12. Ibid.; James M. Trotter to Edward W. Kinsley, July 18, 1864, Kinsley Papers.

13. Andrew J. Smith to Burt G. Wilder, December 22, 1917, Wilder Papers; James M. Trotter to Edward W. Kinsley, July 18, 1864, Kinsley Papers; James D. Thurber to Burt G. Wilder, March 9, 1901, Wilder Papers; Ripley, *Siege Train*, 191–192.

14. Hartwell Memoir, 14.

15. Ibid.; [Fox], *Record of the Service*, 31; Wilder Diary, July 6, 1864; Ripley, *Siege Train*, 194; *OR*, 35–1:158, 166.

16. [Fox], *Record of the Service*, 32; *OR*, 35–1:14; Ripley, *Siege Train*, 192.

17. *OR*, 35–1: 86–89; *OR*, 35–1:14–15.

18. Ibid.; *OR*, 35–1:84–86; *OR*, 35–1:166–171; *OR*, 35–1:15, 84–85; H. David Stone Jr., *Vital Rails: The Charleston and Savannah Railroad and the Civil War in Coastal South Carolina* (Columbia: University of South Carolina Press, 2008), 192–193.

19. [Fox], *Record of the Service*, 31–32; *OR*, 35–1:15; Wilder Diary, July 6, 1864; Andrew J. Smith to Burt G. Wilder, February 19, 1918, Wilder Papers; Emilio, *Brave Black Regiment*, 205.

20. General Orders 94, 55th Massachusetts Order Book; 55th Massachusetts Company B Order Book, RG 94, NARA; *OR*, 39–3:740; *OR*, 35–2:328; *OR*, 44:525–526; *OR*, 44:505, 517–

518, 535; *OR*, 44:547; Charles C. Soule, "Battle of Honey Hill: A Federal Account of the Fight on Broad River, S. C., in 1864," *Philadelphia Weekly Times*, May 10 and 16, 1884, printed in Trudeau, *Voices of the 55th*, 193–222; *OR*, 44:64. Companies G and H of the 55th remained on duty at Charleston.

21. *OR* Navy, 16:57–58; *OR*, 44:543, 564; *OR*, 44:570; Soule, "Battle of Honey Hill," May 10, 1884; *OR*, 35–2:328.

22. [Fox], *Record of the Service*, 40; Wilder Diary, November 27, 28, 1864.

23. Fox Letters, 3: November 28, 1864; [Fox], *Record of the Service*, 41; Wilder Diary, November 28–29.

24. Fox Letters, 3: November 28, 1864; [Fox], *Record of the Service*, 41; Wilder Diary, November 28–29, 1864; *OR*, 44:421; Soule, "Battle of Honey Hill," May 10, 1884.

25. *OR* Navy, 16:73; Madeleine Vinton Dahlgren, *Memoir of John A. Dahlgren Rear-Admiral United States Navy* (Boston: James R. Osgood, 1882), 479–480.

26. Account of Sergeant John. A. Moore, 3rd South Carolina Cavalry, reprinted from the *Hampton Guardian*, in James Harvey McKee, *Back "In War Times:" History of the 144th Regiment, New York Volunteer Infantry* (New York: Lieut. Horace E. Bailey, 1903), 195; William A. Courtenay, "Fragments of War History Relating to the Coast Defense of South Carolina, 1861–1865 and the Hasty Preparations for the Battle of Honey Hill, November 30, 1864," *Southern Historical Society Papers* 26 (1898): 62–87.

27. *OR*, 44:422. Bolan's Church was Bethel Episcopal Chapel, a church for slaves built by planter James Bolan in 1861.

28. *OR*, 44:422, 431–432, 433; [Fox], *Record of the Service*, 41–42; Soule, "Battle of Honey Hill," May 10, 1884; Emilio, *Brave Black Regiment*, 245.

29. *OR*, 44:422, 431; [Fox], *Record of the Service*, 41–42; Soule, "Battle of Honey Hill," May 10, 1884; Emilio, *Brave Black Regiment*, 245.

30. *OR*, 44:431; [Fox], *Record of the Service*, 42; Soule, "Battle of Honey Hill," May 10, 1884.

31. *OR*, 44:426, 431–432.

32. *OR*, 44:431–432; Soule, "Battle of Honey Hill," May 10, 1884.

33. Soule, "Battle of Honey Hill," May 10, 1884, mistakenly placed the stream at 150 yards from the Confederate works. The error was widely spread after the war in the writings of Charles Colcock Jones. The correct distance was less than one hundred yards. See report of Captain H. M. Stuart, Stuart's Battery, S.C. Light Artillery, Beaufort Volunteer Artillery, John Jenkins Personal Papers, South Carolina Department of Archives and History, Columbia, SC, in *Supplement to the Official Records of the Union and Confederate Armies*, Part 1, Reports, 12 vols., ed. Janet B. Hewett et al. (Wilmington, NC: Broadfoot, 1998), 7:653–665. Researcher G. Marshall Naul paced the distance between the remains of the breastworks and the location of the stream in a survey conducted on February 22 and 23, 1959, and found it to be 275 feet, nearly 92 yards. G. Marshall Naul Research Collection, 1961–1995, South Caroliniana Library, University of South Carolina, Columbia. The distance is also put at one hundred yards by [Fox], *Record of the Service*, 43, and Franklin McGrath, ed., *History of the 127th New York Volunteers, "Monitors," in the War for the Preservation of the Union—September 8, 1862, June 30, 1865* (N.p.: n.p., 1898), 125.

34. Courtenay, "Hasty Preparations," 76; Soule, "Battle of Honey Hill," May 10, 1884; McKee, *Back "In War Times,"* 187–188; Emilio, *Brave Black Regiment*, 242; Steven D. Smith, et al., *Mapping the Charleston and Savannah Railroad Defenses Phase II* (Columbia: South Carolina Institute of Archaeology and Anthropology, 2011); Major George T. Jackson, Charles Colcock Jones Papers, Rare Book, Manuscript, and Special Collections Library, Duke University.

35. *OR*, 44:432; [Fox], *Record of the Service*, 43; Soule, "Battle of Honey Hill," May 10, 1884; James M. Trotter to Edward W. Kinsley, December 18, 1864, Kinsley Papers.

36. *OR*, 44:428.

37. Captain H. M. Stuart, Jenkins Papers, South Carolina Department of Archives and History; Charles Alfred de Saussure, "The Story of My Service in the Confederate Army," in possession of Mrs. Nancy Peeples, Charleston, SC.

38. *OR*, 44:428–429; McGrath, *History of the 127th New York Volunteers*, 126–127.

39. *OR*, 44:432; Jordan M. Bobson to Burt Wilder, May 14, 1917, Wilder Papers, places Bobson's Company C, the color company, and the color guard at the front of the charge. Henry Hall and James Hall, *Cayuga in the Field: A Record of the 19th N. Y. Volunteers, All the Batteries of the 3d New York Artillery, and 75th New York Volunteers* (Auburn, NY: Truair, Smith, Printers, Syracuse, 1873), 212, and Samuel W. Mason, *New York Herald,* December 9, 1864, both specifically mention that Hartwell moved the colors to the front of the column.

40. Emilio, *Brave Black Regiment*, 248; James M. Trotter to Edward W. Kinsley, December 18, 1864, Kinsley Papers. There were six guns, not seven, as Trotter mistakenly recorded. Henry Hall, *Cayuga in the Field*, 212; McKee, *Back "In War Times,"* 198.

41. *OR*, 44:432; James M. Trotter to Edward W. Kinsley, December 18, 1864, Kinsley Papers; [Fox], *Record of the Service*, 43; Soule, "Battle of Honey Hill," May 10, 1884.

42. [Fox], *Record of the Service*, 43. The account of the 3rd New York Artillery supports Smith's account of the charge nearly reaching the guns. Hall and Hall, *Cayuga in the Field*, 212. The dispatch of correspondent Samuel W. Mason in the *New York Herald,* December 9, 1864, supports the account of the 3rd New York Artillery. For Confederate testimony, see that of Confederate Charles Alfred de Saussure in this chapter. See also Jordan M. Bobson to Burt G. Wilder, May 14, 1917, Wilder Papers. Thirty years after the war, Mathew McFarlan wrote that Sergeant King "was touching elbows with me on my right when he fell." Possibly due to the serious wounds ending his military career, McFarlan's memory of the charge was faulty, unsupported by all other eyewitness accounts. Furthermore, McFarlan's prescribed position in the color guard, as the ranking corporal (date of promotion December 2, 1863), was to the right of the color sergeant, while Smith's was to the left. McFarlan enlisted in the 55th Massachusetts under the name of his grandfather, with whom he was living, but his name also appears in regimental records as McFarlin and McFarland. Years after the war, the US Pension Office incorporated his correct surname, Lewey, into his records (see his Compiled Military Service Record, RG 94, NARA). Thus, it was as M. M. Lewey that he wrote to Luis F. Emilio, January 11, 1896, with his account of the charge. Nearly a year later, in a second letter to Emilio, he wrote, "I was color bearer, Corporal." M. M. Lewey to Luis F. Emilio, December 16, 1896. If by this statement he meant he was a color bearer at the Battle of Honey Hill, he was incorrect. He was only a member of the color guard during the battle. Both letters are contained in Records of Association of Officers of the 55th Massachusetts Volunteer Infantry, MHS, microfilm. These letters, edited, may also be found in Trudeau, *Voices of the 55th,* 170–172.

43. Smith, "Adventures." For Patterson's wound, see John Patterson, Compiled Military Service Record, RG 94, NARA; Lewey to Emilio, January 11, 1896, MHS.

44. De Saussure, "Story of My Service," 9–10.

45. In both of his letters to Emilio, Mathew McFarlan Lewey compressed the sequence of events in the charge: "It appears to me just now, and I am quite sure it is correct, that Col. Hartwell, Capt. Crane . . . Lt. Boynton, Sergeant King fell simultaneously—before the flag could be recovered from King's lifeless form." Lewey to Emilio, January 11, 1896, MHS. In his second letter to Emilio, Lewey recalled, "I saw Sergeant King fall immediately by my

side, and within ten and fifteen feet of me. Capt. William D. Crane and Lieut. Boynton fell dead." Lewey to Emilio, December 26, 1896, MHS. All four men fell before the flag could be recovered, but they did not fall simultaneously. Hartwell's horse went down, and Crane was killed just beyond the turn in the road; Boynton was killed while crossing the creek, and King was killed thereafter, but far beyond the creek. The final charge of the 55th Massachusetts is most accurately measured in seconds. Discrepancies of time and distance and compression of events are common in battle accounts, especially in those written decades after a war. Being severely wounded at the time may also have adversely affected Lewey's memory of events. The accounts of the 3rd New York artillerymen in Hall and Hall, *Cayuga in the Field*, 212; of Mason in the *New York Herald*, December 9, 1864; of de Saussure in his memoir; and of Andy Smith are mutually supportive and all contradict Lewey's recollection of the charge.

46. [Fox], *Record of the Service*, 44; Fox compiled a meticulous list of the 55th's casualties at Honey Hill, which he recorded in the manuscript of his regimental history, providing the names of each soldier. In addition to the casualties incurred in the regiment's final charge, three enlisted men were killed, and three officers and twenty-three enlisted men were wounded in other actions at Honey Hill. One soldier was captured and survived the war. Fox, "55th Massachusetts," 1:107–111.

47. [Fox], *Record of the Service*, 43–44; Soule, "Battle of Honey Hill," *Philadelphia Weekly Times*, May 17, 1884; Andrew J. Smith to Burt G. Wilder, January 31, 1917, Wilder Papers.

48. *OR*, 44:423, 426–427; [Fox], *Record of the Service*, 44; Soule, "Battle of Honey Hill," May 17, 1884; Foster reported the Union casualties at Honey Hill as 88 men killed, 623 wounded, and 43 missing. *OR*, 44:420, 425. The Confederates placed their casualties at eight killed and forty-two wounded, but with only a few of their units reporting. *OR*, 44:416.

49. *OR*, 44:420, 422–425, 426–427.

50. Fox, "55th Massachusetts," 1:112.

CHAPTER 6: BOYD'S LANDING TO CHARLESTON

1. Dr. Henry O. Marcy, Diary of a Surgeon, 1864–1899, South Carolina Historical Society, Charleston.

2. [Fox], *Record of the Service*, 44–45.

3. Ibid.; *OR*, 44:636; Fox Letters, 3: December 15, 1864.

4. [Fox], *Record of the Service*, 45.

5. Ibid.; Wilder Diary, December 6, 1864; Emilio, *Brave Black Regiment*, 256.

6. Wilder Diary, December 8, 1864; Emilio, *Brave Black Regiment*, 256. Colonel Silliman commanded the 26th USCT.

7. Emilio, *Brave Black Regiment*, 257; [Fox], *Record of the Service*, 45, 47; Fox Letters, 3: December 15, 1864; Wilder Diary, December 3, 5, 7, 4, 5, 9, 15, 17, 28, 30, 1864, January 2, 10, 1865.

8. Wilder Diary, December 9, 12, 1864.

9. [Fox], *Record of the Service*, 46; Wilder Diary, December 4, 1864; William Warren Marple to his brother, December 5, 1864, accessed September 10, 2019, http://www.marple.com/usctletter.html.

10. [Fox], *Record of the Service*, 48.

11. Ibid., 48–49; Wilder Diary, January 11–15, 1865.

12. [Fox], *Record of the Service*, 49–51; General Orders No. 3, January 31, 1865, 55th Massachusetts Order Book; 55th Massachusetts Company B Order Book, RG 94, NARA.

13. [Fox], *Record of the Service*, 51–52.

14. Ibid., 52–53; Fox Letters, 3: February 7, 1865; *OR*, 47–2:162.

15. William Tecumseh Sherman, *Memoirs of General W. T. Sherman* (1875; New York: Library of America, 1990), 754–755.

16. *OR*, 47–2:96–97, 411–412; Sherman, *Memoirs*, 754–757.

17. [Fox], *Record of the Service*, 53; *OR*, 47–2:1142. See also, Ripley, *Siege Train*, 243.

18. Ripley, *Siege Train*, 243–244.

19. [Fox], *Record of the Service*, 53. Foster returned to Washington to receive medical treatment for his leg wound.

20. Ripley, *Siege Train*, 245; [Fox], *Record of the Service*, 54.

21. Charles F. Lee to his mother, February 11, 1865, Charles F. Lee Papers, 1864–1865, South Caroliniana Library, University of South Carolina.

22. [Fox], *Record of the Service*, 54; Ripley, *Siege Train*, 248.

23. [Fox], *Record of the Service*, 54; *OR*, 47–2:96–97; *OR*, 47–2:411–412.

24. Johnson, *Defense of Charleston Harbor*, 249–250; *OR*, 47–1:1021–1022; Fox Letters, 3: February 17, 1865; Fox, "55th Massachusetts," 1:150–151.

25. *OR*, 47–1:1021; [Fox], *Record of the Service*, 54, 55.

26. *OR*, 47–1:1023–1024; Fox, "55th Massachusetts," 1:148–149; Hartwell Memoir, 15; [Fox], *Record of the Service*, 54–56; Johnson, *Defense of Charleston Harbor*, 250–251.

27. [Fox], *Record of the Service*, 55; Hartwell Memoir, 15; Johnson, *Defense of Charleston Harbor*, 250–251.

28. Potter's report to Gillmore, *OR*, 47–1:1024; [Fox], *Record of the Service*, 55.

29. [Fox], *Record of the Service*, 56; Potter's report to Gillmore, *OR*, 47–1:1024–1025; Fox Letters, 3: February 20, 1865.

30. [Fox], *Record of the Service*, 56; see also, Fox, "55th Massachusetts," 1:152–154.

31. [Fox], *Record of the Service*, 56; Fox Letters, 3: January 20, 1865.

32. Fox, "55th Massachusetts," 1:155–156; [Fox], *Record of the Service*, 57.

33. Fox, "55th Massachusetts," 1:156; [Fox], *Record of the Service*, 57.

34. Fox, "55th Massachusetts," 1:156.

35. Ibid., 1:156–157; [Fox], *Record of the Service*, 57–58.

CHAPTER 7. WAR'S END

1. [Fox], *Record of the Service* 58. The expedition also included the 32nd USCT, 54th New York, and 144th New York. The 21st USCT and other reinforcements arrived at St. Stephens.

2. [Fox], *Record of the Service*, 58–60; Fox, "55th Massachusetts," 1:158–167.

3. [Fox], *Record of the Service*, 58; Fox, "55th Massachusetts," 1:159–160; *Supplement to the Official Records*, pt. 2, vol. 77:725, 730.

4. [Fox], *Record of the Service*, 61–62; Fox, "55th Massachusetts," 2:3.

5. Fox Letters, 3: March 14, 1865; Louis P. Towles, ed., *A World Turned Upside Down: The Palmers of the South Santee, 1818–1881* (Columbia: University of South Carolina Press, 1996), 451; Arney Robinson Childs, ed., *The Private Journal of Henry William Ravenel* (Columbia: University of South Carolina Press, 1948), 211; 212–213; Fox, "55th Massachusetts," 2:8.

6. [Fox], *Record of the Service*, 62; Childs, *Journal of Henry William Ravenel*, 213–214; Towles, *World Turned Upside Down*, 450.

7. [Fox], *Record of the Service*, 62; Fox, "55th Massachusetts," 2:4; *OR*, 47–2:604–605, 641.

8. [Fox], *Record of the Service*, 63–65; Fox, "55th Massachusetts," 2:8–10, 11.

9. [Fox], *Record of the Service*, 65; Fox, "55th Massachusetts," 2:15.

10. Fox, "55th Massachusetts," 2:15–19, 20, 21, 23, 24; [Fox], *Record of the Service*, 65–68; 55th Massachusetts Regimental Letter Book, March 18, 1865, 74, RG 94, NARA; Fox Letters,

3: March 19, 1865; Wilder Diary, July 4, 1864, March 19, 1865, March 26, 1865; Charles F. Lee to his mother, March 28, 1865, Lee Papers; Douglas Bostick to Sharon S. MacDonald, April 18, 2011, email communication, AJS Papers. See also, Katherine Dhalle, "Scholar Says Union Regiment Never Fought at McLeod," *Charleston (SC) Post and Courier*, April 4, 1996. The authors thank Douglas Bostick, Willis Keith, and Katherine Dhalle for their assistance in identifying the burial site of the soldiers killed at Rivers' Causeway and the location of Battery Means.

11. Wilder Diary, March 30, 1865; 55th Massachusetts Letter Book, March 31, 1865, 75, RG 94, NARA.

12. Testimony of Sergeant Eli Lett, Alfred E. Pelette court-martial records, May 23, 1865, RG 153, NARA.

13. Fox, "55th Massachusetts," 2:26; 55th Massachusetts Letter Book, March 31, 1865, 77, RG 94, NARA; Wilder Diary, March 30, 1865; Emilio, *Brave Black Regiment*, 288.

14. Wilder Diary, March 30, 1865.

15. 55th Massachusetts Letter Book, April 25, 1865, 77, RG 94, NARA.

16. Alfred E. Pelette, court-martial record, May 23, 1865, 5–6, 11–12, 15, RG 153, NARA.

17. Ibid., 9–10.

18. Ibid.

19. Ibid., 16–17.

20. Ibid., 17–18; [Fox], *Record of the Service*, 114, 122.

21. [Fox], *Record of the Service*, 68; *OR*, 47–1:1042, Hartwell's report.

22. [Fox], *Record of the Service*, 68; *OR*, 47–1:1042. For Potter's raid see Emilio, *Brave Black Regiment*, 289–309; Trudeau, *Like Men of War*, 375–395. For "scouts" see Charles F. Lee to his mother, March 19, 1865, Lee Papers. Pettus was the son of Brigadier General Edmund W. Pettus and nephew of Mississippi governor John J. Pettus.

23. [Fox], *Record of the Service*, 68–69; *OR*, 47–1:1042; Fox, "55th Massachusetts," 2:28–30.

24. Fox, "55th Massachusetts," 2:30–32; [Fox], *Record of the Service*, 69; *OR*, 47–1:1042.

25. [Fox], *Record of the Service*, 69–70. See also, Fox, "55th Massachusetts," 2:32; *OR*, 47–1:1042.

26. [Fox], *Record of the Service*, 70; Fox, "55th Massachusetts," 2:32; *OR*, 47–1:1042. Porcher was not charged and was released from arrest after arriving in Charleston. W. Mazyck Porcher, "Memoir," *Charleston (SC) Weekly News*, August 16, 1882. See also William Mazyck Porcher Papers, South Caroliniana Library, University of South Carolina. William H. Torrey to Burt G. Wilder, [September] 1912, Wilder Papers; Charles C. Soule to Burt G. Wilder, [August] 1912, Wilder Papers.

27. [Fox], *Record of the Service*; 70; Fox, "55th Massachusetts," 2:33–34; *OR*, 47–1:1042, Hartwell's report; Charles C. Soule to Burt G. Wilder [August] 1912, Wilder Papers; Porcher, "Memoir."

28. *OR*, 47–1:1043; [Fox], *Record of the Service*, 70–71; Fox, "55th Massachusetts," 2:34–35; Wilder Diary, April 13, 1865.

29. *OR*, 47–1:1043; Fox, "55th Massachusetts," 2:35; [Fox], *Record of the Service*, 71, 73; Hartwell Memoir; Wilder Diary, April 12, 1865.

30. *OR*, 47–1:1043; [Fox], *Record of the Service*, 71–72; Fox, "55th Massachusetts," 2:36–38; *OR*, 47–1:1043.

31. *OR*, 47–1:1043; [Fox], *Record of the Service*, 73; Fox, "55th Massachusetts," 2: 38–42; Wilder Diary, April 13, 1865.

32. Fox, "55th Massachusetts," 2:42; Fox Letters, 3: April 15, 1865. See also [Fox], *Record of the Service*, 74, and Wilder Diary, April 13, 1865.

33. "Fort Sumter Restoration of the Stars and Stripes," *New York Times*, April 18, 1865; Fox, "55th Massachusetts," 2:43; Fox Letters, 3: April 15, 1865.

34. Fox Letters, 3: April 18, 1865; [Fox], *Record of the Service*, 74. See also Fox, "55th Massachusetts," 2:44; Wilder Diary, April 19, 1865.

35. Fox, "55th Massachusetts," 2:44; Charles F. Lee to his mother, April 19, 1865, Lee Papers.

36. [Fox], *Record of the Service*, 74–75; Fox, "55th Massachusetts," 2:45.

37. Charles F. Lee to his mother, May 3, 1865, Lee Papers; Fox Letters, 3: May 2, 1865.

38. Fox, "55th Massachusetts," 2:50–53; [Fox], *Record of the Service*, 76–77.

39. Fox, "55th Massachusetts," 2:53; [Fox], *Record of the Service*, 77–78; *Charleston (SC) Daily Courier*, April 21, April 29, 1865.

40. *OR*, 44–1:540. For identification of Private Smith, 2nd Kentucky Cavalry, as Harrison Smith, see *Trigg County, Kentucky Historical Articles* (Melber, KY: Simmons Historical Publications, 1987), 2:53–54.

41. Charles F. Lee to his mother, May 31, 1865, Lee Papers; [Fox], *Record of the Service*, 79, 82.

42. [Fox], *Record of the Service*, 81–82.

43. *Charleston (SC) Daily Courier*, June 13, 1865; Robert J. Zalimas, "A Disturbance in the City: Black and White Soldiers in Postwar Charleston," in Smith, *Black Soldiers in Blue*, 361–390; [Fox], *Record of the Service*, 83.

44. [Fox], *Record of the Service*, 83.

45. Ibid., 83–84. The photograph of Andy Smith is in the Alfred S. Hartwell Collection at the State Library of Massachusetts, Boston. Originally unnamed, the photograph was identified as that of Smith in 2002 by Sergeant Joe W. Siefferman, crime scene investigator/forensic artist, Illinois State Police Division of Forensic Services, Crime Scene Service Command, Charleston, IL, AJS Papers.

46. Ibid., 84; *Weekly Anglo-African* (New York), October 14, 1865.

47. [Fox], *Record of the Service*, 84.

48. *Weekly Anglo-African* (New York), October 14, 1865; "I got my final discharge at Mt. Pleasant, SC in August, 1865. Shortly afterwards we sailed to Gallop Island, near Boston from whence I returned to Clinton, Ill. in September or October." Smith, "Adventures."

CHAPTER 8: A WORLD TURNED UPSIDE DOWN: KENTUCKY AFTER THE WAR

1. Union Major General John M. Palmer, Kentucky's military commander in 1865, conservatively estimated about sixty-five thousand individuals remained enslaved. Berlin, *Freedom: Destruction of Slavery*, 515. For slavery's turbulent demise in Kentucky see ibid., 493–518; Aaron Astor, *Rebels on the Border: Civil War, Emancipation, and the Reconstruction of Kentucky and Missouri* (Baton Rouge: Louisiana State University Press, 2012), 94–135; Aaron Astor, "'I Wanted a Gun': Black Soldiers and White Violence in Civil War and Post War Kentucky," in *The Great Task Remaining before Us: Reconstruction as America's Continuing Civil War*, ed. Paul A. Cimbala and Randall M. Miller (New York: Fordham University Press, 2010), 30–53; Victor B. Howard, *Black Liberation in Kentucky: Emancipation and Freedom, 1862–1884* (Lexington: University Press of Kentucky, 1983), 29–90; Marion B. Lucas, *A History of Blacks in Kentucky*, vol. 1, *From Slavery to Segregation, 1760–1891* (Frankfort: Kentucky Historical Society, 1992): 146–177.

2. Odell Walker, "Lyon County before and after the War Between the States," in Odell Walker, *Profiles of the Past: A Collection of Writings from Lyon County's Historian* (Kuttawa, KY: Lyon County Historical Press, 1994), 103–104.

3. Thomas J. Pressly and William H. Scofield, eds., *Farm Real Estate Values in the United States by Counties, 1850–1959* (Seattle: University of Washington Press, 1965), 51. The average value of farmland in Livingston and Trigg Counties, both adjoining Lyon County Between the Rivers, also declined from ten dollars an acre in 1860, but by 1870 their average values had recovered far better than Lyon's to seven dollars and nine dollars respectively.

4. Livingston County's 1860 population consisted of 5,955 whites, 36 free blacks, and 1,222 slaves. Trigg County's 1860 population consisted of 7,562 whites, 41 free blacks, and 3,448 slaves. US Census 1860, State of Kentucky, Table No. 1, Population by Age and Sex, accessed January 4, 2010, https://www2.census.gov/library/publications/decennial/1860/population/1860a-15.pdf#.

5. Reports of J. Bond Thompson, April 21, 1866, and February 1867, Microfilm M1904: Roll 130, NARA. The labor shortage was widespread throughout the subdistrict, "The demand for laborers is in excess of the supply, especially for farmhands and numerous applications are made daily for help of all descriptions both male and female." W. James Kay to John Ely, April 3, 1867, Microfilm M1904: Roll 128, NARA.

6. May report of Lyon County agent William C. Noel, May 1866, Microfilm M1904: Roll 130, NARA. There were 304 farms and 178 slave owners in 1860; see US Census, 1860 Kentucky Slave Schedule, Lyon County, Microfilm M653: Roll 404: Lyon County, NARA; William C. Noel to John H. Donovan, May 18, 1866, Microfilm M1904: Roll 129, NARA.

7. William C. Noel to John H. Donovan, May 18, 1866, Microfilm M1904: Roll 129, NARA.

8. Ibid.; William C. Noel to John H. Donovan, May 29, 1866, Microfilm M1904: Roll 130, NARA; John H. Donovan to Lieutenant Levi F. Burnett, Adjutant General for the Commissioner of the State of Kentucky, June 2, 1866, Microfilm M1904: Roll 128, NARA. Donovan, summarizing agent Noel's report, failed to distinguish clearly between events in Lyon and Trigg Counties, thus attributing to Lyon County abuses Noel reported only for Trigg. Historian George C. Wright followed Donovan's misstatement to assert that "in Lyon and Trigg counties an undetermined number of blacks were still being held in slavery," but Noel never reported freedmen were being kept as slaves in Lyon County. George C. Wright, *Racial Violence in Kentucky, 1864–1940: Lynchings, Mob Rule, and "Legal Lynchings"* (Baton Rouge: Louisiana State University Press, 1990), 20.

9. William C. Noel to John H. Donovan, June 14, 1866, Microfilm M1904: Roll 130, NARA; Report of A. Benson Brown, August 31, 1868, Microfilm M1904: Roll 128, NARA. Noel also reported being at a loss to know what he could do for orphans who had moved into empty buildings at the abandoned Tennessee Rolling Mill, near the Lyon/Trigg County line and the Empire ironworks in Trigg County. The bureau did not intervene on behalf of the orphans, but families of freedmen living nearby may have done so.

10. Report of J. Bond Thompson, April 21, 1866, Microfilm M1904: Roll 130, NARA; William C. Noel to John C. Donovan, May 18, 1866, Microfilm M1904: Roll 129. Agent Noel's strongest accusation was limited in scope: "The Rebel Citizens [of Lyon County] are disposed to treat the law of Freedmen with utter Contempt (I mean those that have refused to come forward)"; William C. Noel to John H. Donovan, June 14, 1866, Microfilm M1904: Roll 130, NARA.

11. John H. Donovan to John Ely, April 30, 1866, Microfilm M1904: Roll 128, NARA.

12. Ibid., August 4, 1866, Microfilm M1904: Roll 128, NARA.

13. For conditions in the Paducah subdistrict west of Lyon County, see Patricia A. Hoskins, "The Freedmen's Bureau in the Jackson Purchase Region of Kentucky, 1866–1868," *Register of the Kentucky Historical Society* 110, no. 3/4 (2012): 503–531.

14. Captain Herbert S. Broun, Freedmen's Bureau [for Brevet Major General Clinton B.

Fisk, assistant commissioner for Tennessee and Kentucky] to A. M. York, Paducah, February 24, 1866, Microfilm M1904: Roll 132, NARA. Broun's letter to York included a newspaper clipping of a letter to the editor from the *Chicago Tribune*, February 19, 1866, with the heading, "HORRIBLE BARBARITY: A Slave Whipped to Death in Kentucky." Brigadier General Fisk directed that an investigation and report be made of the incident. H. W. Cobb, general agent, Freedmen's Aid Commission, Chicago, had written the letter to *Tribune* editors. According to Cobb, Reuben Harris's family fled from Kentucky to Chicago, where they received shelter and related their story to Cobb. No other record of the incident has been found in bureau papers. The 1860 Kentucky Slave Schedule records Isaac Rucker as a slave owner in Livingston County but not in Lyon County. Livingston County and Lyon County, Kentucky Slave Schedules, 1860, Microfilm M653: Roll 4: Livingston County and Lyon County, NARA.

15. Report to Benjamin Runkle, June 5, 1868, Microfilm M1904: Roll 129, NARA; A. Benson Brown to Benjamin Runkle, August 31, 1868, Microfilm M1904: Roll 128, NARA. For conditions east of Lyon County see J. Michael Crane, "'The Rebels are Bold, Defiant, and Unscrupulous in Their Dementions of All Men': Social Violence in Daviess County, Kentucky 1861–1868," *Ohio Valley History* 2, no. 1 (2002): 17–29; Michael J. Rhyne, "'We are Mobed and Beat': Regular Violence against Free Black Households in Kentucky's Bluegrass Region, 1865–1867," *Ohio Valley History* 2, no. 1 (2002): 30–42.

16. A. Benson Brown to Benjamin Runkle, October 31, 1868, Microfilm M1904: Roll 128, NARA.

17. Henry Bond to W. James Kay, May 7, 1868, Microfilm M1904: Roll 130, NARA.

18. Conventional data derived from the federal slave schedules counted slaves based on ownership, not residency, ignoring the schedules' listings of "Fugitives from the State" and "manumitted slaves." The total number of these slaves was not large in 1860, nearly 5 percent (at least 952) of the 19,577 slaves in the twelve-county region of western Kentucky, but these numbers, when taken into consideration, correct conventional census totals and provide a more nuanced description of black demographic changes at the county level. Most notably, at least 1,030 black residents, not 78, left western Kentucky between 1860 and 1870, and while seven counties (Ballard, Caldwell, Calloway, Crittenden, Graves, Hickman, and Trigg) had only small adjustments of less than 1 percent when accounting for fugitive and manumitted slaves in 1860, five other counties (Fulton, Livingston, Lyon, Marshall, and McCracken) incurred significant declines in their 1860 slave populations of between 12.7 and 23.24 percent and thereafter experienced greater population growth than is recognized by conventional tabulations. For example, conventional census data understates Lyon County's growth by nearly 50 percent. The 1870 census may have undercounted the black population. See Kelly Miller, "Enumeration Errors in Negro Population," *Scientific Monthly* 14, no. 2 (February 1922): 168–177; 1860 Kentucky Slave Schedule, Microfilm M653: Roll 401: Ballard, Caldwell, Calloway; Roll 402: Crittenden; Roll 403: Fulton, Graves, Hickman; Roll 404: Livingston, Lyon, McCracken; Roll 405: Marshall; Roll 406: Trigg, NARA; 1870 US Census, vol. 1., The Statistics of the Population of the United States, Table 2: Population of Each State and Territory, by Counties, in the Aggregate, 1790–1870, State of Kentucky, 31–33, accessed January 4, 2020, https://www2.census.gov/library/publications/decennial/1870/population/1870a-07.pdf?#.

19. Records of the Assistant Commissioner for the State of Tennessee, Bureau of Refugees, Freedmen, and Abandoned Lands, 1865–1869, August 28, 1866: "Reports of Outrages, Riots and Murders, January 15, 1866–August 12, 1868"; J. R. Lewis to Major General C. B. Frisk, August 26, 1866, Microfilm M999: Roll 34, NARA. J. R. Lewis reported: "Geo. M. Stewart,

Supt, Stewart Co. . . . Aug 3d[.] He reports the abduction of two freed colored children, by their former owners, parties from Trigg Co. Ky. [T]he names of the children Ellen and Lewis Woods, and of the parties who carried them off by force Thos and John Greenwoode who live two miles from Roaring Spring Trigg Co. Ky. The matter was referred to the Asst Comr of Ky. and Richard Woods the father of the children directed to apply to the Bureau Agent of Trigg Co." Accessed January 4, 2020, https://www.genealogymagazine.com/tennessee-outrages-reports-to-the-freedmens-bureau-part-iii/.

20. 1860 Kentucky Slave Schedules, Microfilm M653: Roll 404: Livingston County; Roll 405: Marshall County; Roll 406: Trigg County, NARA; 1870 US Census, accessed January 4, 2020, https://www2.census.gov/library/publications/decennial/1870/population/1870a-07.pdf?#.

21. 1870 US Census accessed, January 4, 2020, https://www2.census.gov/library/publications/decennial/1870/population/1870a-07.pdf?#; 1860 Kentucky Slave Schedule, Microfilm M653: Roll 404: Lyon County, NARA. The fugitives reflected the age distribution of Lyon County's slaves as a whole. Children made up 50 percent or more of those enslaved in these counties. It is interesting to note two of the slaves who had escaped were age seventy.

22. Donovan to Ely, January 30, 1866, Microfilm M1904: Roll 128, NARA.

23. 1860 Kentucky Slave Schedules, Microfilm M653: Roll 404: Lyon County, NARA.

24. Christopher Waldrep, "Kentucky's Slave Importation Law in Lyon County: A Document," *Filson Club History Quarterly* 65, no. 4 (1991): 505; Records Pertaining to Slavery, Lists of Slaves, 1856–1859, Lyon County Clerk's Office.

25. Waldrep, "Kentucky's Slave Importation Law," 505–506. The estimation that roughly half the slave owners may have possessed slave families was derived by Brenda Joyce Jerome, ed., "1860 Lyon County Kentucky Slave Schedule," *Western Kentucky Journal* 8, no. 4 (2001): 16–21, and reprinted in Walker, *In Lyon County*, 68–74. The slave schedule lists the age and gender of each slave, and in publishing the list, Jerome gave the number of slaves over and under age twenty belonging to each owner.

26. Waldrep, "Kentucky's Slave Importation Law," 505–506. In 1860, Lyon County slave owners claimed 551 slaves under age twenty and 433 under age fifteen. Trigg County owners claimed 1,984 slaves under age twenty, and Livingston owners claimed 697 slaves. These figures represent ownership only and are not adjusted to account for fugitive or manumitted slaves. 1860 Kentucky Slave Schedules, Microfilm M653: Roll 404: Livingston County and Lyon County; Roll 406: Trigg County, NARA.

CHAPTER 9: BOTTOM RAIL ON TOP NOW

1. Smith, "Adventures."

2. Joseph T. Glatthaar, *Forged in Battle: The Civil War Alliance of Black Soldiers and White Officers* (New York: Free Press, 1990), 246–248; Donald R. Shaffer, *After the Glory: The Struggles of Black Civil War Veterans* (Lawrence: University Press of Kansas, 2004), 40–43, 56–59; Loren Schweninger, *Black Property Owners in the South, 1790–1915* (Urbana: University of Illinois Press, 1990), 160. The average value of real estate per family or head of household in the Lower South was $746. The term "urban" encompasses both the few large southern cities and the many small towns and settlements. Landholdings of the comparatively small numbers of free blacks are not distinguished from those of former slaves.

3. Schweninger, *Black Property Owners*, 145–146, 147–148. The average value of real estate in the Lower South was $544 per rural family and $1,229 per urban family.

4. Ibid., 153–154, 157. By 1870, one rural black family in seventeen (6,538 families out of a total of 112,721) owned land in Missouri, Tennessee, and Kentucky. The average value of

rural real estate per family was $693 in Missouri, $709 in Tennessee, and $580 in Kentucky. The combined average value of rural and urban real estate in Kentucky was $684.

5. Ibid., 160.

6. Shaffer, *After the Glory*, 16–21, discusses how military service enhanced the development of young black men who had previously been denied the experiences of participating as equals in a free society. The first of these experiences was education, but we have no evidence Smith ever learned to read or write. While it is possible he may have learned to read at some level, the evidence suggests he did not learn to write or at least does not seem to have used the skill: he signed his deeds and other legal documents by making his mark, and later in his life, Smith dictated his correspondence. Certainly the development of leadership skills and the psychological benefits of military service Shaffer describes were a boon to young Andy Smith. To illustrate the importance military service might contribute to the life of a former slave, Shaffer quotes Kentucky native Robert Anderson, who suffered serious financial reverses after the war but eventually achieved success: "It is to that determination, formed when a soldier, that I owe my independence today" (57). Smith and Anderson were both determined, hard-working individuals who prevailed through difficult times and ultimately achieved financial success, but on the whole Smith's life does not easily conform to patterns typical of the lives of other veterans identified in Shaffer's study. These black veterans were more likely than black nonveterans to move to the North, live in cities, and die before their fiftieth birthday. As a group, they were more prosperous than nonveterans, and while they sought to own land, "it is difficult to say whether veterans were more successful than [black] nonveterans in acquiring real property," and "the vast majority of them remained poor" (ibid., 59). Smith returned to the rural South, acquired large tracts of land, operated rural businesses to enhance the profits of his land acquisitions, and lived until age eighty-nine. While he did suffer financial reverses in the early twentieth century, he did not revert to poverty, and he recovered financially.

Black veterans took an active role in the movement for suffrage, some engaged in armed resistance to white mobs, and a few did hold political office during Reconstruction, but their numbers were small: veterans made up about 16 percent of black adult males, but 10 percent of black officeholders (ibid., 73). As a loyal slave state during the war, Kentucky's government did not undergo Reconstruction and was not required to admit blacks to political office. Thus, Kentucky's blacks did not have the same access to the political process as did their fellow blacks in states experiencing Reconstruction. There are no sources revealing Smith's thoughts on black suffrage or other political issues. He does not appear to have confronted the political establishment, managing instead to live in peace with local whites while he built his life. Instead of resorting to confrontation, he relied on the courts to resolve disputes. Like other veterans, he was highly regarded in his local community, but this was likely due in large part to his ability and willingness to provide jobs, farmland, and support to his neighbors when needed. Shaffer places Smith among those veterans who did try to maintain contact with their Civil War comrades, citing the correspondence between Smith, other veterans of the 55th Massachusetts, and with Burt Wilder (ibid., 165–168).

7. For the bounty on the fox, see Lyon County Circuit Court Order Book 1864–1868, June 9, 1868, Kentucky Department for Libraries and Archives, Public Records Divisions, Frankfort, Kentucky (hereafter cited as KDLA).

8. In response to an inquiry from the Bureau of Pensions dated January 15, 1898, Smith gave the date of his marriage as September 3, 1866 (which was also his birthday). The form was signed on June 6, 1898. Andrew Jackson Smith Pension File, Certificate no. 488.807, RG 15, NARA. The marriage bond of Andy Smith and Amanda Young was, however, signed

on September 4, 1866, Lyon County Clerk's Office and copy in the AJS Papers. The date of their marriage license is given as September 4, 1866, and the Minister's Return is dated September 5, 1866, entry no. 8 (repeated in entry no. 11), Lyon County Marriage Books, Roll 7003464, KDLA. The original marriage bond and marriage license are housed among the records of the Lyon County Clerk's Office. Owen Benberry (public officials frequently misspelled the Benbray surname as Benberry, Benbrey, or Benbry, and the new spellings became permanent) secured the bond for Smith. Nearly twenty years later, Andy and Amanda Smith took her six-year-old cousin, Will Benberry, into their home. That her family may have lived in Birmingham was related to Andrew S. Bowman by descendants of the Young family. Her date of birth is given on her tombstone.

9. US Census, 1870, 1880. Dora's surname is not clearly spelled on the census form.

10. US Census, 1880; William Benberry included personal information in a deposition, Lyon County Circuit Court, Deposition of W. H. Benberry, August 4, 1902, Interrogatories filed August 6, 1902, Andrew Smith vs. R. L. Delaney, KDLA. Will was one of several children of Kitty and Owen Benberry. Why they sent Will to live with Andy and Amanda Smith is not known; Andrew Smith and Amanda Smith, Deed of Conveyance to William Hughey Benbrey [Benberry], November 10, 1892, Deed Book U: 606–607, Lyon County Clerk's Office; Lyon County Tax Assessment Book 1887, KDLA.

11. Lyon County Tax Assessment Book 1867, KDLA. That the Smiths might have farmed land belonging to a relative of Amanda was related to Andrew S. Bowman by a descendant of the Young family.

12. Ibid., 1868, 1869.

13. For an informative description of tobacco cultivation in Lyon County, from which this account is derived, see Walker, *In Lyon County*, 134–142.

14. Ibid.; Hambleton Tapp and James C. Klotter, *Kentucky: Decades of Discord, 1865–1900* (Frankfort: Kentucky Historical Society, 1977), 296; James O. Nall, *The Tobacco Night Riders of Kentucky and Tennessee, 1905–1909*, Kentucky Bicentennial Edition, 1792–1992 (1939; Kuttawa, KY: McClanahan House, 1991), 5; Henry, *Land Between the Rivers*, 69–70.

15. Lyon County Tax Assessment Book 1870, KDLA; US Agricultural Census of 1870, Lyon County, Kentucky, KDLA.

16. Lyon County Tax Assessment Book 1871, KDLA.

17. Between the Rivers residents Ray and Shara Parish guided the authors to the remains of Smith's house and farm in March 2007.

18. Walker, *In Lyon County*, 131.

19. Ibid., 171–174.

20. Lyon County Tax Assessment Books 1872, 1873, KDLA.

21. H. M. Hanson vs. Andy Smith, Lyon County Circuit Court, 1874, KDLA.

22. Lyon County Tax Assessment Book 1874, KDLA.

23. Ibid., 1875.

24. Andrew Smith vs. N. C. Gray and James Shuff, November 1875, Lyon County Circuit Court, KDLA.

25. Ibid.; Lyon County Circuit Court Order Book E: 1872–1876:456–457, 459, KDLA.

26. Ibid.

27. Lyon County Tax Assessment Book 1879, KDLA.

28. Ibid., 1880.

29. Andrew Jackson Smith Pension File, Certificate no. 488.807, RG 15, NARA. The occasion of Smith's hip injury is described in a general affidavit dated July 19, 1890.

30. Ibid. The dates for Smith's medical treatment for war-related ailments between 1868

and 1888 are given on an undated form, possibly for the year 1888, "Claimant's Statement in Compliance with Circular No. 62 of the Pension Office." Smith or his physicians attributed the hearing loss in his left ear to having been hit in the head by a minié ball at Shiloh, but it is far more likely the hearing loss resulted from his frequent proximity to artillery fire while serving on Morris and Folly Islands.

31. In 1882, Congress provided full and prorated pensions for Union soldiers "disabled by reason of any wound received or disease contracted while in the service of the United States, and in the line of duty." The maximum disability payment for noncommissioned officers and privates was eight dollars per month. For officers, maximum monthly payments extended from fifteen dollars for second lieutenants to thirty dollars for lieutenant colonels, colonels, and general officers. *Statutes at Large*, 12:566–569. The Bureau of Pensions instructed that miscellaneous disabilities be rated in fractions of eighteen dollars. Smith was originally given a disability rating of four-eighteenths on December 31, 1887. His disability rating was increased to six-eighteenths and his monthly pension to six dollars on July 26, 1890. Andrew Jackson Smith Pension File, RG 15, NARA.

32. Lyon County Tax Assessment Books 1881–1882, 1884–1892, 1895, KDLA.

33. Ibid., 1881–1891.

34. Ewing Benberry to Andrew S. Bowman, July 3, 1995; Newt Benberry, contributing to an interview of Ewing Benberry by W. Robert Beckman and Sharon S. MacDonald, August 8, 2001. Newt Benberry joined the interview of Ewing Benberry in progress; Kentucky County Court Order Patent no. 54825, Land Office, Kentucky Secretary of State; Willard Rouse Jillson, *The Kentucky Land Grants* (Louisville: Standard Printing, 1925), 1711.

35. Deed Commissioner's Book, 1:438–440, Lyon County Clerk's Office. The $1 difference in the purchase price of $858 and the payment of $857 is the result of an accounting error in the bank notes.

36. Lyon County Tax Assessment Books 1881–1886, KDLA.

37. Ibid., 1887–1890.

38. Ibid., 1891–1900.

39. A description of the Smiths's new homesite and farm, which came to be called the Andy Smith tract in subsequent land transactions, is given in, *D. L. Nowlin vs. Andrew Smith*, 1909, Lyon County Circuit Court, KDLA; [Fox], *Record of the Service*, handwritten notation opposite p. 118, Association of Officers of the 55th Massachusetts Volunteer Infantry Records, 1864–1904, MHS.

40. Documentation for most of Andy Smith's land transactions in Lyon County is missing. Only those deeds recorded in the office of the county clerk survive, eight documenting the purchase and twelve the sale of land. Before the advent of modern transportation, the recording of deeds for those living Between the Rivers could be arduous, entailing hours of travel, perhaps a day or more, and crossing the Cumberland River. Furthermore, there was no compulsion to do so beyond the legal protection gained by registering one's deed. Deeds might not be presented to the county clerk for weeks, months, or even years, and sometimes never.

41. We have no record of these individual land transactions, nor do we know the profit Smith derived, but his increased valuations reveal he was selling land and using some of the proceeds to purchase land of greater value. Even in the years for which Smith's land deeds were recorded, it is evident from the tax assessments that other, unrecorded land transactions continued to be made. Smith's 1886 tax assessment, for example, reveals he held 267 acres of land, 10 fewer acres than in 1885, but no deed accounts for this decline in acreage. Meanwhile, the valuation of his remaining land increased by $70 to $1,164, sug-

gesting he might have sold land and purchased a similar amount of greater value. In August, more than one month after the 1886 tax assessment, Smith purchased 258 acres for $1,000 and sold 69¾ acres for $69.75, transactions for which deeds survive, yielding an interim total of 447¼ acres. But the records for the following year reveal the figure is too low to account for all of Smith's acreage. In April 1887, prior to that year's tax assessment, a deed documents Smith's sale of 366½ acres of his own land for $2,932 and an additional 239 acres belonging to a third party for $956. Smith's remaining land, based on the evidence in the deed and the county tax book, would have totaled only 80¾ acres, but the land in his possession just two or three months later, at the time of his annual tax assessment, was 332 acres, an increase of 55 acres over his 1886 assessment. Meanwhile, the assessed value increased by $460 to $1,584. The pattern continues for the remainder of the years Smith held land in Lyon County.

42. Deed Book K: 69–70, August 15, 1891, Lyon County Clerk's Office.

43. Lyon County Tax Assessment Books 1880–1911, KDLA.

44. *John Kimmel and Felix Rudolph vs. Andy Smith*, 1888, Lyon County Circuit Court, KDLA

45. Ibid.

46. *Sligo Iron Stove Company vs. Andrew Smith and T. J. Nickell*, 1895, Lyon County Circuit Court, KDLA.

47. *Andrew Smith vs. R. L. Dulaney*, 1895, Lyon County Circuit Court, KDLA.

48. Ibid.

49. *Andrew Smith vs. Alfred Doom*, 1901, Lyon County Circuit Court, KDLA.

CHAPTER 10: HARD TIMES

1. Lyon County Tax Assessment Books 1900, 1904, 1907, 1909, 1911, KDLA. The other tax assessment books from the early decades of the century do not survive. His homestead, part of the land he purchased in 1889, came to be known as the Andy Smith Tract and comprised 164 acres.

2. Nall, *The Tobacco Night Riders,* was the standard work for decades; Christopher Waldrep, *Night Riders: Defending Community in the Black Patch, 1890–1915* (Durham, NC: Duke University Press, 1993) is a subtle treatment of the night rider phenomenon placed in the context of social history.

3. Waldrep, *Night Riders,* 140–149. For night rider activity in the vicinity of Lyon County, see Wright, *Racial Violence in Kentucky,* 136–141. In George C. Wright, *A History of Blacks in Kentucky,* vol. 2, *In Pursuit of Equality, 1890–1980* (Frankfort: Kentucky Historical Society, 1992), 5, the author mistakenly asserts, "By 1908 no blacks remained in Lyon." The 1908 tax assessment for Lyon County does not survive, but the 1909 assessment recorded 333 black heads of households, of whom 142 owned land. The 1910 Census recorded 1,799 blacks in Lyon County. US Census, https://www2.census.gov/library/publications/decennial/1910/volume-2/volume-2-p7.pdf.

4. Newt Benberry, contributing to an oral history interview of Ewing Benberry by W. Robert Beckman and Sharon S. MacDonald, August 8, 2001; Nancy J. Dawson, taped interview of former residents of Grand Rivers, July 1, 2006, AJS Papers.

5. *D. L. Nowlin vs. Andrew Smith,* 1909, Lyon County Circuit Court, KDLA.

6. Ibid. Andy Smith's childhood friend, sometimes business partner, and first cousin B. F. (Benjamin Franklin) Smith (a son of Andy's uncle Edward J. Smith) also secured the sale bond for the property on July 29, 1909. J. M. Smith was a son of B. F. Smith and the nephew of W. D. (William Albert) Smith, one of B. F. Smith's younger brothers. B. F. Smith, J. M. Smith, and George. W. Dixon were among the signers of a sterling character reference for

Andy Smith, dated June 3, 1913, that Smith had sent to Burt G. Wilder. J. M. Smith should not be confused with his uncle, James Maison Smith. George W. Dixon's name was misspelled as Dickson in the court document describing the property's changes of ownership.

7. Lyon County, Kentucky, Tax Assessment Books, 1909, 1911, KDLA. The 1911 book is the last surviving tax assessment record dating from the years Smith lived in Lyon County.

8. W. E. Jolly et al. to W. H. Benberry, Lot 7 with House, Block 20 Northwest, Grand Rivers, June 26, 1905, J. M. Worter to William Benberry, Lots 1–6, Block 20 Northwest, Grand Rivers, October 7, 1905, Deed Book 35, pp. 588–591; Edward H. and Maude Walker to Andy Smith, Lot 5, Block 21 Northwest, Grand Rivers, Kentucky, April 28, 1910, Deed Book 50, page 338, Livingston County, Kentucky Clerk's Office. Certificate of Character from Neighbors of Andrew J. Smith, June 3, 1913, Wilder Papers. In part, it is difficult to date precisely Smith's move to Grand Rivers because Grand Rivers had been his mailing address since the 1890s. A pension form dated September 6, 1912, gives his residence as Lyon County. Andrew Jackson Smith Pension File, RG 15, NARA. An unsigned letter from the Hillman Land Company to E. H. Simmons, October 3, 1926, reveals that the Andy Smith Tract was in the company's possession in 1917, seemingly for the entire year. Hillman Papers, University Archives & Special Collections, Woodward Library, Austin Peay State University, Clarksville, TN.

9. Andrew J. Smith to The County Board of Education, Lyon County, Kentucky, May 9, 1915, Deed Book Z, 590–591, Lyon County Clerk's Office; Ray Parish, "Civil War Hero Buried at Oakland Cemetery," *Between the Rivers* 7 (Spring 2000): 5–6.

10. Andrew S. Bowman, interview, September 29, 2001, AJS Papers; the date of Amanda Smith's death is given on her tombstone; Gertrude Catlett to Andy Smith, Letters, AJS Papers.

11. Andrew S. Bowman, interview, September 29, 2001, AJS Papers; the dates of Laculian's and Gertrude's births and deaths are given on their shared tombstone.

12. The 1910 US Census records identify Ruth (as Caruth was often called as a child and young woman) Smith, granddaughter, living with the Catlett family in Princeton, Indiana. The census taker for Lyon County recorded Geneva's name as America and listed Nellie Meyers, eighteen, as a servant, private family housekeeper, and Will as a hired man, a description no more appropriate for Will's relation to Smith than that used by the 1880 census taker who categorized Dora as a servant.

13. Andrew Jackson Smith Pension File, October 1892–January 1907, RG 15, NARA. The length of Smith's pensionable service was two years, three months, and four days.

14. Ibid.; Dependent and Disability Pension Act, June 27, 1890, *Statutes at Large*, 26:182.

15. An Act Granting Pensions, February 6, 1907, *Statutes at Large*, 34:879. For the experiences African American and immigrant veterans encountered as they engaged the pension system, see Larry M. Logue and Peter Blank, *Race, Ethnicity, and Disability: Veterans and Benefits in Post–Civil War America* (New York: Cambridge University Press, 2010). To gain appreciation of the variety and depth of information found in the pension files of black Civil War veterans, see Elizabeth Regosin and Donald R. Shaffer, eds., *Voices of Emancipation: Understanding Slavery, the Civil War, and Reconstruction through the U. S. Pension Bureau Files* (New York: New York University Press, 2008).

16. The new pension law was approved to commence on March 13, 1907. Declaration for Pension, March 11, 1907, with approval given on the form, Act of February 6, 1907, signed October 31, 1907, Andrew Jackson Smith Pension File, RG 15, NARA.

17. Declaration for Pension, September 6, 1912; letter, Commissioner [Bureau of Pensions] to Andrew Smith, January 10, 1913; Affidavit of Andrew Smith, January 20, 1913, Andrew Jackson Smith Pension File, RG 15, NARA.

18. Affidavit of Andrew Smith, January 20, 1913, Andrew Jackson Smith Pension File, RG 15, NARA.

19. Form letter, Commissioner [Bureau of Pensions] to Andrew Smith, February 15, 1913. Willis E. Jolly, Smith's notary, affirmed that the Roster of Enlisted Men, as published in *Record of the Service of the 55th Regiment of Massachusetts Volunteers,* gave Smith's age as twenty on his enlistment in May 1863. Willis E. Jolly to Commissioner of Pensions, July 3, 1913. The form letter may have been sent in response to Jolly's letter. G. M. Saltzgaber, Commissioner of Pensions to Andrew Smith, October 15, 1913. No reply to Jolly is in Smith's pension file. All sources in Andrew Jackson Smith Pension File, RG 15, NARA.

20. Andy Smith to G. M. Saltzgaber, Comm. of Pensions, [no date]; [G. M. Saltzgaber] Commissioner to Director of the Census, November 7, 1913; William J. Harris, Director, Bureau of the Census to The Commissioner of Pensions, December 13, 1913; Pension forms, Act of May 1912. All sources in Andrew Jackson Smith Pension File, RG 15, NARA.

21. Smith's monthly pension increase at age seventy-five, under the Pension Act of May 11, 1912, was to have been thirty-five dollars, but the Pension Act of June 10, 1918, raised the payment to forty dollars. US Department of the Interior, *Report of the Commissioner of Pensions to the Secretary of the Interior for the Fiscal Year ended June 30, 1918* (Washington, DC: US Government Printing Office, 1918), 11–12. The Pension Act of July 3, 1926, increased his monthly pension that year to sixty-five dollars, but it also provided for pensions of seventy-two dollars for veterans so nearly helpless or blind as to need or require the regular aid and attention of another person, and to ninety dollars if totally helpless or blind. On October 4, Smith's pension increased to seventy-two dollars. US Department of the Interior, *Report of the Commissioner of Pensions to the Secretary of the Interior 1926* (Washington, DC: US Government Printing Office, 1926), 3. The Pension Act of July 3, 1926, increased to ninety dollars the disability pension set at seventy-two dollars in the Pension Act of May 1, 1920. US Department of the Interior, *Report of the Commissioner of Pensions to the Secretary of the Interior for the Fiscal Year ended June 30, 1921* (Washington, DC: US Government Printing Office, 1921), 4–5. Andrew Jackson Smith, Certificate of Death, gave his age as eighty-eight years, six months, one day, March 4, 1932, Bureau of Vital Statistics, Commonwealth of Kentucky, March 4, 1932. Smith's pension increases are given on forms, Act of May 11, 1912, and Act of May 1, 1920, and Andrew Jackson Smith Pension File, RG 15, NARA.

22. Edward H. Beardsley, "The American Scientist as Social Activist: Franz Boas, Burt G. Wilder, and the Cause of Racial Justice, 1900–1915," *Isis* 64, no. 1 (March 1973): 50–66; Richard M. Reid, ed., *Practicing Medicine in a Black Regiment: The Civil War Diary of Burt G. Wilder, 55th Massachusetts* (Amherst: University of Massachusetts Press, 2010), 13–16.

23. For Wilder's refuting the writings of popular writers Owen Wister and Margaret Deland and scientists Robert E. Bean and Robert W. Shufeldt, see Beardsley, "American Scientist," 55–58. Beardsley noted that when Wilder sought to publish a critical review of Shufeldt's book, *America's Greatest Problem: the Negro* (1915), in *Science,* the editor, James McKeen Cattell, required Wilder to shorten the review's length and "also thought it improper 'to take up in *Science* the social relations, etc. of the Negro.'"

24. Burt G. Wilder, "The Brain of the American Negro," in *Proceedings of the National Negro Congress,* May 31–June 1, 1909 (New York: National Negro Congress, 1909): 22–66, quotations on pp. 21 and 40.

25. Ibid., 22.

26. Burt G. Wilder, "Two Examples of the Negro's Courage, Physical and Moral," address at the Garrison Centenary, December 10, 1905 (Boston: Charles Alexander, 1906), repr. from *Alexander's Magazine* 1 (January 1906): 22–28.

27. Wilder had never ceased gathering information about the regiment. Over the decades, he had corresponded with fellow veterans, both officers and enlisted men, to fill in missing facts and clarify ambiguities. He had traveled to Charleston to map the battlefield at Rivers' Causeway and consult with Confederate veterans of the engagement. Upon retirement, he edited, annotated, and made a typescript of his wartime letters to his fiancée.

28. Andrew J. Smith to Burt G. Wilder, February 12, 1913, Wilder Papers.

29. Burt G. Wilder to Andrew J. Smith, February 15, 1913, AJS Papers.

30. Ibid.; Burt Wilder to Andrew J. Smith, June 8, 1913, AJS Papers. In this letter, Wilder notes that he had written Smith on March 23 and 26, 1917, but had received no reply. No letters from Wilder with these dates are in the AJS Papers.

31. Andrew J. Smith to Burt Wilder, March 22, 1913, Wilder Papers.

32. The sketch of Smith's life dated June 1913, Wilder Papers, was not dictated by Smith. It is a third-person account that contains numerous errors of fact about Smith's life in the army and must be used carefully as a source.

33. Certificate of Character from Neighbors of Andrew J. Smith, June 3, 1913, Wilder Papers. "P. M." after the name T. T. Handberry likely stands for postmaster.

34. Burt Wilder to Andrew J. Smith, August 17, 1913, AJS Papers.

35. Andrew Jackson Smith to Burt Wilder, November 9, 1914, Wilder Papers.

36. Burt Wilder, "The 55th Massachusetts Volunteer Infantry, Colored," address presented to the Brookline Historical Society, May 8, 1914, Wilder Papers. The address was printed as a leaflet in 1914 and later revised with the addition of footnotes.

37. Burt Wilder, letter to the editor, *National Tribune*, December 10, 1914. Wilder was correcting the contents of an address delivered by Charles Colcock Jones Jr. before the Survivors' Society of Augusta on April 26, 1884, and printed in the *National Tribune* on November 26, 1914.

38. *National Tribune*, April 27, 1916.

39. No government official was designated to receive Medal of Honor recommendations, and it is understandable that Wilder wrote Saltzgaber. Wilder wanted his recommendation to be received not by the Bureau of Pensions but by the War Department's Records and Pensions Office that housed the military service records used to verify both Medal of Honor recommendations and pension applications. Saltzgaber, as commissioner of pensions, retained oversight of all federal pensions, civilian and military, and forwarded Wilder's recommendation. By 1916, when Wilder submitted the recommendation, the Records and Pension Office and the Adjutant General's Office had merged.

40. Wilder's letter to Smith does not survive. Andrew Jackson Smith to Burt Wilder, December 14, 1916, Wilder Papers. The Record and Pension Office, as a branch of the US War Department, maintained government service records for decades. From 1889 to 1904, it handled records for veterans of the Civil War, Indian Wars, and Spanish-American War. Unlike Smith, Wilder's intent in recommending him for the Medal of Honor was twofold: "to secure for him a medal of gallantry and an extra ten dollars a month pension." Burt G. Wilder to Charles E. Grant, February 19, 1917, Wilder Papers.

41. Andrew Jackson Smith to Burt Wilder, January 18, 1917, and June 20, 1917, Wilder Papers. The last army Civil War Medals of Honor were awarded in 1917. US Army Center of Military History, Medal of Honor Recipients Statistics, accessed January 4 2020, http://www.history.army.mil/moh/mohstats.html. The last navy Medal of Honor was awarded for a Civil War action in 1916.

42. In addition to Lieutenant Ellsworth, Captain George E. Gouraud, a member of Major General Foster's staff, and Lieutenant O. W. Bennett, 102nd USCT, received the Medal of Honor for actions at Honey Hill.

43. Burt G. Wilder to G. M. Saltzgaber, Commissioner of Pensions, December 21, 1916, File #2511990, RG 94, NARA and AJS Papers.

44. Adjutant General Henry P. McCain to Burt G. Wilder, January 5, 1917, File #2511990, RG 94, NARA and AJS Papers.

45. For Hartwell's report, see *OR*, 44:432.

46. Burt Wilder to Andrew Jackson Smith, January 13, 1917. A copy of the letter is preserved in the Wilder Papers. Before learning of the Adjutant General's rejection of his application, Smith wrote Wilder, January 5, 1917, providing the names of Captain Thomas Ellsworth and Corporal Richard Warrick as witnesses to his saving the colors. Smith's reply to Wilder's January 13, 1917, letter is dated January 18, 1917. Wilder Papers.

47. Burt Wilder to Andrew Jackson Smith, February 5, 1917, AJS Papers.

48. Burt Wilder to Andrew Jackson Smith, January 23, 1917; James Thurber to Burt G. Wilder, January 25, 1917; William DuPree to Burt Wilder, January 25, 1917; David Lee to Andrew Jackson Smith, April 8, 1917, AJS Papers. Wilder forwarded Thurber's and DuPree's letters to Smith.

49. Vespasian Warner to Burt Wilder, March 10, 1917, Wilder Papers.

50. Burt G. Wilder to Andrew Jackson Smith, April 17, 1917, reporting he had written a fourth letter to Grant; Charles E. Grant to Burt G. Wilder, April 20, 1917, AJS Papers. Wilder forwarded Grant's letter to Smith.

51. Burt Wilder to Andrew Jackson Smith [no date, but not written before April 23, 1917], retained copy, Wilder Papers.

52. Jordon M. Bobson affidavit, May 14, 1917, Wilder Papers.

53. Andrew Jackson Smith to Burt Wilder, June 20, 1917, Wilder Papers.

54. Andrew Jackson Smith to Burt Wilder, March 4, 1918, Wilder Papers. "Dr. Burt G. Wilder, Famous Member of Cornell's First Staff, Dies in Massachusetts," *Cornell Alumni News* 27, no. 18 (January 29, 1925): 223–224.

55. Burt G. Wilder, *The 55th Massachusetts Volunteer Infantry, Colord* [sic], *June, 1863 September, 1865* (Brookline, MA: Riverdale Press, August 1917), n10. A third edition revised by the addition of an appendix appeared in 1919, n21, Wilder Papers.

CHAPTER 11: THE SECOND TIME AROUND: GRAND RIVERS

1. Andrew J. Smith to Burt Wilder, February 12, 1913, Wilder Papers. Smith's purchase of a house on February 26, 1914, establishes the approximate time of his move to Grand Rivers. C. W. Bell to Geneva and Ruth [Caruth] Smith, February 26, 1914, Deed Book 41:394, Livingston County Clerk's Office, Smithland's Landing, KY.

2. Henry, *Land Between the Rivers*, 174–175; Frank E. Smith, *Land Between the Lakes* (Lexington: University Press of Kentucky, 1971), 39–41; Betty Joe Wallace, *Between the Rivers: History of the Land Between the Lakes* (Clarksville, TN: Austin Peay State University, Center for Field Biology, Dept. of History and Philosophy, 1992), 171; Shelley Nickell, "The Town That Could not Prosper," *Between the Rivers*, no. 12 (Summer 2002): 19–21.

3. W. Jolly and others to W. H. Benberry, June 26, 1905, Deed Book 35:588; J. M. Worten to Wm. Benberry, October 7, 1905, Deed Book 35:590–591; W. H. Benberry to Nelson Gibson, February 5, 1909, Deed Book 35:236–237, Livingston County Clerk's Office.

4. C. W. Bell and Fannie Bell to Geneva and Ruth [Caruth] Smith, February 26, 1914, Deed Book 41:394; George W. Dixon to Jennie [Geneva] and Ruth [Caruth] Smith, May 18, 1914, Deed Book 41:396; George W. Dixon to Jennie [Geneva] and Ruth [Caruth] Smith, May 20, 1914, Deed Book 42:118; George W. Dixon to Jennie [Geneva] and Ruth [Caruth] Smith, December 21, 1916, Deed Book 41:398, Livingston County Clerk's Office.

5. The estimate of approximately twenty-five families resident in Grand Rivers was given in an interview of former residents who lived there as children in the 1920s and 1930s, one of whom, Hattie Benberry, knew Andy Smith. A video copy of the interview, conducted by Nancy J. Dawson, on July 1, 2006, is in the AJS Papers.

6. C. W. Bell to Andy Smith, August 14, 1920, Deed Book 50:337; E. E. Redd and Minnie Redd to Andy Smith, June 6, 1923, Deed Book 50:376, Livingston County Clerk's Office.

7. L. E. Hurt to E. E. Redd, Deed Book 41:498; for land in Block 4 belonging to Andy Smith described as being within an enclosure, see Ruth Lawson, Henry Lawson, Geneva Lawson, Henry Lawson to United States of America, October 11, 1938, Deed Book 61:458–464, beginning at GIR–702, Livingston County Clerk's Office.

8. Andy Smith, Ruth [Caruth] Robinson, Geneva Shelton, and Henry Shelton to Arthur Benberry, December 14, 1928, Deed Book 59:293, Livingston County Clerk's Office.

9. Andrew S. Bowman, interview, September 29, 2001, AJS Papers.

10. Dolores Shelton Brown, interview by Sharon S. MacDonald, August 16, 2007, AJS Papers.

11. Ewing Benberry, interview by W. Robert Beckman and Sharon S. MacDonald, August 8, 2001; Dolores S. Brown, interview, August 16, 2007, AJS Papers.

12. Golda Bell Ramage Beaman, interview by Sharon S. MacDonald, May 21, 2003, AJS Papers.

13. Mary White, interview by Andrew S. Bowman, September 19, 2004, AJS Papers.

14. Hattie Benberry, interview by Nancy J. Dawson, July 1, 2006, AJS Papers.

15. Dolores S. Brown, interview, August 16, 2007, AJS Papers.

16. Ibid.

17. J. W. Robinson, Affidavit of Attending Physician, October 13, 1926, Andrew Jackson Smith Pension File, RG 15, NARA.

18. Andrew Jackson Smith to the Commissioner of Pensions, December 19, 1928, Andrew Jackson Smith Pension File, RG 15, NARA.

19. William Benberry, Affidavit of Attendant, October 4, 1926, Andrew Jackson Smith Pension File, RG 15, NARA; Ewing Benberry, interview August 8, 2001, AJS Papers.

20. Andrew Jackson Smith, Certificate of Death, Bureau of Vital Statistics, Commonwealth of Kentucky, March 4, 1932; Dolores S. Brown, interview, August 16, 2007, AJS Papers.

CHAPTER 12: RECLAIMING THE LEGACY

1. Caruth Smith Washington, Biographical Introduction, 9. Caruth wrote her introduction in the third person. Caruth Smith Washington, videotape interview, July 16, 2001, AJS Papers.

2. Andrew S. Bowman, interview, September 29, 2001, AJS Papers.

3. Marriage certificate of Henry Shelton and Geneva Smith, November 28, 1923, Clay County, Indiana; marriage certificate of Richard Robinson and Ruth Smith, July 30, 1923, Clay County, Indiana. A deed of April 13, 1929, between Ruth Smith Robinson, Geneva Smith Shelton, Andy Smith, and Henry Shelton identified "Ruth Robinson" as "a single lady, Detroit Michigan." AJS Papers. As a child and young woman, Caruth used the name Ruth.

4. Caruth Smith Washington, Biographical Introduction, 9, AJS Papers.

5. Wardner H. Jones Funeral Home, 417 Jefferson Avenue, Buffalo, NY.

6. As late as 1971–72, Caruth served as New York Department president for the Ladies of the Grand Army of the Republic.

7. Norman Hodges to W. Robert Beckman, March 10, 2003, email correspondence, AJS Pa-

pers. Norman Hodges, PhD, was an associate professor of Africana studies and history at Vassar College from 1969 to 1998.

8. Ibid.

9. Geneva's "Journal," AJS Papers.

10. Hodges to Beckman, March 10, 2003, AJS Papers.

11. Andrew S. Bowman, Journal, entry under Susan Geneva Smith Shelton, AJS Papers.

12. Andrew S. Bowman, interview, September 29, 2001, AJS Papers. This interview is the source for the remainder of this chapter.

CHAPTER 13: PASSING THE TORCH

1. Andrew S. Bowman, interview, September 29, 2001, AJS Papers.

2. Andrew S. Bowman, interview, September 29, 2001, AJS Papers; *National Tribune*, December 10, 1914.

3. A letter from Katherine Dhalle to Sharon S. MacDonald, March 24, 2013, AJS Papers, and the accounts of Andrew and Esther Bowman are the sources for the following paragraphs continuing until Dhalle's and the Bowmans' first meeting at the National Archives.

4. The Andrew Bowman interview, September 29, 2001, AJS Papers, is the source for most of the remainder of this chapter. It is supplemented by other sources that are identified by notes.

5. Reports of Clerks, Adjutant General's Office, File #2511990, RG 94, NARA.

6. Wilbert H. Luck, *Journey to Honey Hill* (Washington, DC: Wiluk Press, 1976), 84. An early work, perhaps the first written about the battle, it was not subjected to professional review and editing and must be used with caution. Nonetheless, it played a notable role in advancing Andrew Bowman's search for the missing evidence. The citation in the notes to Andy Smith's saving the flag, while crediting C. B. Fox, did not identify Lieutenant Colonel Fox nor adequately reference Fox's regimental history, so those unfamiliar with the regiment or its records would have difficulty finding the source.

7. [Fox], *Record of the Service*, Preface, 43.

8. Katherine Dhalle to Sharon S. MacDonald, April 6, 2013, AJS Papers.

9. Ibid.

10. US Department of Defense, *Manual of Military Decorations and Awards*, DOD 1348.33–M, July 30, 1990. Time limitations were established in 1918: *Statutes at Large*, 40, pt. 1: 871, Act of July 9, 1918.

11. David Bowman, Reflections about Andrew Jackson Smith, October 2, 2019, AJS Papers.

12. Brigadier General Adelbert Ames recommended Anderson for the Medal of Honor as part of a group of thirteen volunteers who advanced to clear palisading from their regiment's path at Fort Fisher, January 15, 1865, but the recommendation was soon lost, only to be found around 1890. In 1914, Anderson and the three other remaining survivors of the group, represented by an attorney, petitioned to receive the medal.

13. Ibid.

14. Andrew S. Bowman, Journal, entry under Cynthia Middleton, AJS Papers; Entry no. 86, 55th Massachusetts Descriptive Book, RG 94, NARA.

15. General Orders No. 3, January 31, 1865, 55th Massachusetts Order Book, RG 94, NARA; Andrew S. Bowman, interview, September 29, 2001, AJS Papers.

16. Special Order No. 17, February 8, 1865, 55th Massachusetts Order Book, RG 94, NARA.

17. National Defense Authorization Act for Fiscal Year 1996, Public Law 104–106, Section 526: Procedure for Consideration of Military Decorations Not Previously Submitted in Timely Fashion, *Statutes at Large* 110 (February 10, 1996): 186, 313–314.

18. Andrew S. Bowman, Journal, AJS Papers.

19. Ibid.

CHAPTER 14: THE QUEST FOR RECONSIDERATION

1. *Statutes at Large*, 33, pt. 1:274–275, April 23, 1904.

2. Reports of Clerks, Adjutant General's Office, and File #2511990, RG 94, NARA.

3. Sergeant Robert King, Co. K, 55th Massachusetts Infantry (Col'd.), Compiled Military Service Record, RG 94, NARA.

4. The clerk made careless recording errors. His complete notation read, "Robert King is reported sgt of Co B [*sic*, Co. K] Killed in action while carrying the Colors Nov. 30, [18]64 at Honey Hill[.] Claimant is reported as sgt 'D. D. [detached duty] Color' Sgt on April 30, [18]64 [*sic*, February 28, 1865] roll." Reports of Clerks, Adjutant General's Office, File #2511990, RG 94, NARA.

5. Sergeant Andrew Smith, Co. B, 55th Massachusetts Infantry (Col'd.), Compiled Military Service Record, RG 94. NARA; Reports of Clerks, Adjutant General's Office, File #2511990, RG 94, NARA.

6. Entry no. 86, 55th Massachusetts Descriptive Book, RG 94, NARA.

7. General Orders No. 3, January 31, 1865, 55th Massachusetts Order Book; 55th Massachusetts Company B Order Book, RG 94, NARA.

8. Special Order No. 17, February 8, 1865, 55th Massachusetts Order Book, RG 94, NARA.

9. Department of Defense, *Manual of Military Decorations and Awards*, DOD 1348.33–M (September 1996), 17: C2.2.3.1.

10. Ibid.

11. Arthur S. Link, *Wilson: The New Freedom* (Princeton, NJ: Princeton University Press, 1954), 243–254.

12. Thomas W. Ewing, Republican, represented the Fifteenth Congressional District of Illinois from July 2, 1991, until he retired January 3, 2001.

13. Thomas W. Ewing to Robert Beckman, July 29, 1997, AJS Papers.

14. Statement of Carol Fraker, October 25, 2004, AJS Papers.

15. Michelle Y. Cromwell, Congressional Coordinator, to the Honorable Thomas W. Ewing, September 8, 1997, AJS Papers. Medal of Honor legislation in the 1918 Army Appropriations Act established time limitations for awards of the US Army Medal of Honor. Medals of Honor, Distinguished Service-Crosses, and Distinguished Service-Medals, Act of July 9, 1918, *Statutes at Large*, 40, pt. 1:871. For the history of the Medal of Honor, see Dwight S. Mears, *The Medal of Honor: The Evolution of America's Highest Military Decoration* (Lawrence: University Press of Kansas, 2018).

16. National Defense Authorization Act for Fiscal Year 1996, Public Law 104–106, Section 526: Procedure for Consideration of Military Decorations Not Previously Submitted in Timely Fashion, *Statutes at Large* 110 (February 10, 1996): 186, 313–314.

17. Hearings on H.R. 2561/S. 1122, Before the Senate Subcommittee of the Committee on Appropriations, 106th Congress, 1st sess., May 11, 1999, 504.

18. Andrew S. Bowman, interview, September 29, 2001, AJS Papers.

CHAPTER 15: THE MEDAL OF HONOR

1. 106th Congress, 1st sess., September 14, 1999, H.R. 2858.

2. Waiving Time Limitation on Awarding Medal of Honor to Robert R. Ingram, H.R. 2813, 105th Cong., 1st sess., Congressional Record 143, pt. 17 (November 8, 1997): 25292–25294; Cong. Rec. 143, no. 156, daily ed. (November 8, 1997): H10406—H10409.

3. Bill Summary & Status, 106th Cong., 1st sess., H.R. 2858, All Congressional Actions (ac-

cessed January 4, 2010), accessed January 4, 2020, http://thomas.loc.gov/cgi-bin/bdquery/z?d106:HR02858:@@@X.

4. Mitchell Yockelson, "'I Am Entitled to the Medal of Honor and I Want It': Theodore Roosevelt and His Quest for Glory" *Prologue Magazine* 30, no.1 (Spring 1998): 7–19, https://www.archives.gov/publications/prologue/1998/spring/roosevelt-and-medal-of-honor-1.html.

5. Hearing Before the House Military Personnel Subcommittee of the Committee on National Security on The Awarding of the Medal of Honor to Theodore Roosevelt, 105th Cong., 2nd sess., 20 (September 28, 1998) (statement of Representative Rick Lazio).

6. House Military Personnel Subcommittee hearing, 25–26 (September 28, 1998); Bill Bleyer, "TR Wins Last Battle: Congress OKs Medal of Honor," *Newsday* (Melville, NY), Oyster Bay Edition, October 22, 1998.

7. H.R. 105–2263, July 25, 1997; Bleyer, "TR Wins Last Battle."

8. House Military Personnel Subcommittee hearing, 6–75 (September 28, 1998). For insight into the events surrounding the denial of Theodore Roosevelt's recommendation for the Medal of Honor in 1898, see Edward M. Coffman and Allan R. Millett, "Was Congress and President Bill Clinton Justified in Posthumously Awarding the Medal of Honor to Theodore Roosevelt? Two of America's Leading Military Historians Offer Their Opinions," *MHQ: The Quarterly Journal of Military History* 14, no. 3 (Spring 2002): 60–67.

9. Authorizing Award of Congressional Medal of Honor to Theodore Roosevelt, H.R. 2263, 105th Cong., 2nd sess., Cong. Rec. 144, pt. 17 (October 8, 1998): 24737–24742, 24766; Cong. Rec. 144, no. 140, daily ed. (October 8, 1998): H10121–H10126, H10149.

10. Senator Strom Thurmond of South Carolina, speaking on a proposal of a letter to the president to accompany H.R. 2263. Awarding the Medal of Honor Posthumously to Theodore Roosevelt, H.R. 2263, 105th Cong., 2nd sess., Cong. Rec. 144, pt. 19 (October 21, 1998): 27594; Cong. Rec. 144, no. 151 daily ed. (October 21, 1998): S12916–S12917.

11. H.R. 2263 became Public Law 105–371, November 12, 1998.

12. Representative Rick Lazio, press release, November 12, 1998. Enrico A. Lazio, Republican, represented New York's 2nd Congressional District from January 3, 1993, to January 3, 2001.

13. Sharon S. MacDonald to The Honorable Steve Buyer, November 11, 1999, AJS Papers.

14. Azura Domschke, "Family Fights for Medal for Civil War Hero: Relatives Puzzled by Buyer's Delays on Legislation," *Lafayette (IN) Journal and Courier*, November 6, 1999. See also Pete Falcone, "Medal of Honor for Black Civil War Soldier Stuck in Backlog," *Bloomington (IL) Pantagraph*, November 6, 1999.

15. Steve Buyer, "Medal will come in Proper Order," *Lafayette (IN) Journal and Courier*, November 16, 1999. This article was also published in the *Kokomo (IN) Tribune*, November 26, 1999, and the *Indianapolis Star*, December 5, 1999.

16. Richard Walton, "A Final Battle: Grandson Fights to Get Civil War Veteran the Medal of Honor," *Indianapolis Star*, November 12, 1999; Azura Domschke, "Medal of Honor Delay Upsets Vets," *Lafayette (IN) Journal and Courier*, November 6, 1999.

17. National Defense Authorization Act for Fiscal Year 2001, Sec. 531, Authority for Award of the Medal of Honor to Ed W. Freeman for Valor during the Vietnam Conflict; Sec. 532, Authority for Award of the Medal of Honor to Andrew J. Smith for Valor during the Civil War, H.R. 4205, 106th Congress, 2nd sess., Cong. Rec. 146, pt. 6 (May 17, 2000): 8152–8153; Cong. Rec. 146, no. 61, daily ed. (May 17, 2000): H3215.

18. Senator Daniel K. Akaka speaking in support of Award of Medal of Honor to Ed W. Freeman, James K. Okubo, and Andrew J. Smith, S. 2722, 106th Congress, 2nd sess., Cong.

Rec. 146, pt. 8 (June 13, 2000): 10491; Cong. Rec. 146, no. 73, daily ed. (June 13, 2000): S5057–S5058.

19. Ibid.; "Army Lists 21 Asian-Americans Who Will Receive Medal of Honor," Associated Press, May 13, 2000.

20. Award of Medal of Honor to Ed W. Freeman, James K. Okubo, and Andrew J. Smith, S. 2722, 106th Congress, 2nd sess., Cong. Rec. 146, pt. 8 (June 13, 2000): 10491; Cong. Rec. 146, no. 73, daily ed. (June 13, 2000): S5057–S5058.

21. Representative Steve Buyer speaking in support of Recognizing Award of Medal of Honor to President Theodore Roosevelt, 106th Cong., 2nd sess., Cong. Rec. 146, pt. 8 (June 13, 2000): 10603–10604; Cong. Rec., 165, no. 73, daily ed. (June 13, 2000): H4330.

22. "Teddy Roosevelt May Get Medal He Sought after Fighting in Cuba," *Pittsburgh Post-Gazette,* July 21, 2000.

23. Theodore Roosevelt Association, "Quest for the Medal of Honor," accessed January 4, 2020, http://archive.is/McTQ8.

24. Ibid.

25. Ibid.

26. Bill Bleyer, "Long, Rough Ride to the Medal: Roosevelt Will at Last Get Top Military Honor," *Newsday,* January 12, 2001.

27. Ibid.

28. There are a number of errors in Andrew Jackson Smith's official citation. Note that Smith served in the 55th Massachusetts Volunteer—not "Voluntary"—Infantry. The 55th Massachusetts advanced in the morning and charged around noon, not in "the late afternoon," nor did it pursue enemy skirmishers and conduct a "running fight." That was the work of Brigadier General Potter's division. Colonel Hartwell's 2nd Division, including the 55th, advanced, trailing in Potter's wake. The 55th and 54th Massachusetts did not form "columns to advance on the enemy position in a flanking movement," and "the 55th and 54th regiments" did not continue "to move into flanking positions." The 55th advanced forward toward the center front, while the 54th had been broken up before the 55th's charge at the Battle of Honey Hill: four companies at the intersection of the Boyd's Landing and River Road, two companies guarding the intersection at Bolan's Church, and two companies at the front, all having been separated from Hartwell's command. Smith did not carry the colors "throughout the battle"; he carried them after Sergeant Robert King had been killed. Confederate artillerists fired canister, not "grape," at Honey Hill. Finally, the charge of the 55th Massachusetts is not "called the Battle of Honey Hill."

29. Ibid. In November 2014, President Barack Obama awarded the Medal of Honor to Union Army First Lieutenant Alonzo Cushing for his actions at the Battle of Gettysburg, now the longest delay of the award at 151 years. David Vergun, "Obama: Medal of Honor Recipient Cushing's Courage Lives On in Soldiers Today," November 6, 2014, US Army, https://www.army.mil/article/137786.

30. White House, Office of the Press Secretary, Medal of Honor Ceremony Remarks of the President, January 16, 2001, accessed January 4, 2020, https://clintonwhitehouse6.archives.gov/.

31. Theodore Roosevelt Association, "Quest for the Medal of Honor," accessed January 4, 2020, http://archive.is/McTQ8.

BIBLIOGRAPHY

UNPUBLISHED PRIMARY SOURCES

Association of Officers of the 55th Massachusetts Volunteer Infantry records, 1864–1904. Massachusetts Historical Society, Boston.

De Saussure, Charles Alfred. "The Story of My Service in the Confederate Army." Nancy Peeples, private collection, Charleston, SC.

Emilio, Luis F. Records of the 54th Massachusetts Volunteer Infantry Regiment, 1863–1915. Massachusetts Historical Society, Boston.

Floyd, C. H. Letters. Abraham Lincoln Presidential Library, Springfield, IL.

41st Illinois Volunteer Infantry Papers. Kip A. Johnson, private collection, Effingham, IL.

Fox, Charles Barnard. "Records of the 55th Regiment Massachusetts Volunteer Infantry," manuscript, 2 vols. Records of the Association of Officers of the 55th Massachusetts Volunteer Infantry, 1864-1904. Massachusetts Historical Society, Boston.

———. "Extracts from Letters to my Wife during my connection with the 55th Regiment Massachusetts Volunteers," 3 vols. Charles Barnard Fox Papers, 1861–1865. Massachusetts Historical Society, Boston.

———. Papers, 1861–1865. Massachusetts Historical Society, Boston.

G. Marshall Naul Research Collection. South Caroliniana Library, University of South Carolina, Columbia.

Hartwell, Alfred S. Memoir. Miscellaneous Collections. US Military History Institute, Carlisle Barracks, Pennsylvania.

Hartwell, Colonel Alfred S. Papers. State Library of Massachusetts, Boston.

Henry, Dr. Joseph Milton. Papers. Austin Peay State University, University Archives & Special Collections, Woodward Library, Clarksville, Tennessee.

Hillman Company Papers. Austin Peay State University, University Archives & Special Collections, Woodward Library, Clarksville, Tennessee.

Jenkins, John. Personal Papers. South Carolina Department of Archives and History, Columbia.

Jones, Charles Colcock. Papers. Duke University, Rare Book, Manuscript, and Special Collections Library, Durham, North Carolina.

Kentucky County Records
  Caldwell County Deed Books, County Clerk's Office, Princeton, KY.
  Livingston County Deed Books, County Clerk's Office, Smithland, KY.
  Lyon County Deed Books, County Clerk's Office, Eddyville, KY.
  Lyon County Deed Commissioner's Books, County Clerk's Office, Eddyville, KY.
  Lyon County Marriage Books, County Clerk's Office, Eddyville, KY.
  Lyon County Marriage Register, County Clerk's Office, Eddyville, KY.
  Lyon County List of Slaves 1856–1859, County Clerk's Office, Eddyville, KY.
  Lyon County Will Books, County Clerk's Office, Eddyville, KY.
Kentucky County Court Order Patents, Kentucky Secretary of State, Land Office, Frankfort, KY.
Kentucky Department for Libraries and Archives (KDLA)
  Lyon County Tax Assessment Records:
        Microfilm: 1863–1875, 1879–1882, 1884–1892.
        Books: 1895, 1899, 1900, 1904, 1907, 1909, 1911.
  Lyon County Circuit Court Case Records.
  Lyon County Circuit Court Order Books.
Kinsley, Edward W. Papers. Duke University, Rare Book, Manuscript, and Special Collections Library, Durham, North Carolina.
Lee, Charles F. Papers, 1864–1865. South Caroliniana Library, University of South Carolina, Columbia.
Marcy, Dr. Henry O. "Diary of a Surgeon," 1864–1899. South Carolina Historical Society, Charleston.
Mrs. D. C. Freeman to Milo Custer, October 17, 1916. McLean County Museum of History, Bloomington, IL.
National Archives and Records Administration (NARA), Washington, DC
  Record Group 15, Records of the Veterans Administration
        Records of the Bureau of Pensions and its Predecessors 1805–1935.
  Record Group 29: Records of the Bureau of the Census
        Eighth Census of the United States, 1860, Microfilm M653.
        Slave Schedule 1860, Eighth Census of the United States, Microfilm M653.
        Ninth Census of the United States, 1870, Microfilm M593.
        US Agricultural Census, 1870, Lyon County, Kentucky, M1528: Roll 13.
        Tenth Census of the United States, 1880, Microfilm T9.
        Thirteenth Census of the United States, 1910, Microfilm T624
  Record Group 94: Records of the Adjutant General's Office, 1780s–1917
        African Brigade Order Book
        Compiled Military Service Records
        55th Massachusetts Volunteer Infantry Regimental Books
            Regimental Order Book.
            Company B Order Book.
            Descriptive Book.

Day Book.

Letter Book.

Record Group 105: Records of the Bureau of Refugees, Freedmen, and Abandoned Lands.

    Microfilm Publication 1904: Records of the Field Offices for the State of Kentucky, Bureau of Refugees, Freedmen, and Abandoned Lands, 1865–1872. Washington, DC: NARA, 2003.

Record Group 153: Records of the Office of the Judge Advocate General (Army) Records of the White House Office: Archived Clinton White House Virtual Library White House. Office of the Press Secretary. Medal of Honor Ceremony Remarks of the President, January 16, 2001. Accessed January 3, 2020. https://clintonwhitehouse6.archives.gov/.

Porcher, William Mazyck. Papers. South Caroliniana Library, University of South Carolina, Columbia.

Record of the Service of the 55th Regiment of Massachusetts Volunteer Infantry: Printed for the Regimental Association (1866). Massachusetts Historical Society, Boston.

Smith, Andrew Jackson. Papers. Abraham Lincoln Presidential Library, Springfield, Illinois

Stone, William Johnson. Papers. 1864–1953. University of Kentucky Library, Special Collections, Lexington.

Telegram from Secretary of War Edwin Stanton to William Schouler, Adjutant General of Massachusetts, July 16, 1863. Massachusetts National Guard Military Museum and Archives, Concord.

US Census Office. The statistics of the population of the United States : embracing the tables of race, nationality, sex, selected ages, and occupations ... compiled from the original returns of the ninth census, (June 1, 1870) under the direction of the Secretary of the Interior. Washington, DC: US Government Printing Office, 1872.

US Congress. 105th Cong., 1st sess., Congressional Record 143, pt. 17 (November 8, 1997).

US Congress. 105th Cong., 2nd sess., Congressional Record 144, pt. 17 (October 8, 1998); pt. 19 (October 21, 1998).

US Congress. 106th Congress, 2nd sess., Congressional Record 146, pt. 6 (May 17, 2000); pt. 8 (June 13, 2000).

US Congress. Senate Subcommittee of the Committee on Appropriations, Hearings on H.R. 2561/S. 1122, 106th Congress, 1st sess., May 11, 1999, 504. U.S. Government Printing Office, 1999.

US Department of Defense, *Manual of Military Decorations and Awards*, DOD 1348.33-M, September 1996, 17: C2.2: *Procedures Involving Recommendations for the MOH*: C2.2.3.1.

US Department of the Interior. *Report of the Commissioner of Pensions to the Secretary of the Interior for the Fiscal Year ended June 30, 1918.* Washington, DC:

US Government Printing Office, 1918.

US Department of the Interior. *Report of the Commissioner of Pensions to the Secretary of the Interior 1926.* Washington, DC: US Government Printing Office, 1926.

US Department of the Interior. *Report of the Commissioner of Pensions to the Secretary of the Interior for the Fiscal Year ended June 30, 1921.* Washington, DC: US Government Printing Office, 1921.

US Statutes at Large, 1789–1873.

Wilder, Burt Green. Papers. Cornell University, Carl A. Kroch Library, Division of Rare and Manuscript Collections, Ithaca, New York.

PUBLISHED PRIMARY SOURCES: ARTICLES

Bowditch, Charles B. "War Letters of Charles B. Bowditch." *Massachusetts Historical Society Proceedings* 57 (1924): 414–495.

Courtenay, William A. "Fragments of War History Relating to the Coast Defense of South Carolina, 1861–1865 and the Hasty Preparations for the Battle of Honey Hill, November 30, 1864." *Southern Historical Society Papers* 26 (1898): 62–87.

Garner, Chaplain John M. "History of the 18th Missouri Volunteer Infantry." *Unionville Republican,* 1892–1894. Putnam County Public Library, Unionville, Missouri.

Porcher, W. Mazych. "A Personal Memoir of W. Mazyck Porcher." *Charleston (SC) Weekly News,* August 16, 1882.

Soule, Charles C. "Battle of Honey Hill: A Federal Account of the Fight on Broad River, S.C., in 1864." *Philadelphia Weekly Times,* May 10 and 17, 1884.

Wilder, Burt G. "The Brain of the American Negro." *Proceedings of the National Negro Congress, May 31– June 1, 1909.* New York: National Negro Congress, 1909: 22–66.

———. "Two Examples of the Negro's Courage, Physical and Moral." Address at the Garrison Centenary, December 10, 1905. Boston: Charles Alexander Publisher, 1906. Reprinted from *Alexander's Magazine* 1 (January 1906): 22–28.

PUBLISHED PRIMARY SOURCES: BOOKS

Adams, Virginia Matzke, ed. *On the Altar of Freedom: A Black Soldier's Civil War Letters from the Front: Corporal James Henry Gooding.* Amherst: University of Massachusetts Press, 1991, 1999.

Berlin, Ira, Barbara J. Fields, Thavolia Glymph, Joseph P. Reidy, and Leslie S. Rowland, eds. *Freedom: A Documentary History of Emancipation, 1861–1867: Selected from the Holdings of the Archives of the United States.* Ser. 1, vol. 1, *Freedom: The Destruction of Slavery.* New York: Cambridge University Press, 1985.

Childs, Arney Robinson, ed. *The Private Journal of Henry William Ravenel.* Columbia: University of South Carolina Press, 1948.

Dahlgren, Madeleine Vinton. *Memoir of John A. Dahlgren Rear-Admiral United States Navy.* Boston: James R. Osgood, 1882.

Dicey, Edward. *Six Months in the Federal States,* 2 vols. London: Macmillan, 1863.

Douglass, Frederick. *Narrative of the Life of Frederick Douglass, An American Slave. Written by Himself.* Boston: Published at the Anti-Slavery Office, 1845. In *The Frederick Douglass Papers,* ser. 2: *Autobiographical Writings.* Vol. 1, *Narrative.* Edited by John W. Blassingame et al. New Haven, CT: Yale University Press, 1999.

Ferguson, William. *America by River and Rail; or, Notes by the Way on the New World and Its People.* London: James Nisbet, 1856.

Hallowell, Norwood P. *The Negro as a Soldier in the War of the Rebellion.* Boston: Little, Brown, 1897.

Johns, Jane Martin. *Personal Recollections of Early Decatur, Abraham Lincoln, Richard Oglesby and the Civil War.* Edited by Howard C. Schaub. Decatur, IL: Decatur Chapter Daughters of the American Revolution, 1912.

Johnson, John. *The Defense of Charleston Harbor, Including Fort Sumter and the Adjacent Islands, 1863–1865.* Charleston, SC: Walker, Evans & Cogswell, 1890.

Kautz, August V. *The 1865 Customs of Service for Non-Commissioned Officers and Soldiers.* 2nd ed. 1865; Mechanicsburg, PA: Stackpole, 2001.

Kentucky Adjutant-General's Office. *Report of the Adjutant General of the State of Kentucky, Confederate Kentucky Volunteers, 1861–65,* 2 vols. 1915; Hartford, KY: Cook & McDowell, 1979.

Munson, Don, ed. *It Is Begun! The Pantagraph Reports the Civil War.* Bloomington, IL: McLean County Historical Society, 2001.

Rawick, George P., ed. *The American Slave: A Composite Autobiography,* 19 vols., supplements, and index. Westport, CT: Greenwood, 1972–1981.

Reid, Richard M., ed. *Practicing Medicine in a Black Regiment: The Civil War Diary of Burt G. Wilder, 55th Massachusetts.* Amherst: University of Massachusetts Press, 2010.

Ripley, Warren, ed. *Siege Train: The Journal of a Confederate Artilleryman in the Defense of Charleston.* Columbia: University of South Carolina Press, 1986.

Russell, William H. *My Diary North and South.* Edited by Eugene H. Berwanger. 1863; Baton Rouge: Louisiana State University Press, 2001.

Sherman, William Tecumseh. *Memoirs of General W. T. Sherman.* New York: Library of America, 1990. First published 1875 by D. Appleton.

Simon, John Y., ed. *The Papers of Ulysses S. Grant.* Vols. 3–4. Carbondale: Southern Illinois University Press, 1971–1972.

Stillwell, Leander. *The Story of a Common Soldier of Army Life in the Civil War, 1861–1865.* Kansas City, MO: Franklin Hudson.

Towles, Louis P., ed. *A World Turned Upside Down: The Palmers of the South Santee, 1818–1881.* Columbia: University of South Carolina Press, 1996.

Trigg County, Kentucky Historical Articles, vol. 2. Melber, KY: Simmons Historical Publications, 1987.

Trudeau, Noah Andre. *Voices of the 55th: Letters from the 55th Massachusetts Volunteers 1861–1865.* Dayton, OH: Morningside House, 1996.

US Naval War Records Office. *Official Records of the Union and Confederate Navies in the War of the Rebellion*, ser. 1: vols. 1–27. Washington, DC: Government Printing Office, 1894–1917.

US War Department. *The War of the Rebellion: A Compilation of the Official Records of the Union and Confederate Armies*, 4 ser. Washington, DC: Government Printing Office, 1881–1898.

Wallace, Lew. *Lew Wallace: An Autobiography*. New York: Harper and Brothers, 1906.

Wilder, Burt G. *The 55th Massachusetts Volunteer Infantry, Colord* [*sic*], *June 1863–September 1865*. 3rd ed. rev. Brookline, MA: Riverdale, August 1919.

Yacovone, Donald, ed. *A Voice of Thunder: The Civil War Letters of George E. Stephens*. Urbana: University of Illinois Press, 1997.

PUBLISHED SECONDARY SOURCES: ARTICLES

Astor, Aaron. "'I Wanted a Gun': Black Soldiers and White Violence in Civil War and Post War Kentucky." In *The Great Task Remaining before Us: Reconstruction as America's Continuing Civil War*, edited by Paul A. Cimbala and Randall M. Miller, 30–53. New York: Fordham University Press, 2010.

Beardsley, Edward H. "The American Scientist as Social Activist: Franz Boas, Burt G. Wilder, and the Cause of Racial Justice, 1900–1915." *Isis* 64, no. 1 (March 1973): 50–66.

Belz, Herman. "Law, Politics, and Race in the Struggle for Equal Pay in the Civil War." *Civil War History* 22 (September 1976): 197–213.

Boyd, Mark F. "The Federal Campaign of 1864 in East Florida." *Florida Historical Quarterly* 29 (July 1950): 3–37.

"Capt. Ben Dyer Terry." *Confederate Veteran* 14 (1906): 516–517.

Coffman, Edward M., and Allan R. Millett. "Was Congress and President Bill Clinton Justified in Posthumously Awarding the Medal of Honor to Theodore Roosevelt? Two of America's Leading Military Historians Offer Their Opinions." *MHQ: The Quarterly Journal of Military History* 14, no. 3 (Spring 2002): 60–67.

Crane, J. Michael. "'The Rebels are Bold, Defiant, and Unscrupulous in Their Dementions of All Men': Social Violence in Daviess County, Kentucky 1861–1868." *Ohio Valley History* 2, no. 1 (2002): 17–29.

"Dr. Burt G. Wilder, Famous Member of Cornell's First Staff, Dies in Massachusetts." *Cornell Alumni News* 27, no. 18 (January 29, 1925): 223–224.

Futch, Ovid Leon. "Salmon P. Chase and Civil War Politics in Florida." *Florida Historical Quarterly* 32 (January 1954): 163–188.

Gillmore, Quincy A. "The Army before Charleston in 1863." In *Battles and Leaders of the Civil War*, edited by Robert Underwood Johnson and Clarence Clough Buel, 4:52–71. Secaucus, NJ: Castle, 1982.

Hicks, Brevet-Major Henry G. "Fort Donelson." In *Glimpses of the Nation's Struggle: Papers Read before the Minnesota Commandery of the Military Order of the Loyal Legion of the United States, 1892–1897*, edited by Edward D. Neill. Vol. 4:437–453. St. Paul, MN: H. L. Collins, 1898.

Hoskins, Patricia A. "The Freedmen's Bureau in the Jackson Purchase Region of Kentucky, 1866–1868." *Register of the Kentucky Historical Society* 110, no. 3/4 (2012): 503–531.

Jerome, Brenda Joyce, ed. "1860 Lyon County Kentucky Slave Schedule." *Western Kentucky Journal* 8, no. 4 (2001): 16–21.

Keith, Willis J. "Fort Johnson." *Civil War Times Illustrated* 14, no. 7 (November 1975): 32–39.

Miller, Kelly. "Enumeration Errors in Negro Population." *Scientific Monthly* 14, no. 2 (February 1922): 168–177.

Nickell, Shelley. "The Town That Could Not Prosper." *Between the Rivers*, no. 12 (Summer 2002): 19–21.

Parish, Ray. "Civil War Hero Buried at Oakland Cemetery." *Between the Rivers*, no. 7 (Spring 2000): 5–6.

Rhyne, Michael J. "'We are Mobed and Beat': Regular Violence against Free Black Households in Kentucky's Bluegrass Region, 1865–1867." *Ohio Valley History* 2, no. 1 (2002): 30–42.

Stryker, William S. "The 'Swamp Angel.'" In *Battles and Leaders of the Civil War*, edited by Robert Underwood Johnson and Clarence Clough Buel, 4:72–74. Secaucus, NJ: Castle, 1982.

Taylor, Captain Jesse. "The Defense of Fort Henry." In *Battles and Leaders of the Civil War*, edited by Robert Underwood Johnson and Clarence Clough Buel, 1:368–372. Secaucus, NJ: Castle, 1982.

Theodore Roosevelt Association. "Quest for the Medal of Honor." Accessed January 4, 2020, http://archive.is/McTQ8.

Waldrep, Christopher. "Kentucky's Slave Importation Law in Lyon County: A Document." *Filson Club History Quarterly* 65, no. 4 (1991): 505–512.

Walke, Rear Admiral Henry. "The Gun-Boats at Belmont and Fort Henry." In *Battles and Leaders of the Civil War*, edited by Robert Underwood Johnson and Clarence Clough Buel, 1:358–367. Secaucus, NJ: Castle, 1982.

———. "The Western Flotilla at Fort Donelson, Island Number 10, Fort Pillow and Memphis." In *Battles and Leaders of the Civil War*, edited by Robert Underwood Johnson and Clarence Clough Buel, 1:430–452. Secaucus, NJ: Castle, 1982.

Zalimus, Robert J. "A Disturbance in the City: Black and White Soldiers in Postwar Charleston." In *Black Soldiers in Blue: African American Troops in the Civil War Era*. Edited by John David Smith, 361–390. Chapel Hill: University of North Carolina Press, 2002.

PUBLISHED SECONDARY SOURCES: BOOKS

Astor, Aaron. *Rebels on the Border: Civil War, Emancipation, and the Reconstruction of Kentucky and Missouri*. Baton Rouge: Louisiana State University Press, 2012.

Berwanger, Eugene H. *The Frontier Against Slavery: Western Anti-Negro Prejudice and the Slavery Extension Controversy*. Urbana: University of Illinois Press, 1967.

The Biographical Record of DeWitt County, Illinois. Chicago: S. J. Clarke, 1901.

Casstevens, Frances H. *Edward A. Wild and His African Brigade in the Civil War.* Jefferson, NC: McFarland, 2003.

Cimprich, John. *Slavery's End in Tennessee.* Tuscaloosa: University of Alabama Press, 1985.

Cornish, Dudley Taylor. *The Sable Arm: Negro Troops in the Union Army, 1861–1865.* Lawrence: University Press of Kansas, 1956.

Fraker, Guy C. *Lincoln's Ladder to the Presidency: The Eighth Judicial Circuit.* Carbondale: Southern Illinois University Press, 2012.

Glatthaar, Joseph T. *Forged in Battle: The Civil War Alliance of Black Soldiers and White Officers.* New York: Free Press, 1989.

Gould, William B., IV. *Diary of a Contraband: The Civil War Passage of a Black Sailor.* Stanford, CA: Stanford University Press, 2002.

Guelzo, Allen C. *Lincoln's Emancipation Proclamation: The End of Slavery in America.* New York: Simon & Schuster, 2004.

Hannan, Nancy H. *Readville: A Mysterious Providence.* Hyde Park, MA: Albert House, 1990.

Haskins, James. *Pinckney Benton Stewart Pinchback.* New York: Macmillan, 1973.

Henry, J. Milton. *The Land Between the Rivers.* N.p.: Taylor, 1970s.

Hess, Earl J. *Field Armies and Fortifications in the Civil War: The Eastern Campaigns, 1861–1864.* Chapel Hill: University of North Carolina Press, 2005.

Hewett, Janet B., et al., eds. *Supplement to the Official Records of the Union and Confederate Armies.* 100 vols. Wilmington, NC: Broadfoot, 1994–2001.

History of DeWitt County, Illinois. Philadelphia: W. R. Brink, 1882.

Howard, Victor B. *Black Liberation in Kentucky: Emancipation and Freedom, 1862–1884.* Lexington: University Press of Kentucky, 1983.

Jillson, Willard Rouse. *The Kentucky Land Grants.* Louisville: Standard Printing, 1925.

Josyph, Peter, ed. *The Wounded River: The Civil War Letters of John Vance Lauderdale, M. D.* East Lansing: Michigan State University Press 1993.

Klingman, Peter D. *Josiah Walls: Florida's Black Congressman of Reconstruction.* Gainesville: University Press of Florida, 1976.

Link, Arthur S. *Wilson: The New Freedom.* Princeton, NJ: Princeton University Press, 1954.

Logue, Larry M., and Peter Blank. *Race, Ethnicity, and Disability: Veterans and Benefits in Post-Civil War America.* New York: Cambridge University Press, 2010.

Lucas, Marion B. *A History of Blacks in Kentucky.* Vol. 1, *From Slavery to Segregation, 1760–1891.* Frankfort: Kentucky Historical Society, 1992.

Luck, Wilbert H. *Journey to Honey Hill.* Washington, DC: Wiluk Press, 1976.

McPherson, James M. *The Negro's Civil War: How American Negroes Felt and Acted During the War for the Union.* Urbana: University of Illinois Press, 1965, 1982.

Mears, Dwight S. *The Medal of Honor: The Evolution of America's Highest Military Decoration.* Lawrence: University Press of Kansas, 2018.

Miller, Edward A., Jr. *Gullah Statesman: Robert Smalls from Slavery to Congress, 1839–1915*. Columbia: University of South Carolina Press, 1995.

Nall, James O. *The Tobacco Night Riders of Kentucky and Tennessee, 1905–1909*. Kentucky Bicentennial Edition, 1792–1992. Kuttawa, KY: McClanahan House, 1991. First published 1939.

Pressly, Thomas J., and William H. Scofield, eds. *Farm Real Estate Values in the United States by Counties, 1850–1959*. Seattle: University of Washington Press, 1965.

Quarles, Benjamin. *The Negro in the Civil War*. Boston: Little, Brown, 1953.

Regosin, Elizabeth, and Donald R. Shafer, eds. *Voices of Emancipation: Understanding Slavery, the Civil War, and Reconstruction through the U.S. Pension Bureau Files*. New York: New York University Press, 2008.

Rollin, Frank A. *Life and Public Services of Martin R. Delany*. New York: Arno Press, 1969. First published 1868, 1883.

Schweninger, Loren. *Black Property Owners in the South, 1790–1915*. Urbana: University of Illinois Press, 1990.

Shaffer, Donald R. *After the Glory: The Struggles of Black Civil War Veterans*. Lawrence: University Press of Kansas, 2004.

Slagle, Jay. *Ironclad Captain: Seth Ledyard Phelps & the U.S. Navy, 1841–1864*. Kent, OH: Kent State University Press, 1996.

Smith, Frank E. *Land Between the Lakes*. Lexington: University Press of Kentucky, 1971.

Smith, John David, ed. *Black Soldiers in Blue: African American Troops in the Civil War Era*. Chapel Hill: University of North Carolina Press, 2002.

———. *Lincoln and the U.S. Colored Troops*. Carbondale: Southern Illinois University Press, 2013.

Stone, H. David, Jr. *Vital Rails: The Charleston and Savannah Railroad and the Civil War in Coastal South Carolina*. Columbia: University of South Carolina Press, 2008.

Trudeau, Noah Andre. *Like Men of War: Black Troops in the Civil War 1862–1865*. Boston: Little Brown, 1998.

Voegeli, V. Jacque. *Free but Not Equal: The Midwest and the Negro During the Civil War*. Chicago: University of Chicago Press, 1967.

Waldrep, Christopher. *Night Riders: Defending Community in the Black Patch, 1890–1915*. Durham, NC: Duke University Press, 1993.

Walker, Odell. *In Lyon County, Saturday Was Town Day: A Collection of Writings from Lyon County's Historian*. Kuttawa, KY: Lyon County Historical Press, 2002.

———. *Profiles of the Past: A Collection of Writings from Lyon County's Historian*. Kuttawa, KY: Lyon County Historical Press, 1994.

Wallace, Betty Joe. *Between the Rivers: History of the Land Between the Lakes*. Clarksville, TN: Austin Peay State University, Center for Field Biology, Dept. of History and Philosophy, 1992.

Wilson, Keith P. *Campfires of Freedom: The Camp Life of Black Soldiers During the Civil War*. Kent, OH: Kent State University Press, 2002.

Wise, Stephen R. *Gate of Hell: Campaign for Charleston Harbor, 1863*. Columbia: University of South Carolina Press, 1994.

Wright, George C. *A History of Blacks in Kentucky*. Vol. 2, *In Pursuit of Equality, 1890–1980*. Frankfort: Kentucky Historical Society, 1992.

———. *Racial Violence in Kentucky, 1864–1940: Lynchings, Mob Rule, and "Legal Lynchings."* Baton Rouge: Louisiana State University Press, 1990.

NEWSPAPERS

Bloomington (IL) Daily Pantagraph
Bloomington (IL) Pantagraph
Bloomington (IL) Weekly Pantagraph
Charleston (SC) Daily Courier
Charleston (SC) Weekly News
Chicago Daily Tribune
Christian Recorder (Philadelphia)
Clinton (IL) Central Transcript
Clinton (IL) Public
Clinton (IL) Weekly Register
Columbia (SC) Sun
Greenville (SC) Daily News
Honolulu Star-Bulletin
Indianapolis Star
Kokomo (IN) Tribune
Lafayette (IN) Journal and Courier
National Tribune (Washington, DC)
New Bedford (MA) Mercury
New York Herald
Newsday (Melville, NY)
Philadelphia Weekly Times
Pittsburgh Post-Gazette
Unionville (MO) Republican
Weekly Anglo-African (New York)

REGIMENTAL HISTORIES

Ambrose, Daniel Leib. *History of the Seventh Regiment Illinois Volunteer Infantry*. Springfield: Illinois Journal Company, 1868.

Blanchard, Ira. *I Marched with Sherman: Civil War Memoirs of the 20th Illinois Volunteer Infantry*. San Francisco: J. D. Huff, 1992.

Emilio, Luis F. *A Brave Black Regiment: The History of the 54th Regiment of Massachusetts Volunteer Infantry*. 1894; New York: Da Capo, 1995.

[Fox, Charles B.] *Record of the Service of the 55th Regiment of Massachusetts Volunteer Infantry*. Cambridge, MA: Press of John Wilson and Son, 1868.

Hall, Henry, and James Hall, *Cayuga in the Field: A Record of the 19th N. Y. Volunteers, All the Batteries of the 3d New York Artillery, and 75th New York Volunteers.* Auburn, NY: Truair, Smith, Printers, Syracuse, 1873.

McGrath, Franklin, ed. *A History of the 127th New York Volunteers, "Monitors," in the War for the Preservation of the Union—September 8, 1862, June 30, 1865.* N.p.: n.p., 1898.

McKee, James Harvey. *Back "In War Times": History of the 144th Regiment, New York Volunteer Infantry.* New York: Lieut. Horace E. Bailey, 1903.

Morrison, Marion. *A History of the Ninth Regiment Illinois Volunteer Infantry.* Monmouth, IL: John S. Clark, Printer, 1864.

Newton, A. H. *Out of the Briars: An Autobiography and Sketch of the Twenty-Ninth Regiment Connecticut Volunteers.* Philadelphia: A.M.E. Book Concern, 1910.

ARCHAEOLOGICAL STUDIES

Smith, Steven D., Stephen R. Wise, Jeff Grigg, Tamara S. Wilson, Mathew Luke, and Spencer Baker. *Mapping the Charleston and Savannah Railroad Defenses Phase II.* Columbia, SC: South Carolina Institute of Archaeology and Anthropology, 2011.

MAP

Plats of Grand Rivers, Kentucky, 1838. Tennessee Valley Authority. US Government.

VIDEO INTERVIEWS

Caruth Smith Washington videotape interview, July 16, 2001. Andrew Jackson Smith Papers.

Dawson, Nancy. Interview of Former Residents of Grand Rivers, KY, July 1, 2006. Andrew Jackson Smith Papers.

ACKNOWLEDGMENTS

I CANNOT BEGIN TO THANK MY WIFE, Esther, enough for fifty-seven years of love, devotion, and partnership, truly the love of my life; and my three wonderful children, Catherine, Andrew Jr., and David; and my grandkids, including my Civil War running buddy, Ebone Clara Jones, for understanding and enduring twenty years of roller-coaster emotional drama and listening to my nearly daily adventures in the Civil War.

I am forever grateful to my mother, Susan Geneva Smith Shelton, and my aunt, Caruth Smith Washington, for their storytelling and bringing our family history to life, and for Aunt Caruth's preservation of the documents Andy Smith entrusted to her; to the Benberry family, especially Charles Leon, Dwayne, Ewing, Hattie, Newton, and Randy, together with Golda Beaman and Mary Louise White, all of whom shared their memories of Andy Smith and the community he helped to build in Grand Rivers.

Many others came forward to support Andy Smith: fellow FAA colleagues Jerry Nelson, Debbie Anderson, and Daniel Reid; Vernice Williams, Indianapolis; historian Kathy Dhalle; Jerry Orton, Sons of Union Veterans, New York Department, and Lorraine Orton, New York Department, Daughters of Union Veterans; John Shonaker, Carlisle Barracks; and especially archivist Cynthia Middleton at the National Archives who guided Esther and me to the missing records and thereby provided the final piece to our puzzle. Our research efforts in Washington, DC, were significantly aided by the hospitality of Mr. and Mrs. Will Caldwell (thank you for the key to your home). Dr. Stephen Wise led us across the Honey Hill Battlefield. Gilbert Taylor, Crispus Attucks High School, helped shape our public message. Members of the Indianapolis Civil War Round Table, including McClernand B. Crawford, Nikki Schofield, and Tom Krasean, were steadfast supporters, as was Jacqueline D. Wright, Daughters of Union Veterans,

Springfield, Illinois. Our Steel Magnolias, aunties Carla Long, Barbara J. Toler, Mary Alice Walton, and Barbara Ann Martin, tracked reporting in the press and on the airwaves; Randal Pinkston interviewed Caruth on CBS's *Sunday Morning*, Father's Day 1996.

I will always remember Carol Fraker and Representative Thomas Ewing for placing Andy Smith's records with the US Army's Awards and Decorations Branch and Senator Richard Durbin for intervening when the Medal of Honor recommendation was delayed in the Department of Defense. I thank Sandra Roberts, Normal, Illinois, for contacting Senator Durbin on behalf of Andy Smith, Patrick Souders of Senator Durbin's office, and Joe Alexander of Representative Ewing's office, for their effectiveness and consideration.

For their support as the recommendation made its slow journey through the Department of Defense I thank US Representative Julia Carson, US Senator Evan Bayh, and US Senator Richard Lugar, all of Indiana, and their staffs. US Army Colonel Curtis B. Taylor, Fort Benjamin Harrison, wrote letters of support, and Indianapolis business executive John H. Horner drew on his years of public service to help us coordinate with governmental agencies and wrote letters of support; Duane Alexander submitted a proclamation of support from the American Legion; Pete Falcone's article in the *Bloomington (IL) Pantagraph* caught the essence of our struggle. Richard Walton, *Indianapolis Star*, and Azura Domschke, *Lafayette (IN) Journal and Courier*, reported on the causes of delays in Congress.

It is with appreciation that I recognize those who helped us share Andy Smith's legacy with thousands of schoolchildren through performances of "The Major and the Color Sergeant" with Khabir Shareef (Major Martin R. Delany), Charles Poindexter (Garland White), and our songbirds, Anna Marie and Virginia Westley, and Ryan McDaniel, who will carry on the tradition as the new Andy Smith. Crown Hill Cemetery sustained performances of "The Major and the Color Sergeant" through their Spirit of Freedom Foundation. Don and Sarah Heitman of Indianapolis School 45 were early believers who supported us with a newspaper article and provided Civil War uniforms for presentations. The continuing support of Patricia Brown Payne, Indianapolis Public Schools, and of Annette Henderson have helped us reach out to increasing numbers of children year after year. For many years, Orville Uggen organized Hartford City, Indiana Civil War Days. Reenactor Mike Lozano, 55th Massachusetts Infantry, was an early champion of Andy Smith, and to reenactor James Floyd, 11th South Carolina Infantry, CSA, my appreciation for his salute at the 2001 Honey Hill reenactment. Indian Creek Middle School history teacher Thomas Haywood endorsed us and brought black Civil War history to his rural Indiana school. Bennie McRae Jr. continues to support black military history through his website Lest We Forget.

Ray and Shara Parish endeavored to do whatever was needed to recognize Andy Smith's presence in the Land Between the Rivers. Ray, as president of Between the Rivers Inc., obtained a Medal of Honor headstone for Andy Smith's grave and also worked with the Kentucky Historical Society to erect a historical highway marker on the Woodlands Trace Parkway by Oakland Cemetery.

In 2003, John M. Trowbridge, Kentucky Military History Museum, was instrumental in organizing the state of Kentucky's recognition of Andy Smith by dedicating two miles of Kentucky Highway 453 near Grand Rivers as the Andrew Jackson Smith Memorial Highway. In 2014, under the leadership of Judge/Executive Wade White, a memorial to Andy Smith was among those raised in Lyon County's new Veterans Plaza, located at the entrance to the Lyon County Judicial Center.

The authors and I are especially appreciative of Mr. Dan Acker of ASALH, the Association for the Study of African American Life and History, for his introduction to Janell W. Agyeman, who guided the preparation of our manuscript for publication and directed us to Westholme Publishing. Publisher Bruce H. Franklin immediately grasped the significance of Andy Smith's story and enthusiastically applied his considerable talents to producing the book. Copy editor Ronald Silverman's practiced and incisive eye enhanced our text in many places, and graphic artist Trudi Gershenov designed the remarkable book cover that will introduce Andy Smith's image to the reading public.

—Andrew S. Bowman

We first express our appreciation to the librarians of Illinois State University's Milner Library. Their expertise enabled us to conduct research with an ease equaling that enjoyed at larger universities. In particular, Garold Cole and Van Schwartz helped to build the history collection; Joan Winters, Angela Bonnell, and Maureen Brunsdale facilitated access to resources; and Chris Young was marvelous at Interlibrary Loan.

Aaron Astor, Maryville College, Kentucky; Stanley D. Buckles, Mount Pulaski, Illinois; Kelli Christiansen, Chicago; Georgia Cravey, Indianapolis; Willis J. Keith, James Island, South Carolina; Susan Hawkins, National Park Service, Fort Donelson National Battlefield, Tennessee; Greg Koos, McLean

County Museum of History, Bloomington, Illinois; William Reger and Carl J. Wenning, Illinois State University; Timothy B. Smith, University of Tennessee, Martin; Ginger Stubbs, Dunlap High School, Illinois; and Stephen Wise, director, Parris Island Marine Corps Museum, South Carolina, read and commented on parts or all of the manuscript.

The authors express their appreciation to the following individuals, each of whom contributed significantly to the completion of this work:

Historians: Aaron Astor, Kentucky; Michael Coker, Charleston, South Carolina; Bill Cunningham, Kentucky; Corlin R. Ferguson, Illinois State University; Susan Hawkins, National Park Service, Fort Donelson National Battlefield, Tennessee; David Lowe, National Park Service, Washington, DC; David L. Nickell, Between the Rivers Inc., Kentucky; Michael Rhyne, Ohio; Bryce Suderow, Washington, DC; Joey Woolridge, Clinton, Illinois.

Archivists/librarians: DeAnne Blanton, Claire Kluskens, and Rebecca Sharp, National Archives and Records Administration; Elizabeth Carroll-Horrocks, State Library of Massachusetts; Kent DeGroott, Massachusetts National Guard Museum and Archives, Concord, Massachusetts; Elaine Engst and Laura Linke, Cornell University; Laura Elder and Mary Jo Fairchild, South Carolina Historical Society; Harlan Greene, College of Charleston; Lori Duff, Clerk of Lyon County, Kentucky; Lance Hall, Kentucky Department for Libraries and Archives; Gina Garber, Austin Peay State University; Francie LaCamera, Illinois State Library; Bill Kemp, McLean County Museum of History; Melanie Robbins, Putnam County Public Library, Unionville, Missouri.

Cartographers Bill Nelson and Jill Thomas, and archaeologist Jim Legg, who contributed his knowledge of the war along the South Carolina coast, each provided quality maps. Cartographer Dana MacBean incorporated the curvature of the battle line to draw the most accurate map to date of the Honey Hill battlefield. Mark Garland mapped the boundaries of Andy Smith's land purchases. Paul Rossmann created original maps and redrew others to produce a uniformity of style among all maps. Julia Denise Smith, Tennessee Valley Authority, and Tammy L. Kirk, US Army Corps of Engineers, helped provide maps of Grand Rivers and the Cumberland River. Mayor Tom Moodie helped us prepare the Grand Rivers map.

Ronald Clark, Springfield, Illinois, Civil War Round Table, directed the authors to McClernand B. Crawford, president of the Indianapolis Civil War Round Table. Kip Johnson, Effingham, Illinois, opened his extensive files on the 41st Illinois Volunteer Infantry. Historian Gretchen Knapp, Illinois State University, guided us to Cynthia van Ness, Buffalo History Museum, for research assistance. Graduate students Kelley LeJuene and Valarie

Sherman, Illinois State University, organized and provided insightful analysis of Andy Smith's law cases. Attorney Robert J. Lenz, Bloomington, Illinois, provided professional guidance into Andy Smith's enigmatic, final law case; Denise Preller, Hudson, Illinois, contributed impressive skills as she researched genealogical and twentieth-century subjects. Ronald Timmerman, Carlock, Illinois, contributed many hours of research support. John Warner IV, Clinton, Illinois, shared family memories of Andy Smith and provided the photograph of Dr. John Warner. Odell Walker, Lyon County historian, generously shared his knowledge of life Between the Rivers.

Dr. Stephen R. Wise, director, Parris Island Marine Corps Museum, guided the authors across the Honey Hill battlefield; Willis J. Keith, James Island, contributed his editorial skills, unending assistance, and deep knowledge of Civil War history. Nancy Peeples, Charleston, provided Charles Alfred de Saussure's memoir. Staci Richey, graduate student, University of South Carolina, researched the G. Marshall Naul Collection. Douglas Bostick, Charleston, identified the location of Battery Means. Jeremy Pluckett, graduate student, University of Kentucky, searched collections within the state. Sergeant Joe Siefferman, Illinois State Police, conducted the forensic analysis establishing that Andy Smith was the unidentified soldier in the 1865 photograph from the Hartwell Collection housed at the State Library of Massachusetts.

Joanne Smith Evans Carnes, Paducah, Kentucky, and Larry Walton, Hopkinsville, Kentucky, shared their knowledge of Smith family history. Judy Boaz, George Coon Public Library, Princeton, Kentucky, and Richard P'Pool, Princeton, Kentucky, helped us locate Larry Walton. Betty Stiles provided insight into the twentieth century history of Grand Rivers.

Finally, without academic direction afforded years ago by Dr. Paul L. Holmer, Southern Connecticut State University, and, subsequently, by Professor William W. Haddad and Professor Louis G. Perez, Illinois State University, we would never have been in position to help Andy Smith obtain his Medal of Honor.

—W. Robert Beckman and Sharon S. MacDonald

INDEX